P9-ARG-845

# Contents

# THE NATURE OF THE GAME

# THE NATURE OF THE GAME

## LINKS GOLF AT BANDON DUNES AND FAR BEYOND

## Mike Keiser

### *with Stephen Goodwin*

 ALFRED A. KNOPF · NEW YORK · 2022

THIS IS A BORZOI BOOK
PUBLISHED BY ALFRED A. KNOPF

Published in the United States by Alfred A. Knopf, a division
of Penguin Random House LLC, New York, and distributed in Canada
by Penguin Random House Canada Limited, Toronto.

www.aaknopf.com

Knopf, Borzoi Books, and the colophon
are registered trademarks of Penguin Random House LLC.

Pages 303–305 constitute an extension of this copyright page

Library of Congress Cataloging-in-Publication Data
Names: Keiser, Mike, author. | Goodwin, Stephen, author.
Title: The nature of the game: links golf at Bandon Dunes and far beyond /
Mike Keiser with Stephen Goodwin.
Description: First edition. | New York, NY: Alfred A. Knopf, 2022.
Identifiers: LCCN 2021031454 (print) | LCCN 2021031455 (ebook) |
ISBN 9780525658597 (hardcover) | ISBN 9780525658603 (ebook)
Subjects: LCSH: Golf resorts—Oregon—Bandon—Design and construction. |
Bandon Dunes Golf Resort (Bandon Or.) | Golf—Oregon—Bandon—History. |
Golf—Social aspects—Oregon—Bandon.
Classification: LCC GV982.O74 K45 2022 (print) | LCC GV982.O74 (ebook) |
DDC 796.35206/879523—dc23
LC record available at https://lccn.loc.gov/2021031454
LC ebook record available at https://lccn.loc.gov/2021031455

Jacket photographs by Nathan Kahler, courtesy of Bandon Dunes Golf Resort
Jacket design by Chip Kidd

Manufactured in Germany

First Edition

For my mother, Louise, who grew up in New Jersey
and played golf at Ridgewood Country Club. When I was a boy,
she encouraged me to play and caddy as much as I wanted to
at the sublime East Aurora Country Club, near Buffalo, New York.
And that's what I did every day for six straight summers.

# THE NATURE OF THE GAME

# Introduction

THIRTY YEARS AGO, when I was just starting to feel my way into the golf business, I flew out to Oregon with Steve Lesnik, the president of KemperSports. I'd found a piece of oceanfront property that looked to me like an ideal site for a golf course, and I wanted Steve's opinion before going all in. Even though we didn't have a formal business agreement, I was counting on him to steer me through the development process.

We drove to the property in a downpour. Wind rocked the car, and the windshield wipers could hardly keep up with the sheets of rain. Finally, we left the highway and turned onto a small lane that led us through a meadow and right out to the edge of the Pacific Ocean. Big waves were crashing on the rocks, and a gust of wind nearly ripped off the door when Steve tried to get out of the car. "If you think people are coming here to play golf," he yelled, "you're out of your fucking mind."

To be fair, he was trying to save me from an expensive mistake. Other golf consultants were more polite, but they all warned me about trying to build any kind of golf resort on the south coast of Oregon. The place was too remote and too raw, a rugged stretch of mostly empty coastline dotted with small towns that had seen better days. The main tourist attraction—the Oregon Dunes National Recreation Area, where ATVers came to ride the giant sandhills—was an hour away by car. The nearest big city, Portland, was five hours, and San Francisco was ten. Sometimes I thought the consultants might be right and my obsession would turn out to be a costly, embarrassing folly. But I'd made enough money to build a golf course, and the course I wanted to build was a seaside links course.

No one, including me, foresaw at the time how deeply Bandon Dunes would tap into an appetite for a different kind of golf. I knew that I loved links golf, and I suspected that there were others, like me, increasingly disenchanted with the kind of golf that was served up to the American public— long, difficult, "championship courses" (as Jack Nicklaus said, "the emptiest phrase in golf"). Forgettable, formulaic design. Fairways lined with houses. Golf carts on paved paths that made you feel like a token in a giant board game. Lush, overwatered fairways. Pretentious clubhouses. Name-brand architects. Signature holes. Man-made lakes with fountains. Flower beds with the name of the course spelled out in pansies and begonias. A pervasive air of commercialism.

That was the prevailing model, and I was determined to do everything differently at Bandon Dunes. My goal was to get back to a simpler, purer game—to golf that still felt like an outdoor adventure. "When golfing, you want to be alone with Nature," C. B. Macdonald wrote a century ago, and the location for my course was wild and beautiful, on high bluffs overlooking the Pacific. No carts, cart paths, or real estate. At Bandon Dunes, golf would be what it had always been, a walking game. You could carry your own bag, pull your own cart, or take a caddy, but you had to walk. The architect I hired was an unknown who said, "My strongest qualification in those days was probably my Scottish accent." The courses—there was soon a second course, Pacific Dunes—had firm, fast playing conditions. The clubhouse was modest and intimate, and the landscaping consisted mostly of gorse, shore pines, beach grass, and bunkers that had been sculpted by the wind.

We described the golf at Bandon Dunes in several different ways—as dream golf, as throwback golf, as American links. I'd always been aware that it was risky to try to transplant links golf to this country; you couldn't just roll up an ancient Scottish links like a length of sod and unroll it in a new location thousands of miles away. Somehow, Bandon Dunes had to combine the ancient and modern. Golf is a game deeply rooted in tradition; we had to find out how to preserve its rituals, its character, and its customs, in a new setting.

I say that as though we set about this task with a deliberate plan. But in the early days, the focus was on trying to get a golf operation to run smoothly. We were overwhelmed by the initial response to the resort, and it was clear that the allure of Bandon Dunes encompassed more than golf. My original partner, Howard McKee, wasn't a golfer; an architect and land planner, he approached his work as an exercise in place-making. In his view, golf was a part of a larger endeavor to create a spot that drew upon the location's natural and cultural resources to encourage health, contentment, and well-being. Before "authenticity" became a buzzword, Howard was driven to create a place that was one with its environment. He used local materials in building and design, sited structures so they harmonized with the landscape, and integrated the buildings into an overall design that had the comforting scale and intimacy of a village.

In short, Bandon Dunes evolved into its own kind of resort where the most traditional form of the game—walking golf on a links course—acquired a fresh, local personality. Success builds on success, and within a few years we had added new courses, additional lodging, new clubhouses and restaurants. The courses won so many awards and accolades that we didn't have space on the walls of the Bunker Bar to display them all. Bandon Dunes was recognized as one of golf's top resorts.

Today, there are six courses at Bandon Dunes, occupying a three-mile stretch of unbroken coastline. And I've learned that under the right conditions, the Bandon Dunes model can be reproduced. I've been involved in the development of resorts at Barnbougle Dunes in Australia; Cabot Cape Breton in Nova Scotia; and most recently, Sand Valley in Wisconsin. All except Sand Valley are located on the ocean, and they all offer a local version of familiar elements: links golf reimagined in a new environment, an ancient game whose appeal is burnished in a twenty-first-century setting.

Bandon Dunes was not simply a "pioneering one-off," wrote Josh Sens in a recent *Golf Magazine* article that addressed its influence since opening twenty years ago: "The ripple-effects of Bandon have reached far beyond its grounds. Even as it helped revive the economic fortunes of a flagging region, Bandon helped awaken a larger, slumbering market. It might be a stretch to say that Bandon rescued golf. But for those—and there were many—who felt that golf had lost its way, Bandon got the game on track again. Its popularity shattered tired assumptions about golfers and freshened worn ideas about what a course should look like and where a course could be."

While Bandon Dunes has brought an infusion of energy to the game, the resorts have been a bright spot in a picture that has been far from rosy. Anyone who reads the trade magazines knows that the golf industry at large has struggled. As I write now, in the fall of 2020, the industry is coming off its best year in decades; during the Covid-19 pandemic, millions of people flocked to golf courses for a breath of fresh air. The game offers plenty of room for social distancing. Golf facilities everywhere quickly instituted policies to ensure the safety of players and staff, and they provided a welcome, much-needed escape and stress reliever for people who were otherwise confined.

This burst of activity underscored the fact that the game had been in decline since the "Tiger boom" in the early 2000s. In the United States, courses have been closing at the rate of about 100 per year for the last ten years. Many are now on the market at fire-sale prices—and still can't attract buyers. The number of rounds played annually has declined from a high of slightly more than 30 million in 2000 to about 24 million in 2019—and rose by 14 percent in 2020, the pandemic year. Even some young people were attracted to the game; for years, they'd been drifting away, or as head-lines have screamed, "Millennials Are Killing Golf!" The moving average of golf's TV ratings has been on a long downward slide. Private clubs are struggling to hold on to their members, and hardly a month goes by without out a report on the implosion of another residential golf community. At a great many conferences and in countless articles and studies, the problems of golf in the twenty-first century have been described and dissected, with much hand-wringing and foreboding. Seth Waugh, CEO of the Professional Golfers' Association of America, one of the game's custodial institutions, summed up the situation: "Over the last twenty-five years we've done a lot to try to kill golf. We've made it too hard, too expensive, and . . . too long. The one thing we haven't done is make it too fun." The major governing bodies have all introduced programs aimed at "growing the game." For everyone who cares about the future of golf, the last few years have been a period of soul-searching.

I am not a prophet. I'm a businessman, and I'd never claim that we've found all the answers at our resorts. I will say, though, that we have done our best to put the fun back into playing. We've tried to build beautiful courses, and we've created a product—a golf experience—that seems to fill a deep-seated need. Golfers often describe their Bandon experience in superlatives or religious terms, or both. While trends show a game that has been losing its popular appeal, I see in our resort guests the same fascination and delight that golf has always inspired. What golfers want, I believe, is a game that hasn't lost its power to thrill, exasperate, absorb, and exhilarate.

Links golf does all of the above. I've often thought of myself as its Johnny Appleseed, a guy who would plant the seed of a links course whenever he had a chance, and it's been a great satisfaction to see some of those seeds grow into fine, healthy trees. I've said, only half joking, that I intend to go right on doing what I've always done, developing new courses, until I die or run out of money.

I need to make it clear that I don't see them as mine exclusively. Whenever I play a round at Bandon Dunes or Cabot Links, I'm reminded at every turn of the brilliance of the designers. My name might be on the deed of the resorts, but the names on the golf courses are those of the architects: David Kidd, Tom Doak, Bill Coore, Ben Crenshaw, Jim Urbina, Rod Whitman. Some of them were young men when I first hired them, and they are now the stars of their profession. They have gone on to design marvelous courses not just in this country but all over the world. Their work is admired and imitated—and in that respect, the influence of Bandon Dunes has certainly made itself felt throughout the golf world.

My son Michael, a true student of the game, likes to talk about the emergence of a "new canon" as the merits of a new generation of courses become more widely recognized and appreciated. I think he might be right. Fashions in golf, as in all fields of design, are always evolving, but these changes seem to go deeper than fashion. The Bandon courses are more than an alternative to the manufactured layouts that marked the mid-century American style. Drawing their inspiration from ancient sources, from the links, this "throwback" golf is more rugged and wild. The depth and breadth of change bespeak a paradigm shift—a revival, a renaissance, a return to classic design principles that allow for variation, individuality, and mystery.

While this book is a personal story, its real subject is a movement that has tried to both restore the pleasures of a game that has been around for centuries and to reposition it so it can thrive for generations to come. As a boy, I was fortunate to live near a course where I often spent the entire day, playing with my pals as we tried to break 50 for nine holes, roaming around a magical place that seemed a world unto itself, heaven on earth. Now that I am getting on in years, there's nothing I'd rather be doing than building golf courses so others can feel that same abiding joy.

•  •  •

The first nudge for writing this book came from my sons, Michael and Chris, who have joined me in the golf business. They pointed out that many things have changed in the twenty years since the opening of Bandon Dunes and the publication of *Dream Golf,* a book about that experience. Wasn't it time for a book about our new resorts, Barnbougle Dunes, Cabot Links, and Sand Valley? About the new courses at Bandon, the Preserve and the Sheep Ranch?

Though I was skeptical at first, the idea had staying power, and what evolved in our discussions was the narrative you're now reading—not a memoir, but more like a group portrait in which I am surrounded by many others. If a new book was going to tell anything close to a complete story, it would have to include all the people who've worked alongside me—my sons, architects and business partners, the caddies, greenkeepers, and staff members who give the resorts their personality. To do justice to such a rich cast of characters, some parts of the book are written as oral histories in order to bring a multitude of individual voices to the page.

Success has many fathers, and failure is an orphan. That maxim is usually invoked to question anyone who wants to claim star billing. Here I mean it literally: success really does have many fathers, and I see myself as only one of them.

Since some of the most important people in my life haven't played a direct role in any of the golf operations, I want to acknowledge them here, starting with my parents. Growing up in East Aurora, New York, a suburb of Buffalo, I had a Tom Sawyer childhood. In memory, there is a succession of long summer days when my three younger brothers and I played outside, inventing our own games until daylight faded. Thanks to my mom, née Louise Belcher, a lifelong golfer, we belonged to the East Aurora Country Club. My dad, Pap, would never have joined on his own behalf; his pride and joy was a two-acre stand of white pines and Scotch pines behind our house, where he was always tending his beloved trees, trimming, lopping, planting. He'd been an Eagle Scout and a pilot, a winner of the Navy Cross, and every summer he took us camping in the Adirondacks. He never missed an opportunity to instill in us a sense of stewardship. We were expected to leave things better than we found them.

From my parents I learned to love golf, the outdoors, and the freedom to explore and discover my own interests, talents, and passions. I have to smile when I find myself repeating my father's familiar sayings, and realize how much I have come to resemble him as I try to teach my own children the importance of stewardship. My parents made an effort to send me to the Nichols School, on the other side of Buffalo, a boys' school where students were often reminded of another precept that has stuck with me: from those to whom much is given, much is expected.

In today's throwaway culture, these values might seem antiquated. I consider them bedrock precepts that will never be out of fashion. My wife, Lindy, shares my views. We met when she was a freshman at Smith College and I was a senior at Amherst. My roommate, Phil Friedmann, was with me that night, and he saw the look on my face—that of a young man who'd just found the woman he wanted to marry. More than fifty years later, I still marvel at her grace and generous instincts. Lindy has been a loving partner in every significant venture in my life, including the start-up of our first business. We've also been partners in many philanthropic endeavors that

*With Lindy, my first and lifelong partner*

have brought us a circle of friends and associates who see the world as we do and aspire to leave it a little better than we found it. Education has been one focus of our philanthropy; another has been the Shirley Ryan Ability-Lab, one of the leading physical medicine and rehabilitation facilities in the nation. I've also had a long, rewarding association with the Evans Scholar Foundation, which awards four-year, full-ride scholarships to caddies. Early in our marriage, Lindy and I agreed that we would always donate to charities at least as much as we spend on ourselves. As our circumstances have improved, that ratio has changed: spend $1, give $4.

We have two daughters, Leigh and Dana, and they along with Michael and Chris grew up in Chicago, where we have lived for years in a spacious apartment in a Beaux Arts building on Lakeview Avenue, in Lincoln Park. When the children were growing up, the center of our social life was attending their performances and games. Now, with both boys in the golf business and our daughters leading their own lives, one in Chicago and the other in California, where we spend two months every winter, we remain a close family. And our eight grandchildren have given Lindy's days and mine a new emotional focus.

Several principles and values carry over from our family life into the way that I've approached my work as a golf developer. The game itself encourages and reinforces these values, with the importance of stewardship that's drummed into every young golfer. Repair your divots. Rake the bunker. Walk carefully on the green. Leave the course in the same condition as you would like to find it. You have a responsibility to those who follow you, and also to those who preceded you—to those who created the rules, traditions, and ethos of a game of honor. Yes, a game of honor. Non-golfers might shrug off any such claim, but to me the fact that players call penalties on themselves has always been an essential part of golf's character.

My sons share these views, and I'm honored to work with partners who have taken to heart their role as stewards of an ancient and beloved game. I didn't expect them to follow me into the business, and I encouraged them to find careers all their own. As millennials, they're aware that their peers are seen as having lost interest in golf—and they want to find ways to bring them back into the fold. They also share their generation's concern for the health of the planet, and they have actively sought to augment the conservation efforts that have always been a part of our golf operations. At Sand Valley, in Wisconsin, we have the lofty goal of someday restoring 100,000 acres of primeval sand barrens that have been destroyed by commercial logging.

Unrealistic? Maybe. Not so long ago, all the experts were telling me that Bandon Dunes was unrealistic. One of Michael's favorite sayings, and now mine, is the advice of Daniel Burnham: "Make no little plans. They have no magic to stir men's blood."

Every time we build a golf course, we are carrying on Pap's legacy and building another legacy of our own. I hope this book will be a part of that legacy too, my attempt to explain how I have tried to bring dream golf into reality, and why I want to do everything I can to secure the future of the game. When I talked to the crew that was about to start building the first course at Bandon Dunes, I told them to regard it as though their work would still exist five hundred years from now.

Too much to ask? Anything else would have been too little.

1

# The Call of the Links

*The impression of the true old game is indescribable. It was like the dawn or the twilight of a brilliant day. It can only be felt. The charm, the fascination of it all, cannot be conveyed in words. Would that I could hand on unimpaired the great game as it was my good fortune to know it!*

—CHARLES BLAIR MACDONALD

*Painting of the links of North Berwick by Sir John Lavery, 1919*

THERE ARE TWO KINDS OF GOLF, links golf and all the others, and they're as different from each other as a caddy is from a golf cart.

I haven't always been a links purist. Like most Americans, I grew up with a fuzzy idea of what links golf was all about. To the best of my youthful knowledge, "links" was just a slightly fancier way of saying "golf course." In my teens, I realized that links courses were found mostly in Scotland, where everybody's hero, Arnold Palmer, showed up annually on black-and-white TV, slashing the ball out of waist-high rough or staggering through the crowds thronging the fairways on his way to winning the British Open. All the spectators seemed to be wearing rain slickers and carrying umbrellas, and the whole event, from the galleries and the gloomy weather to the pot bunkers and the gorse, looked foreign and dank. The shaggy, bumpy, treeless courses certainly didn't bear much resemblance to the green, groomed, tree-lined country clubs around Buffalo, New York, which to my mind set the standard of beauty.

If you'd told me then that I would someday consider links golf the most exciting, authentic form of the game, I would've laughed at you. I just didn't understand the mystique that had grown up around what seemed to me an antiquated version of the sport. There is a famous old saying that the links were created by the hand of God, and expressly designed to provide the ideal grounds for golf. My initial reaction to statements like that: *Really?*

Yet I have become a believer. When playing a links course, I throw cynicism to the fresh winds blowing off the sea. This game feels foreordained, and I sense, as golfers have for countless generations, that there is something mystical and eternal about the links—"something more deeply interfused," to quote William Wordsworth, a poet whom I've revered since college. A round on ancient links where golfers have walked for centuries brings out the poet in almost everybody.

In me, the links also brought out the developer. My first journeys to Scottish and Irish links happened to coincide with my first forays into the golf business. I can't single out a lightning-bolt moment when the clouds parted and the gods of links golf spoke to me, but at some point it occurred to me that other American golfers might fall in love with it just as I had—so why not transport the links to the United States?

The idea seemed so far-fetched that I instinctively regarded it as a day-dream and pushed it aside. This was in the 1980s, when there weren't any true links in the country. Even the famous courses that called themselves links, like Pebble Beach, were not true links.

A century ago, in the early days of American golf, several of our great courses were designed and built by men who'd learned the game in Scotland. Many of them were actually Scots who'd grown up on the links. But there were many Americans, too, who'd made a careful study of the Scottish models. Inspired by these originals, they sought to adapt traditional design principles to a new set of conditions. On this side of the Atlantic, there was no linksland comparable to that on the coast of Fife. Golf architects worked on different terrain, in a different climate, and on different soils. Some of the pioneering architects, like C. B. Macdonald, tried to create faithful reproductions of famous holes in Scotland. Others, like A. W. Tillinghast and George Crump, were less concerned with any particular holes or courses but devoted to capturing the spirit of the links.

Macdonald, Tillinghast, Crump—they were all part of an era that is often called the Golden Age of Golf Architecture. In the years between 1910 and 1930, this profession of golf architecture was brand-new, and the game itself was catching on as a popular, exciting new pastime. Some writers thought it wouldn't be long before every man, woman, and child was bitten by the golf bug. Between the courses built here during that period and the links of Scotland, there is a striking family resemblance. They are members of the

THIS CLASSIC DESCRIPTION OF LINKSLAND, written by Sir Guy Campbell, a British architect and historian, appeared in the *WORLD ATLAS OF GOLF,* a landmark book that awakened interest in course design when published in 1976.

"British golf was first played over links or 'green fields.' . . . Nature was their architect, and beast and man her contractors. In the formation and overall stabilization of our island coastlines, the sea at intervals of time and distance gradually receded from the higher ground of cliff, bluff, and escarpment from which the tides once flowed and ebbed. And as during the ages, by stages, the sea withdrew, it left a series of sandy wastes in bold ridge and significant furrow, broken and divided by numerous channels . . . dried out by the winds [and] formed into dunes, ridges, and knolls, and denes, gullies, and hollows . . . eventually the whole of these areas became grass-covered [with the] thick, close-growing, hard-wearing sward that is such a feature of true links turf."

same clan. You can take the game out of Scotland, but you can't take Scotland out of the game.

Though I knew that the game had originated in Scotland, I hadn't thought much about the differences between links golf and American golf. I certainly hadn't considered the reasons why our courses had developed so differently, a difference that had only grown more pronounced over the decades. My reaction to links golf was much simpler. Why, I asked myself, don't we have courses like this at home?

Now, twenty years after Bandon Dunes opened, it's apparent that a great many golfers here were asking the same question, because we've witnessed what can be called a links revival. The courses that I've built, working with architects who share my vision, are imbued with the charm and character of the foundational links. They have the seaside locations, the fescue turf, the coastal winds, the design features and shot values of true links courses. People don't come to Bandon Dunes to play the same game they can play at their home courses. They come for the same reason that drew me to the linksland—to play a game that is as close as possible to the one invented by the Scots.

Before I could break ground in America, I had to know something about the original links, and my education began almost as an afterthought on a trip to England. In 1985, Lindy and I went to London to visit Chris and Deedy Ogden, friends and former neighbors from Chicago, and Chris set up a golf trip. His father, Mike, and his son, also Mike, joined us for a trip to Ireland that was immediately christened Three Mikes and a Chris.

Off we went to Royal County Down, Lahinch, and Ballybunion, four Americans folded into a van and speeding along the narrow, winding, terrifying Irish roads. Stone walls, fields of emerald green, fickle weather. I was the best golfer of the bunch, and Chris played mostly to humor his dad. In other words, we were four duffers hacking our way around those challenging courses in wind, mist, sunshine, and rain, sometimes all of those within a few holes. Our weathered caddies were rich with timeless caddy wisdom, rooted in the certainty that a small white ball will inevitably reveal the comedy and tragedy of the human condition.

We stayed at guesthouses or small hotels with creaking floors and antique plumbing. The bathtubs had claw feet and the toilet tanks, mounted high on the wall, had long pull chains. The hosts were delightful and eccentric. The food was plain but hearty. At Lahinch, the ancient barman served us delicious pork cracklins. The Ballybunion clubhouse was a repurposed Quonset hut. We felt as though we were roughing it, but no one missed the luxury and comfort of American golf resorts. On the contrary, the sense of being in a place teeming with local characters and customs made our trip an adventure. The first hole at Ballybunion took us past a cemetery with Celtic crosses—what could be more Irish? A few holes later, we passed a field filled with caravans, or campers, where folks on holiday were sitting out on lawn chairs. Not a sight you'd ever see from the fairways of Pebble Beach or Pinehurst.

As I recall these memories, it seems we might easily have been disoriented and miserable—but we weren't. I was euphoric, as was the senior Ogden, who decided to call it quits after a round at Ballybunion. "I'm ready to retire," he announced. "I have played the greatest course in the world."

That's how I felt, too. Ballybunion is one of the most beloved courses in the world, and one of the most beautiful. Though all true links courses are near the sea, only a few have spectacular holes like the 11th at Ballybunion, a long par-4 with a fairway terraced into billowing seaside dunes. The teeing area juts out over the beach, bringing you right up against the full might and majesty of the North Atlantic.

Was that what won me over, the beauty? Was it the warmth and humor of the people we met at the clubhouses and guesthouses? The caddies? The overall sense of golf as a pursuit that gave meaning and pleasure to every part of the day? Why had we all adopted without a moment's hesitation the mindset that we would play in any kind of weather? What had made us so happy to walk? Why didn't we miss the service and pampering of golf at home? Why did the game here, played with the same implements, feel so ancient and so right?

To put it another way: Where did American golf go wrong?

These and many other questions tugged at me after that Irish trip, and kept tugging on subsequent adventures I had with my regular golfing group. Many of us were classmates from the Nichols School, in Buffalo, and our commissioner, Warren Gelman, organized our trips meticulously. Before we started going to British links courses, we'd visited American clubs and resorts such as Hilton Head and Innisbrook, Firestone and Muirfield Village. The highlight of these extended weekend jaunts was to play a course

OVERLEAF
*The unforgettable 11th at Ballybunion, one of the wonders of links golf*

that had hosted a PGA Tour event. We'd bought into the idea that the tracks where the pros competed for big pots of money had to be the best in the world. Never mind that they were long and relentlessly difficult, with narrow fairways, cavernous bunkers, and numerous water hazards. (I admire the stance of architects Bill Coore and Ben Crenshaw: "We don't do water hazards.") Playing them was like taking an exam that you knew you were doomed to fail but nevertheless had to keep scribbling in your blue book until the bell rang and you were released.

Which led to another question: Since links courses were also difficult, why did I feel cheerful and refreshed after shooting 90 at Ballybunion or Royal Dornoch, as opposed to grumpy and discouraged after shooting the same score at Firestone? On the long summer evenings in Scotland, I wanted to keep on playing until it was too dark to see the ball. At Firestone, even before the round was over, I wanted to slink off the course, have a stiff drink, and forget the whole experience. To admit to myself that I hadn't enjoyed my round on a course designed by Robert Trent Jones, at the time the most acclaimed architect in American golf, felt like a failing on my part.

As I tried to educate myself about the game's design and history, the questions kept multiplying. As is often the case, the conventional wisdom was misleading at best, a convenient justification for doing things the same old way. I became convinced that the heavily engineered courses in the United States weren't designed for golfers like me and my friends. To play them successfully, you had to be able to hit shots that were beyond our abilities— long, straight drives and high, quick-stopping, precise approaches. You had to be able to recover from deep bunkers that gnawed into the greens, and to putt on surfaces as slick as the hood of a car. And yes, you had to stay out of the accursed water hazards. The only people who could manage these feats were pros and a tiny fraction of top amateurs. Why design courses for them? Why inflict misery on everyone else? Who had decreed that a round of golf should be an examination, and the architect should be an examiner intent on exposing the student's every flaw?

Links courses had mostly evolved without architects. If they were created by God, they were built by men—who in the beginning didn't have many tools. The construction was done by hand, with shovel and wheelbarrow. Most of the ridges, hollows, folds, and twists of the ground were left untouched, and golfers had to figure out how to maneuver around the course. Grazing sheep and nibbling rabbits kept the turf open, trimmed,

"IF THERE BE ADDED TO ITS GOLFING CHARMS the charms of all its surroundings—the grand history of St. Andrews and its sacred memories—its delightful air—the song of its numberless larks, which nestle among the whins—the scream of the seabirds flying overhead—the blue sea dotted with a few fishing boats—the noise of its waves—the bay of Eden as seen from the high hole when the tide is full . . . it may truly be said that, probably, no portion of ground of the same size on the whole surface of the globe has afforded so much innocent enjoyment to so many people of all ages from two to eighty-nine, and during so many generations."

—JAMES BALFOUR, describing the links of St. Andrews, 1887

and healthy. The only water hazards were ditches or small streams (burns) that ran through the course. Golf balls were expensive, and the thrifty Scots didn't like to lose them; the most likely place to do so was in the prickly stands of gorse (whins). The keepers of the links did face some of the bunkers with sod to stabilize them, and they built up greens to improve drainage, but the overall effort was to make the links playable for everyone, young and old, crack or duffer. In Scotland, the links were located on commonly owned ground, and the spirit of the game—the national game—was public and inclusive.

The Scots are known as a stern, dour people, but they betray their humor and appetite for amusement in the game they invented. Links golf is meant to be enjoyed.

What soon became apparent was that I was not the only golfer who responded to the call of the links. In truth, I felt as though I was a little late to the party. Every issue of a golf magazine seemed to include another rhapsodic article about yet another traveler's discovery of the joys of the links. On my own trips, the signs of a rapidly developing golf travel industry were hard to miss. Tour operators for traveling golfers had sprung into operation. Larger, more luxurious hotels were being built. New courses opened, and old courses tidied themselves up. After unveiling an impressive new clubhouse, Ballybunion seemed to attract hundreds of overseas members almost overnight. At the best-known links, starting with St. Andrews, tee times had to be made months in advance.

Some of the reasons for this shift in perception were straightforward matters of time and money. In the days of ocean liners, only wealthy golfers could afford the pilgrimage to Scotland, a trip that could last for months. Less expensive air travel had completely changed the calculus: now more and more people could easily get to the British Isles, and they could go for a week or even a weekend. From New York, the flight to Ireland was only a few hours longer than one to Florida. You could board a plane at JFK in the evening, wake up at daybreak at Shannon Airport, and, by eight o'clock, after a full Irish breakfast, be standing on the 1st tee at Ballybunion, miraculously alert and energized. When all the expenses were added up, a links expedition probably cost about the same as a comparable trip to an American resort. If memory serves, the 1985 green fee at Ballybunion was thirty-five Irish pounds, about sixty dollars.

The price wouldn't have mattered, though, if the experience of links golf hadn't touched some nerve. Golfers are sometimes dismissed as self-absorbed, vacuous dullards whose conversation is limited to exhaustive accounts of the shots they played on their most recent round. They can be obsessed with technique, numbers, scoring, equipment, bets, bad bounces—the all-consuming details of the game.

Links golf somehow exists on a different level entirely. It speaks to the inner golfer, and it speaks to the soul. Anyone who doubts this should read *Golf in the Kingdom* by Michael Murphy, a hymn to links golf that has sold over a million copies since its publication in 1971. During the 1980s, it might have been the most ubiquitous golf book in the world, often the only book for sale in pro shops from Myrtle Beach to Pebble Beach. For readers like me, Murphy captured perfectly the strangeness and enchantment of the links experience. As a matter of fact, I was so taken with the book that I used the name of its star character, Shivas Irons, on a bank account that I set up to finance my golf expenses. Except I misspelled it as *Chivas* Irons.

*Golf in the Kingdom* recounts the adventure of Michael Murphy (same as the writer, though this is a novel), a young American who's on his way to India for a year of study. On a detour to the legendary links of Burningbush, in Fife, the "Kingdom" of golf, he falls under the spell of a charismatic pro, Shivas Irons, a golfing genius and a student of the occult. Reading about Murphy's round with Shivas and his dinner with local notables singing the praises of *gowf,* you can almost smell the gorse, breathe in the sea air, and feel in your bones the solid contact of a perfect golf shot.

In form, the book is a vision quest, and golf is the medium through which Murphy seeks meaning, wisdom, and transcendence. (The author once commented on the number of seemingly conservative golfers who'd embraced his work: "Who knew that so many Republicans were mystics at heart?")

Murphy wasn't the first to write such a book. Another of my favorites, *Scotland's Gift: Golf,* published in 1928, is Charles Blair Macdonald's account of his discovery of the game as a young man at St. Andrews and his attempts to transplant it, spirit intact, to America. Many articles and essays about links golf are abbreviated versions of the vision quest. The most eloquent of golf writers, Herbert Warren Wind, wrote lovingly and at length about Royal Dornoch and Ballybunion. More recently, Lorne Rubenstein, Michael Bamberger, and Tom Coyne have become bards of the links, describing this experience so powerfully that their books make even casual golfers want to undertake a quest of their own. The links pilgrimage is a journey for those who want to discover the soul of the game and, as Macdonald said, "find their own soul in the process."

My association with KemperSports dates back to this time when I was not only traveling frequently to the links but also making my first investments in golf. I flirted with buying a tract of land in Virginia's populous Loudon County. I looked up and down the East Coast for suitable venues, chartering helicopters to inspect property on the coast of North Carolina, and even ventured as far as Cuba, where the Russian pilot demanded payment in cash—but that's another story.

One transaction stands out as a symbol, or symptom, of my tentative entry into this new business: I bought a lot in Bloody Point, a highly touted golf community in South Carolina that had everything—marquee architect, oceanfront location, big gates, all the usual trappings of prestige. I never built on that lot, just couldn't pull the trigger, and it took me years to resell it—at a loss, I might add. Bloody Point simply wasn't my kind of place.

What was my kind of place? The answer, it was becoming unavoidably

"FASCINATION IS THE TRUE AND PROPER DISCIPLINE. And gowf is the place to practice fascination. Our feelin's, fantasies, thoughts and muscles, all must join to play. In gowf ye see the essence of what the world itself demands. Inclusion of all our parts, alignment o' them all with one another and with the clubs and with the ball, with all the land we play on and with our playin' partners. The game requires us to join ourselves to the weather, to know the subtle energies and that change each day upon the links and the subtle feelin's of those around us."                                                —SHIVAS IRONS

clear, was Dornoch or Ballybunion. Faraway towns, beautiful seaside links. Remote as they were, I noticed that traveling golfers kept arriving in rental cars, vans, and buses. Americans, Swedes, Germans, Japanese, Koreans. Tears blurred their vision when they arrived at St. Andrews and laid eyes on the Old Course. For golfers from all over the world, the call of the links was evidently irresistible. My entrepreneurial curiosity was fully engaged. Would an American links along the lines of Dornoch or Ballybunion attract the same busloads? Could I or anyone else build such a course?

At first, as I've said, the question itself seemed ridiculous. If nobody had ever built a true links in this country, what made me think I could? I might as well decide that I wanted to become, say, a French Impressionist painter. A particular convergence of historical factors—time, place, culture—was necessary to create the circumstances in which links golf (or Impressionism) could take root and flourish. To replicate those circumstances, I would need a piece of linksland, a tract of sandy, well-drained land that had been rumpled and ridged over the centuries by wind and tides, and was now covered with lean turf that had been conditioned by the grazing of sheep and

the nibbling of rabbits. Furthermore, to create the real thing, I would also have to speak Scots, wear tweed, play *gowf* with hickory shafts and gutta percha balls, and forget the history of the game since 1900—in short, I'd have to channel Old Tom Morris, the patron saint of the links.

This was not a realistic option. Nevertheless, the idea of building a links course had taken hold, and I kept wondering how to go about it. Many traits of the classic links were obviously impossible to reproduce. For example, golf had been played in Scotland for centuries by kings and commoners, and one reason that the Old Course at St. Andrews is so venerated is that it's steeped in history. All golfers feel this the moment they arrive in the Auld Grey Toon. No one can transplant history. In addition, many of the most storied links flow right into the heart of the town, whether at St. Andrews or Dornoch or Carnoustie or North Berwick, and the course has long been an integral part of the community's identity and culture. That wasn't going to happen in any American town.

But other traits might be reproducible. Even if linksland, strictly defined, referred to a specific stretch of the Scottish coast, and even if the geologic

*Sea, sky, and golf— the magnificent view from the 10th hole of Royal Dornoch*

26

WHAT, EXACTLY, CONSTITUTES A LINKS? In 2010 a pair of respected writers, George Peper and Malcolm Campbell, joined forces in an attempt to provide a definitive answer in *TRUE LINKS*, a handsome book that laid out a set of rigorous criteria and offered a list of the 246 courses in the world that met them. Only five courses in North America made the cut. Four of them, I'm proud to say, were courses that I built: Bandon Dunes, Pacific Dunes, and Old Macdonald in Oregon, and Cabot Links in Novia Scotia. I was also a partner in the development of two Australian links, Barnbougle Dunes and Lost Farm.

Full disclosure: I was a consultant for the book. While agreeing with its methods and conclusions, I have to confess that I am not as much of a purist as some of my links-loving friends. To me the links DNA appears to have traveled in complex ways, showing up in many courses that were omitted from the list. They weren't even candidates for inclusion. My working understanding of links golf includes National Golf Links in Long Island, Prairie Dunes in Kansas, Sand Hills in Nebraska, and Sand Valley in Wisconsin, a new Keiser property. Even if they don't have oceans, these courses have the sandy soil, rumpled terrain, fast turf, and other playing qualities of the ancient links. In this book, I'm going to call them inland links.

conditions that sculpted the linksland spanned centuries, I had played enough links courses to know that there was no uniform standard or template. The dunes on Irish links are generally larger than those in Scotland. Some courses, like St. Andrews, are quite flat, while others, like nearby Gullane, are hilly. Some are treeless, while others have groves; some are marshy, or rocky, or drained by ditches, or crisscrossed by stone walls—but these features don't identify or disqualify them.

In short, links terrain is varied, and I thought there had to be places in the United States with the two essential qualities—a seaside location and sandy soil. My favorite links courses, Ballybunion and Royal Dornoch, have glorious views of the sea, and the golf is infused with a sense of space and infinity. As for sandy soil, I liked how links turf felt underfoot, and I knew that the firm, fast playing conditions of the links could be reproduced somewhere in America.

But would Americans be willing to play such courses? They were used to soft courses that encouraged aerial golf, or target golf. The challenge was to hit the ball high, often over a hazard, to a safe, receptive target, whereas links courses were best played close to the ground. To keep the ball from being buffeted by the ocean winds, a golfer needed to hit shots with a lower trajectory, letting them bounce along the ground toward the target. Though bump-and-runs are in some respects easier to execute, it takes a fine hand to play them accurately. Plus, these low, running shots can take funny hops and bad bounces, so better players—those expecting to shoot a low score—generally prefer to play through the air. By definition, links golf is not fair, and American golfers had learned to expect fairness. One of the essential phrases in Scottish golf is "the rub of the green"—acknowledgment that unpredictable bounces are to be expected, and accepted without complaint.

An even more fundamental question: Would Americans walk? Links golf is a walking game. The Scots and Irish have always sneered at golf carts, which they call "buggies," pronounced *boogies*. It's estimated that only 30 percent of the rounds in the United States are played on foot. Carts certainly didn't belong on the course that I hoped to build, but would an American links be required to allow them? Could a course claim to be authentic if carts were trundling down the fairways?

My fantasy links resembled Royal Dornoch, where golfers walked, with or without caddies, and a sparkling wind blew off a foam-flecked sea. Like most grand schemes, mine was vast and changeable, varying from one overseas golf trip to the next, influenced by the courses I'd played most recently.

Yet the core idea had taken root. Golf instinct, business instinct, artistic instinct, cultural instinct—they all chimed in to tell me that Americans would embrace a links course.

## 2

# My Second Career

*Before he established Bandon Dunes in Oregon, recycled-products impresario Mike Keiser created this delightful and devious nine on 68 acres of densely wooded sand dunes off Lake Michigan, just north of the Indiana border. Utilizing the services of architects Dick and Tim Nugent of Chicago as well as mixing in his own armchair-architect ideas, Keiser produced the Pine Valley of nine-hole courses, with vast expanses of exposed sand edging fairways that pitch and roll as if in a storm off the lake, and smallish greens tucked atop sand spits and behind leafy trees.*

—RON WHITTEN, *Golf Digest*

*Dunes Club, No. 6*

**M**Y SECOND CAREER has now lasted longer than my first. It began in 1985 when a realtor in New Buffalo, Michigan, urged me to buy a tract of sixty acres in order to keep developers from putting up a wall of condos near our lakefront house. A perfect, low-key, weekend getaway for Lindy and me and our kids, New Buffalo was about two hours from our apartment in North Chicago, and we liked the place just as it was. The asking price for the land was so low—$315,000—that I did a double take. Within a few days I made a cash offer. I've found that cash without contingencies is a hard offer for sellers to resist. Further, I like the clarity—cash offers require you to work through the complications of a transaction and make a genuine commitment.

Soon we had a new family activity: wilderness golf. In the evenings, we'd all walk over to the new Keiser domain, choose a tree in the distance, and try to hit it with a golf ball. My companions were my three oldest children, Michael, Leigh, and Dana, and sometimes Lindy. Before long I was trimming and thinning the trees to make playing corridors; designing rudimentary golf holes, in other words. The property was heavily wooded, but with a central ridge and a series of smaller humps, hollows, and slopes, it looked like golfing terrain. When the leaf mold and ground cover was scraped away, the soil beneath was light and sandy. The better I got to know this scruffy, scrubby piece of terrain, the more it seemed to resemble Pine Valley.

The comparison felt outrageous. In my mind, Pine Valley was a shrine of American golf, one of the most original, beautiful, and fascinating courses I'd ever played. Thanks to a former teammate from Amherst, Tom Sturges, I'd had this opportunity several times in the late 1970s and early 1980s. Tom was able to get us on Merion, too, and the mighty triumvirate of Shinnecock Hills, Maidstone, and National Golf Links out on Long Island. At Amherst, we'd played several historic and highly ranked courses, but I was too intent on my own game to notice much about them.

Now, as I made my way around these American masterpieces, the balance had shifted, and I had a hard time focusing on my shots. I was far more interested—amazed, really—by how they were designed and built. They were somehow more inviting than more modern courses, but why? What gave them their character, their aura, their appeal?

*Pine Valley, No. 2. With the expanse of untended sand, shaggy rough, hilly terrain, and row after row of gnarly bunkers, this par-4 carved out of the woods was the kind of hole we wanted to create at the Dunes Club.*

To understand my attraction and to learn something about how golf courses were conceived, designed, analyzed, and evaluated, I started reading about their history and architecture. The book on my bedside table was *100 Greatest Golf Courses*, a compilation by the editors of *Golf Digest*. One of the editors, Ron Whitten, soon became my intellectual guide. He was a cowriter of an encyclopedic volume called *The Architects of Golf*, a massive work that attempted to list every architect and every course on his résumé. Ron's descriptions of courses I'd barely heard of made me want to see them.

It's a strange and costly addiction, this urge to visit courses all over the world. I suppose it's no different from the angler's desire to cast a fly in the great salmon rivers, or a traveler's to stay in the grand hotels. In those years, though, it would've been more convenient to play my golf at home. I still wasn't a member of a club in the Chicago area. As a family man and the head of a growing business, Recycled Paper Greeting (RPG), I really didn't have time for golf—but I made time. Many days I left Chicago on an early flight to

Philadelphia or Islip, Long island, and flew home late that night. Many golfers catch the bug when they first discover the game; they can't stop thinking about their swing, their footwork, their weight shift, and they rehearse their shoulder turn while waiting for the elevator. I'd had that bug myself, but this was something different—an intellectual curiosity, an awareness that the game had a scope and complexity I'd only begun to explore.

Until these adventures started, I hadn't paid much attention to course rankings. I knew that Pine Valley was ranked high on the Top 100 lists, usually in the first or second spot, along with the other classics I'd been visiting. They'd been built a century ago, in the first burst of excitement as America embraced the Scottish game. Decades later, they still dominated the lists. Even as the lists proliferated, with several magazines launching their own ranking systems and tinkering with the criteria, those courses retained their lofty spots. Down in the lower brackets, newer courses appeared, and there was plenty of churn and turnover. But in the stratosphere, the rankings were almost as constant as the constellations. Any avid golfer is familiar with the roster: Pine Valley, Augusta National, Pebble Beach, Cypress Point, Shinnecock Hills, Merion, Winged Foot.

What did they have in common? My experience at RPG had taught me the value of lists. They might not be perfect, but they do indicate what people like and suggest some of the complicated reasons for their preferences. The rankings told me that most other golfers responded as I did to these time-honored courses, that they recognized the artfulness of the design, that they had the same feelings of expectation and adventure as their rounds progressed. In ways they might not be able to articulate, they were aware that the courses captured the flow and rhythm of the game, presenting a sequence of surprising, stirring holes that fit together in a pattern that felt right. As you played any one of them, you were passing through a landscape that had been transformed into a work of art. Even if you didn't notice every single detail of your surroundings—how could you?—you were aware of some shifting of inner gears, of leaving behind ordinary cares and worries. Here golf transported you to a different realm, a different state of mind and awareness. Yes, it was still a game, but it had the power to inspire, to exhilarate, to make you forget the usual ticking of the clock. You were playing golf, and that was all that mattered.

The men who built these iconic American courses I regarded as visionaries, artists, and heroes. Drifting ever more deeply into golf, I was still far from imagining exactly what kind of opportunities, if any, this golf business might hold for an entrepreneur whose tastes ran to courses that were a century old.

But that property I'd bought just down the road had set me thinking. What if I built a nine-hole course on that land? Little by little, as I discussed it with friends, the idea took hold. When I realized that sixty acres wasn't big enough, I bought an adjacent twenty acres. Folly or not, I was going to get my hands dirty and build a golf course—specifically, a little tribute to Pine Valley.

I have trouble recalling how I managed to pay enough attention to Recycled Paper Greetings to keep the business on track. Lindy claims that I'm good at compartmentalizing, and during this period I must have been able, when necessary, to put a lid on my growing obsession with golf.

RPG, the company I founded with Lindy and my college roommate, Phil Friedmann, was making us rich, though we'd thrown together our business plan in only a few days. The idea for the company came to me, literally, in a dream at the end of a winter in Vail, Colorado, and within weeks we were launched on what proved to be a lifelong trajectory.

Lindy and I had gone to Vail as a kind of last hurrah. I'd just served a three-year hitch in the Navy, stationed for most of it in Virginia, where Lindy completed her BS in chemistry at William and Mary. After my discharge in January 1971, we had a few months on our hands. I was planning to enter Harvard Business School in September, and since we both loved to ski, Lindy and I decided to spend the rest of the winter as ski bums. We rented an apartment in Vail, supported ourselves with menial jobs, and skied only when the weather was perfect.

Phil Friedmann was jealous. He, too, liked skiing, and was signed up to enter law school at NYU that fall. Having taken an extended round-the-world trip after graduating from Amherst, he was as apprehensive as I was about going back to school. Late in the season, he came out to see us in Vail, and we commiserated with each other about having to return to the classroom. Lindy had a different perspective; she grew up in a family of brilliant academics and looked forward to spending time in Cambridge. Phil and I felt the walls closing in. We saw professional school as a threat to our newfound sovereignty.

On our last night in Colorado, I dreamed that we started a business based on the use of 100 percent recycled paper. I wasn't even sure that such a product existed. That dream surely reflected my growing anxiety during those final weeks in Vail. I just couldn't imagine myself sitting in a lecture hall for the next three years, taking notes and writing case studies. Taking the dream as an omen, we decided then and there to follow our instincts, or at least try to. Where would we base our business? We ruled out Buffalo, my hometown, and decided on Chicago, because Phil's mother owned a house there and we could crash for a while without paying rent.

Lindy and I packed up the car with all our belongings, left Colorado in early April, and drove to Chicago. By April 21, 1971—the first anniversary of Earth Day—Recycled Paper Greetings was up and running. There were three original partners: Phil, Lindy, and me. We'd decided that whatever our product was, it would be made on recycled paper. Environmentalism was gathering force as a political movement, one that we believed in. After exploring the idea of printing textbooks, we learned that it would take years to get this product to market, and we didn't have years. We were in a hurry. So we went with greeting cards. Phil and I put up $500 each, and my father gave us $5,000 in seed money. Soon, we all moved into a two-bedroom apartment—yes, Phil too—and Lindy got a job as a research assistant to pay the rent. For the first two years, she was RPG's only breadwinner, bringing home a paycheck while Phil and I tried to coax our start-up off the ground.

We thought, correctly, that an environmentally minded business would attract favorable coverage in the press. Turn wastepaper into Christmas cards! But we quickly learned that consumers didn't give a damn what kind of paper their cards were printed on. The giants in the card industry at the time, Hallmark and American Greetings, dominated the market in traditional cards—loaded with sentiment, lots of hearts and flowers. We had no desire to compete with them head-on, and RPG would have been crushed if we'd tried. No, our niche would be as a maker of witty, humorous, whimsical cards. Each of our cards told a story, often an irreverent one. The big companies were looking for emotions and tears; we were hoping for smiles and laughter. Instead of working with in-house designers, we relied on freelance artists and writers, and soon we had thousands of cards,

*Our logo at RPG—the crown of a green tree— underscored our environmental mission.*

and many hippo returns

*Sandy Boynton, whose talents have led her into a multitude of creative endeavors, remains a good friend, and sometimes joins me for a round of golf at Bandon Dunes.*

literally, to choose from. RPG cards didn't all look alike—the graphics were fresh, creative, diverse. The press loved us, as we'd hoped, and we did just well enough to keep our heads above water as we kept paddling. Our first office was that little apartment, and our secretary, Lindy's sister Andrea, had a desk in what had once been a closet. In our second year, RPG made a grand total of $40,000.

Then, at a trade show in New York in 1975, we met Sandy Boynton, with whom we hit it off immediately. She was still a Yale student, obviously a creative dynamo, a woman of huge talent and conviction. Brilliant and original, she loved words, puns, stories, and animals. Other companies had turned down her cards; they just didn't get her. We loved her work and immediately gave her a contract. Sandy designed an offbeat birthday card, Hippo Birdie Two Ewes, whose drawing shows a hippopotamus, a tweety bird, and two ewes wearing pointed birthday hats—and it became a phenomenon that has sold over ten million copies. With Sandy's artistic firepower, RPG soared to new levels of success. By the mid-1980s we were billing $100 million annually. My advice to all young entrepreneurs: find a genius like Sandy Boynton.

As RPG grew, Phil and I began to identify our separate roles. He did most of the traveling and marketing, and I stayed in Chicago and chose most of the cards. Within the company, we were sometimes known as Mr. Outside and Mr. Inside, but that's as far as it went. We avoided titles and exact job descriptions. In fact, when asked to state our job titles on some official document, we balked. If forced to choose, we thought we might like to be the Baron and the Earl. Titles set up hierarchies, and that was something we both distrusted. In the end, we both called ourselves vice presidents.

RPG did adopt some administrative policies, but Phil and I believed in a fluid, open-ended, unstructured mode of operation. Our product was a creative product, and we wanted our company culture to encourage creativity. Because we used recycled paper, we'd always attracted motivated employees who wanted more than a paycheck from their job. They liked working for a company that had an environmental mission.

Most days, I left my shoes at the office door and worked in my stocking feet. Whenever possible, we conducted staff meetings with everyone standing—it kept the meetings short and to the point. Our offices were in a building that had once been a dairy, and I liked to show visitors the ramps on which the cows were moved from one level to another; on damp days there was still a faint whiff of the barn. Our Art Room, which also served as our main conference room, was furnished with folding tables and canvas director's chairs. Wasting money on corporate pomp was not our style.

I don't want to leave the impression that RPG was a loose, ragtag operation. In that Art Room, the walls were fitted with racks that displayed several hundred cards, face out, on what we called the Best Seller Wall, or the Money Wall. Long before our competitors, we used a sophisticated digital system that enabled us to chart each and every card—number of units shipped, length of time in circulation, previous sales rank, and so on. With this information, we could monitor buying tastes with precision and keep our retail displays filled with best sellers. The Art Room and the Money Wall—there, in a nutshell, you have the paradox of a business that makes and sells an artistic product. The same paradox applies to the golf trade.

RPG's runaway success didn't escape the attention of the investment bankers. To them we looked quaint, disorganized, and highly profitable, and they soon came knocking on the door. They encouraged us to think bigger, spinning fantasies of conglomerates with RPG at the center, surrounded by a host of satellite companies. This was tempting. I was still a young man, and I knew that before long I'd be ready to do something different. RPG had more than 140 employees in Chicago, an extensive network of artists, and a national sales force. We were an established brand. But as the administrative and managerial requirements kept growing, it became clearer and clearer that I liked starting things more than running them.

Eventually, I realized that I didn't want to become a corporate overlord, either. Make a widget that people want to buy—that's the essence of old-fashioned American capitalism. That's what we'd done at RPG, and it has nothing to do with mergers, acquisitions, leveraged buyouts, corporate restructuring, and the other activities that are the bread and butter of investment bankers. Financial concerns often seem abstract to me, and I've relied on colleagues to decipher contracts and spreadsheets. I'm far more at home with tangible products, objects that can be seen and felt and touched, and much prefer dealing with people rather than documents. My goal has never been to amass a great fortune or to see my name on the Forbes 400. These accomplishments don't last—but golf courses do. The bankers wanted me to diversify the company, but I decided to diversify myself. Deep down, what I wanted to make was a great golf course.

RPG was profitable enough for me to do what I wanted, and I decided to build a golf course that people would still be playing a hundred years from now. It felt like the right decision at the time, and it still does. I've never been prone to second-guessing myself. What kept me awake at night wasn't the fear that I'd made a bad decision but that I wouldn't be able to build a golf course as good as the one I imagined. And the one I imagined was Pine Valley.


Reading about George Crump, the man behind Pine Valley, helped bolster my confidence. Like many leading figures of golf design in early twentieth-century America, Crump had gravitated to the game after making his mark in another business—just as I was contemplating doing. To name just a few others who fit this profile: Hugh Wilson, famously associated with Merion, was a refugee from the insurance business; Alister Mackenzie, designer of Cypress Point and Augusta National, had trained as a doctor; Perry Maxwell, the genius of Prairie Dunes, was a banker who began anew by building a nine-holer on a piece of property he'd acquired (sound familiar?); and Charles Blair Macdonald, sometimes called the Godfather of American Golf, didn't really hit his stride as an architect until after he'd spent decades as a stockbroker.

These luminaries didn't approach their work in golf as a career. They stood at the threshold of American golf when the game seemed exactly that—a game, a pastime, a sporting pursuit in a country that was just getting rich enough to offer time for leisure. Golf was not then (or now) a particularly lucrative business, at least not for the owner of the course. At Pinehurst, Sea Island, Shawnee On Delaware, and other resorts that sprang up early in the century, golf was a loss leader—an attraction that would lure paying guests. Similarly, courses built in residential communities were built to help the developer sell houses, not as profitable operations by themselves.

Most notable American courses of this era—the Golden Age courses that are still revered—belonged to private clubs. Golf was seen as an "adjunct of civilization," as Andrew Carnegie put it, and the wealthy expected to pay for it in the same spirit as they paid for other pastimes. Caught up in the excitement of establishing the ancient game in a new setting, they aspired to create courses that would rival any in Great Britain. The opening of National Golf Links in 1911 was a statement that American golf had come into its own; designed by C. B. Macdonald and heralded as an ideal course, the "National"—talk about an ambitious name!—set a high bar for American golf architecture.

Crump and his many golf companions in Philadelphia were keenly aware of the National and dazzling new courses being built elsewhere in the country. Crump himself was a fine golfer, and his friends were pillars of the game in Philadelphia who had come to believe that the courses in their city were outdated and inferior, with the result that their best players were at a disadvantage in serious competitions. These men became avid students of golf design and supported new projects in their region, with the goal of creating courses of championship caliber. Today, this group is known as the Philadelphia School of Golf Architecture, and Pine Valley is part of their legacy.

George Crump was the prime mover behind Pine Valley. A scion of the family that owned the fashionable Colonnade Hotel in Philadelphia, he'd quietly nurtured his dream to build the course that he and his friends had so often imagined. In 1910, two years after the death of his spirited wife, Belle, Crump took an extended trip to study the links and heathland courses; for budding architects of the Golden Age, the journey to Scotland was an educational requirement. Back home, on a bird hunt, he discovered his ideal site in Clementon, New Jersey, fifteen miles east of Philadelphia. Rugged, isolated, covered with scrub oak and pine, the property had the sandy soil deemed necessary for first-class golf turf. From the outset, the course was recognized as having extraordinary potential, and more than a hundred of Crump's friends contributed to the project.

After acquiring the land, Crump set up a tent so that he could live there as the clearing got under way. Progress reports appeared regularly in the newspapers and sporting journals. When Henry Colt, the preeminent English architect, visited in 1913, he too spent a week in a tent, emerging from the woods to declare that Pine Valley promised to be one of the greatest inland courses in the world. In the following months, Crump welcomed a steady stream of visitors, including C. B. Macdonald, Hugh Wilson, George

Thomas, and A. W. Tillinghast, and invited them to share their comments and ideas, many of which he incorporated into the design. The exact authorship of individual holes has long been a matter of speculation, but the spirit of the course—its beauty, its difficulty, its detail—is beyond doubt the legacy of George Crump, hailed posthumously as the "master man" of Pine Valley.

According to the coroner's report, Crump died of a "Gun shot wound. Head Suicide. Sudden." While no one will ever know why he took his life, the *Philadelphia Evening Ledger* hinted at financial disappointment and distress. As a developer, I know all too well how the building of a golf course can come to dominate every waking moment; it becomes an existential mission, and any setback feels devastating. Pine Valley had been scheduled to open for play in 1914, but massively costly construction and agronomic problems kept causing delays, and by 1918 Crump was broke. "Into it he put $250,000 of his own money. . . . It was to have been his life work, and the tragedy of it is that he did not live to see it completed."

Though I wasn't prepared to camp out in a tent, I saw in Crump's approach a model that was close to my own preferences. He was hands-on. He'd gone to Great Britain to study the best courses and was determined to build one just as good. As the owner, he could have designed Pine Valley himself but chose to work collegially, seeking the advice of friends and experts. He was modest and smart enough to pay attention to their suggestions.

I took special note of Crump's ability to involve others in his project because I like a collaborative working environment, and also because I was trying to determine my own role in such an endeavor. During my rounds of wilderness golf, I'd been designing imaginary holes in New Buffalo. Nobody else would hire me to design a golf course, but since I owned the land, why not hire myself? Did I have the makings of a genuine golf architect? When Ron Whitten, the architecture editor at *Golf Digest*, conducted the first Armchair Architect contest in 1987, I spent hours drawing up a hole to submit. I thought I had a chance of winning—and didn't find out until much later that mine was one of twenty-two thousand entries, along with a drawing by a youngster named Eldrick Woods, later known as Tiger.

Meanwhile, I had sought out Dick Nugent, who was then at the peak of his career after designing Kemper Lakes, which was scheduled to host the 1989 PGA Championship. Even though he belonged to an era when many architects cultivated a recognizable "signature" style, Dick was open-minded and restlessly innovative. After a trip to Ireland, he designed the Golf Club of Illinois using many links features on a layout routed over mostly flat farmland; it could hardly have been more different from Kemper Lakes, noted for its threatening water hazards. I "interviewed" him by playing golf with him at several of Chicago's most respected courses. A Chicagoan born and bred, Dick had an intimate knowledge of many of these old tracks because he'd caddied at them. The moment I was sure that we could work together came at Shoreacres, when I asked, "Why do I like this course so much?"

"Because it breaks all the rules," he replied.

Together we made several trips to study Pine Valley, not only from a strategic and aesthetic point of view. Maintenance also presents a unique challenge when the groomed surfaces of fairway and green must interface with the rugged, sandy scrub. Then we crisscrossed my land in New Buffalo, looking for the best routing. Dick and I drew our plans independently. Since I like doglegs, I included several, leaving myself a daunting problem at the 9th hole. To bring the last hole back to the clubhouse, I proposed a double dogleg that went out for 220 yards, turned at a right angle and continued for another 200 yards, then took another right angle for the approach to the green. Dick took one look at this drawing and said, in a kindly fashion, that it was a disaster.

We used his routing, of course. I christened this maiden project the Dunes Club. The construction supervisor, Pete Sinnott, became a good friend. Another friend, Larry Booth, an architect, designed an exquisite clubhouse, a light, airy, shingled, Lilliputian building that nevertheless had enough room for a couple of mammoth showers. One final touch, also a nod to Pine Valley, was to make the entrance as unobtrusive as possible. Most people drive right by without realizing that there is an entryway behind the wire construction fence and a golf course behind the screen of trees. The Dunes Club has been called the hidden course and the secret course, and that's fine by me. The idea was to make this place feel like a sanctuary, a hideaway for people who wanted to escape urban pressures and decompress for a day.

Word about the Dunes Club began to leak out after it opened for play in the spring of 1989. Local raters were the first to rave about it, and Ron Whitten himself—for me the ultimate authority—paid a visit. Citing the Pine Valley influence, he described the Dunes Club as a "throwback to an earlier era" and called it the best nine-hole course in the country.

The accolades kept rolling in. I was thrilled, and I knew how useful my experience at RPG had been. Instead of competing with much larger, well-established properties, again I'd chosen a niche. I hadn't bothered with a grand, sprawling clubhouse, and the Dunes Club wasn't exactly convenient for most people to get to. Instead of golf carts, I lined up a few locals to serve as caddies. The lunch menu was burgers or bratwurst. Most golfers ate outside, on a shady terrace, where birds flitted between feeders hung from the oaks and maples. The whole place was simple, relaxed, comfortable, a radical alternative to high-profile clubs much closer to Chicago.

Honestly, I hadn't given much thought to running the club as a business. I just wanted to build it. I expected to have a tiny membership, or to absorb the entire expense if nobody wanted to join. But a few neighbors peeked over the fence, liked what they saw, and began a membership that has grown steadily over the years.

I'd found a second career that suited me right down to the ground. This calling combined design and entrepreneurship. The office was often outside, in the open air. The product was tangible. Decisions had immediate results. The golf architect, I realized by looking over Dick's shoulder, not only had to come up with drawings and designs for golf holes; he had to deal with drainage, irrigation, and turf conditions, technical subjects that I preferred to leave to experts. The developer's role was like that of a movie producer—he assembled a team and tried to make sure that all the working parts meshed. He acquired the land, hired the key players, shaped the concept, obtained the permits. After the architect and the construction crew had completed their work, the developer continued to shape the overall experience in ways I'd never really considered—choosing the signage, selecting the logo, hiring the pro and the staff, approving the clubhouse design, cultivating community relations, and casting the decisive vote in everything from the caddy program to the lunch menu to the size of the showerheads.

By the time the Dunes Club opened in 1989, my friend Howard McKee was in Oregon scouting out oceanfront property. I knew I wanted to build another course. It would be another "throwback" course, and this time I wanted to go all the way back to the game's origins.

# BANDON DUNES
## golf resort

1999 **BANDON DUNES**, 6,736 yards, par 72
designed by David Kidd
#44, *Golf Magazine* Top 100 Courses in the U.S. 2020–2021

2001 **PACIFIC DUNES**, 6,633 yards, par 71
Tom Doak
#19, *Golf Magazine* Top 100 Courses in the U.S. 2020–2021

2004 **BANDON TRAILS**, 6,788 yards, par 71
Bill Coore and Ben Crenshaw
#38, *Golf Magazine* Top 100 Courses in the U.S. 2020–2021

2010 **OLD MACDONALD**, 6,944 yards, par 72
Tom Doak and Jim Urbina
#66, *Golf Magazine* Top 100 Courses in the U.S. 2020–2021

2012 **THE PRESERVE**, 1,609 yards, 13-hole par-3 course
Bill Coore and Ben Crenshaw

2020 **SHEEP RANCH**, 6,636 yards, par 72
Bill Coore and Ben Crenshaw
#80, *Golf Magazine* Top 100 Courses in the U.S. 2020–2021
Winner of *Golf Digest*'s 2020 Best New Course Award

3

# Bandon at Twenty

*Bandon at twenty is Mike Keiser's vision, living and breathing.*

—JOSH LESNIK

OVER THE COURSE OF THREE DECADES, I've been to Bandon hundreds of times. Most visits are midweek, three days and two nights, and they begin in Chicago, where I rise early and take a cab to Midway Airport. Wheels up at 7 a.m. I often travel with a contingent from KemperSports or other business associates, and the outbound flight is a three-hour working session. After crossing the Rockies and flying directly over Crater Lake, a perfect sphere of pure blue, our approach to the North Bend airport takes us down the edge of the continent and over the miles and miles of Oregon Dunes, one of the most unspoiled sections of coastline in the Lower 48.

Then we load into a rental car for the half-hour drive to Bandon on Highway 101, passing the mostly empty lumberyards, the hardscrabble town of Coos Bay, the evergreen forests. The urban clamor of Chicago has been left far, far behind. I always feel the old excitement as the Lodge comes into view and the land opens up. The air is fresh as champagne, golf fills the horizon, and this place still feels like a vision—wild, beautiful, and extraordinary, a place that shouldn't exist but somehow does.

It surprises me every time.

The story of Bandon Dunes has been told from many different perspectives in articles, videos, podcasts, blogs, and books. That's as it should be; thousands of people have their own Bandon stories. When I began thinking of how I wanted to present the first twenty years of the resort, I realized this was not exclusively my story and that I wanted to let others who've shaped the concept and character of the place speak for themselves.

I have to begin with Howard McKee, my original Bandon partner, a non-golfer who nevertheless embraced the project as passionately as I did. From the start, our friendship was improbable. We both lived in Lincoln Park, a neighborhood just north of downtown Chicago. Our children attended the same school, and our wives, Lindy and Kennon, had become friends. Though Howard and I were on opposite ends of the political spectrum, we were both conservationists and we spent more than a few Saturday mornings in New Buffalo, arguing and lopping branches off the trees.

*With my friend and partner Howard McKee, who regarded his efforts at Bandon as "soul work"*

He was an architect and land planner whose career had followed a very different trajectory from mine; during several decades with the international firm of Skidmore, Owings & Merrill, he'd been involved in large, high-profile, hugely complicated, and expensive urban projects. In Chicago, he'd tried without success to unite the city's major entities—businesses, government agencies, museums, universities, and foundations—in order to host a World's Fair. In the late 1980s, he left SOM and started looking for something different, something meaningful. He was considering a return to Oregon, where he'd worked for many years, and possibly devoting himself to a year of reading the classics. He was looking for a project that he could regard as "soul work."

One night at dinner, after listening to me describe the kind of golf course I was dreaming about, Howard challenged me to draw up a list of my requirements for a suitable property. A few weeks later, I gave him a couple of handwritten pages that listed my desires in bullet form: five to ten thousand acres, sandy soil, breathtaking scenery, diversity of environment, preferably on a coast or with coastal areas. Howard thought the list was audacious, but it was exactly the kind of daring endeavor he was ready to pursue. Within a few days, he sent me a proposal outlining a systematic approach to finding the sort of land I wanted, and he became my West Coast scout.

At the time, I'd been looking for property on the East Coast. I was willing to extend my search, but I knew nothing at all about Oregon. Howard had spent a good portion of his career in Portland, and he still owned land on the coast, near Cascade Head. Unbeknownst to either of us at the time, the dunesland of Oregon's south coast offered the ideal soil, topography, and climate for links golf. Howard, the non-golfer, had tilted my search in exactly the right direction. How serendipitous is that?

One Saturday morning a couple of years later, out of the blue I got a phone call from a realtor in Gold Beach, Oregon. Her name was Annie Huntamer, and she had a parcel she thought I might be interested in. She didn't know Howard, but his activity had touched off a chain of associations, and I remember thinking at the time that the land I'd been chasing for years had found me.

Serendipity. Howard was a rationalist who believed in the power of karma, an intellectual who had a deep respect for mystery and the unknown. A few years after Bandon Dunes opened, he gave a talk to the resort staff on the subject of serendipity.

**HOWARD MCKEE:** To this day, I continue to be amazed how a series of unexpected circumstances miraculously came together to produce what can only be described as a phenomenon. We all are part of this amazing creation that we experience as Bandon Dunes. Serendipity is defined as the faculty of happening upon or making fortunate discoveries when not in search of them. One might think of it as being in the right place at the right time. The Swiss psychologist Carl Jung referred to a similar phenomenon as synchronicity. These events are outside our control, are not predictable, and cannot simply be explained as chance. They are too meaningful and purposeful to be simply accidental.

**MK:** As the Bandon project grew, so did Howard's role. He became my partner—not an investor but a sweat-equity partner, whose training and expertise as architect and land planner added value to the development. At first, I don't think that either of us realized just how much value he created; as Howard pointed out, nearly all of us involved in making Bandon Dunes were first-timers. No one—not Howard, not David Kidd, the golf architect, not Josh Lesnik, the first general manager, and certainly not me, the developer—had any experience in setting up a destination resort. Our "method" often resembled a group grope. Howard always countered my impatience by pointing out that at every stage of the process we were making sure that we were doing it our way, not following a by-the-book formula that had been used elsewhere.

I was in charge of the golf, and Howard was in charge of almost everything else—the buildings, roads, and paths, the landscaping and parking, the furnishings and fittings in the guest rooms. His abiding principle was to discover, preserve, and express the genius loci, the spirit of the place. Long before "authenticity" was a buzzword, Howard was insisting on it in every single detail of the development, from the Celtic knots in the Lodge's wrought-iron doors to the native cedar used in the window trim of the rooms throughout. The Lodge was designed in the shingle style of the Northwest, all buildings were carefully sited to blend with the landscape, and the master plan called for the creation of a village—a central gathering place. I had started out with the intention of building a golf course; Howard taught me to think of Bandon Dunes in broader terms, as an exercise in place-making.

Howard also directed the campaign to obtain permits for the development, a process that lasted for five years. Oregon is notorious for its strict land-use laws. The previous owners of the Bandon property had also wanted to build a golf resort, but they'd been unable to win approval—which is why they sold me 1,215 acres for the bargain price of $2.4 million. As it happened, Howard, during his time in Portland, had been involved in drafting those same laws, and he developed a detailed, long-term plan to win a special exception to build a destination resort at Bandon. An essential part of the strategy was to win local support, especially from environmental groups—which he'd belonged to when he lived in Oregon—and the Native American tribes that had once occupied the land and still had certain rights. Anyone who spent ten minutes with Howard came away convinced of his sincere determination to honor the land.

DON IVY, cultural resources coordinator for the Coquille Indian tribe: This was never about money. It was about bringing a vision into reality. Howard and Mike were concerned about legacy, and once you're there, a whole different set of values comes into play. The question is whether you're going to build something that will last. Before them, the Euro-American settlers came only to exploit the resources of the place. First they looked for gold, then they logged off the timber. They mined for coal and they looked for chromium. They put their animals on the fields where the camas grew, and the camas disappeared. It was replaced by the gorse that was of no use to anyone. And then they put up the windmills—they were going to harvest the wind. By then the only people who used the place were the ones who came in on their ATVs and ripped up the dunes even more. This land was completely depleted and degraded when Mike bought it. But now it serves many of the same purposes it did when the Indians came here. It's a place for people to gather and visit, and many come in search of renewal and sanctuary. They can find it here because the land has been healed.

MK: Howard was meticulous, thorough, and tough. He tried not to leave anything to chance, and he didn't show his full hand in dealings with state agencies. He knew they'd be looking for flaws in our plans, and he always saved some of his bargaining chips. The environmental impact study that he put together was encyclopedic—he was going to beat them at their own game. In the end, though, when we finally got our approval, Howard was convinced it was the gorse that made the difference. The gorse!

This adds another layer to the theme of serendipity. The gorse was originally brought to Bandon in the 1850s by an Irishman who called himself Lord Bennett, and he used the plant to stabilize the sandy soil and to remind him of the Auld Sod. Since gorse is associated with the links courses of the British Isles—where it is called "the whins," as noted above—I was initially delighted to find it growing in abundance. I took it as a sign that the land was preordained for golf. However, my fondness waned quickly once I discovered what a godawful nuisance gorse is, thorny, dense, and relentlessly invasive. In the spring, it puts on a display of beautiful, canary-yellow flowers that belie its ability to rip the clothes off the back of anyone who tries to walk through it.

I also learned that in the climate of southern Oregon, gorse becomes highly flammable during the dry summers. If a fire gets started, the plants combust like torches that have been drenched with gasoline. The town of Bandon was all but destroyed by a deadly, gorse-fueled fire in 1936. Since then, several other fires had threatened the town. Before I came along, the Nature Conservancy had considered buying the property—and decided against it because the cost of clearing the gorse was so prohibitive. As part of Howard's presentation to the Planning Commission, he made the case that by planting grass and maintaining open fairways, we would help control the gorse and reduce the fire hazard. And that, Howard believed, was what ultimately tipped the balance in our favor and won us our approval.

That was the kind of irony that Howard relished. After all his labors, all his tabbed and indexed studies, the case came down to . . . gorse abatement. As I write these words, I can see Howard's smile and hear his full-throated laugh.

The property I bought in 1991 came with a bonus—a caretaker named Shorty Dow, who billed himself as the "mayor, governor, and sheriff" of Bandon. Shorty had lived there for decades, and he was our original guide, cutting the trails and leading us to spots of special interest. In his own way,

Shorty was a conservationist. He made an inventory of local wildlife, and in his truck he carried a pistol that he used to run off trespassers, poachers, ATVers, and anyone else he saw as a threat. As my friend Bob Peele said, "Shorty is one of the few people who could talk to the president of the United States and the Speaker of the House and dominate the conversation." Shorty liked to entertain out-of-towners at his house, and his wife, Charlotte, always served us her delicious pies. It was a scene that Shorty described as "a bunch of millionaires sitting on the steps." When he passed away in 2016, a plaque was erected in his memory on the spot where he first showed me the full sweep of the Bandon property. For almost five years I'd been looking for the right place to build my course, and when Shorty led me over Back Ridge, I knew instantly that I'd found it.

The force of his personality comes through clearly in his business card.

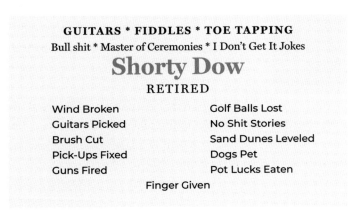

**GUITARS * FIDDLES * TOE TAPPING**
Bull shit * Master of Ceremonies * I Don't Get It Jokes

## Shorty Dow
### RETIRED

| | |
|---|---|
| Wind Broken | Golf Balls Lost |
| Guitars Picked | No Shit Stories |
| Brush Cut | Sand Dunes Leveled |
| Pick-Ups Fixed | Dogs Pet |
| Guns Fired | Pot Lucks Eaten |

Finger Given

In 1996, I hired Josh Lesnik as our first general manager. Only twenty-six, Josh was smart, affable, and ready to take on a new challenge. He moved his young family from Chicago to Bandon and worked out of a trailer that we called the Design Center. His job was to open the resort, and that included marketing, staffing, setting up a reservation system, and recruiting and training a corps of caddies.

Technically, Josh was employed by his father, Steve Lesnik, who as founder of KemperSports was the maestro of golf development and management. Even though we invited other companies to submit bids for the Bandon contract, KemperSports, with Josh as the point man, was far and away the best fit—the most flexible, the most willing to act on my needs as a client, the most creative in solving problems. They didn't insist on imposing

*Josh Lesnik took dirt golf seriously. He was the first to "play" many of the holes at Bandon Dunes.*

a system of their own. In the run-up to the opening, Josh and I talked or emailed every day, sometimes two or three times a day. Together, we came up with a three-word mantra to guide the training of our staff: "friendly, helpful, genuine." Josh understood that I didn't want liveried valets or any other sort of rigamarole when guests arrived at Bandon—no scripted responses, no pomp and circumstance, no confusion. He also understood that I don't like to wait and didn't want our customers to have to either, not at check-in, not at breakfast, not ever. Next time you're at Bandon, you might notice that the pot of coffee hits the table at the same time as you sit down, and the check arrives before you finish that last bite of flapjack. You're there to play golf, and we don't want you to get to the first tee fuming about waiting for the damn check.

**JOSH LESNIK:** To understand the response the course received, you have to put the period of time in context. In 1998 there were very few of these remote, wild, sandy, links golf courses anywhere in North America. Sand Hills in Nebraska was similar, but it was private and had only 150 members. Most people would never see it. There was no advance hype for Bandon Dunes, only curiosity about this course being built in a remote location few had ever heard of. We weren't planning on taking reservations until early in 1999, and there was a lot going on with trying to get everything ready. In the middle of this, Bob Robinson, who was the golf writer for *The Oregonian* and very influential, came to visit in late 1998, and his article was hugely positive. The day his article appeared, the phones started ringing asking about tee times.

Soon after a group from *Golfweek*—Brian Hewitt, Jeff Rude, and Jim Achenbach among them—came to check up on our progress. Out of their visit came an article in March 1999 that said Bandon Dunes was a Top 10 course in the U.S., even though the course wasn't even officially open. *Golfweek* also put a shot of the course on the cover. That had never happened before.

Throughout it all, Mike and I would celebrate every little victory.

MK: While Josh was setting up the resort, another young man, David Kidd, was building its golf course. His father, Jimmy Kidd, the greenkeeper at Gleneagles and a figure in Scottish golf, was also spending time at Bandon; father and son were having a grand time figuring out how to bring links golf to the wilds of the American West, and they were prepared to defend their point of view. The questions asked by some of the people at KemperSports and by Pete Sinnott, whom I hired as the construction manager, went straight to the point: Would American golfers accept this kind of golf? Would they come to a resort where the golf was walking only? Would they accept the sometimes wet, windy conditions of Bandon? Would they complain about bunkers where you had to come out sideways? Would they play on turf that could be brown, or yellow, or some other tawny color, but not the bright green they were used to?

David also had to deal with the "retail golfers" who often accompanied me on those early visits to Bandon. Even if they weren't deeply versed in golf architecture, these friends and playing companions represented a key constituency. I always saw them as something more than just paying customers; they were people who played the game in search of joy and fulfillment. They were looking for dream golf, and if we could give it to them, they wouldn't balk at the price. Rankings are important, but no matter what the experts thought, the retail golfers were the ones who would make or break the resort.

Though my methods were unscientific and I was dealing with a small sample of opinions, I listened carefully to them. Like everyone who knows me for more than a few minutes, they were accustomed to my questioning. I'm often needled for asking, early and often, "What do you think?" Admittedly, those who saw Bandon Dunes in the first stages of construction sometimes thought they were wandering around in a gigantic, chaotic sandbox, but they were unfailingly dazzled by the rugged beauty of the setting. Golf on these cliffs above the Pacific was going to be thrilling—of that there could be no doubt. Since the goal was to give golfers like them a day to remember, I thought we were halfway there; all that remained was to create a course equal to the magnificent location.

Easier said than done, of course. There's simply no such thing as a foolproof site. Though unproven as a designer, David wasn't lacking in boldness and imagination. He probably tired of hearing me say that nobody was going to care if we had nine great holes. We had to have eighteen. That was his objective, too, and he kept pushing, pushing, pushing to make every hole sing. The great example is the 16th, the iconic par-4 with a green perched on the very edge of a cliff. Initially, it was a fine hole with dunes running parallel to the Pacific. Convinced that he could improve on it, David realigned a ridge of dunes so that it is now diagonal to the line of play, and the 16th is one of the most bewitching holes you will ever see, a brilliant combination of beauty and strategy.

Links golf was in David's blood. Every time we might have strayed from the pure Scottish model, he was there to insist on doing it the right way. We had a long-running discussion about whether to include golf carts; David actually tried to draw cart paths and then threw up his hands, saying he'd never done it and didn't want to start now. There was a similar discussion about using the most scenic piece of land—now the 16th hole!—for the location of the clubhouse. David even objected vehemently to a three-story clubhouse, arguing that it would loom over the course and destroy the feeling of solitude. He was right on every count.

DAVID KIDD: No one had any idea that Bandon Dunes would become such a phenomenon, and if they say they did they're lying. It wasn't Bandon Dunes when I worked on it, but rather a course on the remote Oregon coast owned by a greeting card guy from Chicago who hired an unknown kid from Scotland. No one could have known or even suspected what kind of impact the resort would have. Without a doubt Bandon Dunes has educated the golfing public in America and around the world that natural golf is the purest and best example of the game; everything else is a wannabe. Simplicity and minimalism in every facet of design, construction, maintenance, and operations are heralded as a return to a long-gone pastime. People love Bandon Dunes because it's natural, unabashed, simple, honest, uncontrived, beautiful, adventurous, and a thousand other things that man cannot dictate, design, or affect.

MK: We were sold out opening day, and stayed sold out for the rest of that first season.

Everything broke in our favor. In the competition for *Golf Digest's*

1999 Best New Course Award, Bandon Dunes was up against Whistling Straits, a course that had daunting credentials; designed by the leading architect of the era, Pete Dye, it had cost a fortune to build and was clearly destined to host major professional events. In contrast, Bandon Dunes was an outlier whose creator was a brash young man in kilts.

I've had enough business experience to know that even the best product needs a compelling story, and I've wondered whether the course would've had the same impact if David hadn't been Scottish. It's the detail that locks the story into place: oceanfront location, glorious views, cliffs, dunes, sod-faced bunkers, fescue turf, brisk winds . . . this has to be a links. And since the architect is from Scotland, it must be a *true* links.

I think the panel for the 1999 Best New Course Award chose what they saw as the real deal, selecting a natural links on the Pacific Ocean over a manufactured links on Lake Michigan, an upstart Scot over an American wizard. Authenticity brings with it a powerful mystique; it lifts any sporting pursuit into a special, prized category. There's a reason why skiers go to great lengths to make first tracks in the deep powder of the backcountry, or anglers who disdain hatchery fish spend a lifetime in quest of the wild steelhead. As a true links with a pedigree that could be traced back to the source, Bandon Dunes held out a similar promise—a pure, peak experience.

Before discovering Bandon, I'd bought other properties in Oregon—a ranch in southern Oregon, then a house and some acreage down the coast on the beautiful Pistol River. These transactions put me in touch with a realtor, Bob Johnson, who quickly guessed my not-so-secret secret: I like buying and selling and looking at real estate. That ranch Bob sold me was beautiful but mountainous, and I tried to lay a golf course on it; I still hadn't gotten over my architectural ambition. My routing was walked exactly once, by a group of friends who told me politely that it was suited only for billy goats. But I sold the ranch at a nice profit, and Bob has handled my real estate dealings ever since. His persistence and initiative have been crucial to the golf at Bandon Dunes.

BOB JOHNSON: I started working with Mike before the first Bandon course was built. He owned more than 1,200 acres, but some of it was

OVERLEAF
*The iconic 16th at*
*Bandon Dunes*

off-limits to golf, and he coveted a parcel to the north—a horse farm owned by a lawyer who didn't want to sell. He had a reputation for running people off his property at gunpoint. I kept trying to meet with him, but he wouldn't see me until he got into legal trouble himself, and then, very quickly, we were able to make a deal to acquire four hundred acres—which provided the 5th, 6th, 7th, and 8th holes at Bandon Dunes. The day we closed the deal, David and Jimmy Kidd were out there staking the new holes. People think Mike must have owned all the land to start with, but he didn't. He wasn't satisfied with the original routing, and he bought land that he knew would make a difference in the quality of the course. Can you imagine Bandon Dunes without the 5th and 6th holes? It would be a completely different course, and nowhere near as great.

MK: I'd known all along that I wanted to build at least two courses. One course is a curiosity, two are a destination—that's a Keiser mantra. A few avid golfers might go to the trouble of playing one superb course in a remote location, but two courses are exponentially more tempting. 1 + 1 = 3.

To design the second course, Pacific Dunes, I hired Tom Doak, the iconoclastic young architect who'd made a name for himself as an advocate for classic design. He'd named his firm Renaissance Design, and he was convinced that the architects of the 1990s were building less interesting courses than those of the 1920s—and believed that he could do better. Tom was also known as the high priest of minimalism, a philosophy that emphasizes moving as little dirt as possible and using the unique characteristics of a site to fashion the golf holes. The minimalist architect studies the land with respect and close attention, trying to absorb its moods, its features, its character. In other words, this approach is comparable to Howard McKee's; both are searching for the genius loci.

Tom believed that he had a better site than David Kidd's. The dunes were taller, the land was more undulating, the blowout bunkers were larger, and the ground was punctuated with stands of shore pines. Some have compared Bandon Dunes to a Scottish links, and Pacific Dunes has been described as having the spirit of an Irish links. I agree. What mattered most, though, was that the two courses, side by side, were entirely different. Tom saw Pacific Dunes as his breakthrough opportunity, and he and his crew lavished every bit of their creative imagination and technical know-how on creating it.

TOM DOAK: Working on a site so different from David's, I decided that I was going to do most things differently. . . . If Bandon Dunes was Pebble Beach, then we were going to be Cypress Point.

MK: That's classic Tom, invoking Cypress Point, the masterpiece of masterpieces, the Sistine Chapel of American golf. I don't blame him. Pacific Dunes is that good. I confess that, privately, I have always compared Bandon Dunes to Pebble Beach. How could I not? Anyone who builds a golf resort on the Pacific Coast has to be aware of Pebble Beach. I'm not suggesting that any new course can truly rival Pebble, with its storied past and championship history, but when somebody mentioned it, I wanted the response to be "Yes, if you like Pebble, you have to go to Bandon."

And it costs half as much.

That's been a rule of thumb: at Bandon we have kept our green fee at 50 percent of what they charge at Pebble. Furthermore, the second round at Bandon is half-price. For those who have the stamina, the third round is free. And if anyone can get in a fourth round, we pay them $100.

All five regulation courses cost the same, by the way. I would consider it a failure if we'd had to price them differently, as is done at many resorts, singling out a "best" course and relegating the others to a lesser status.

A business analyst might suggest that Bandon Dunes fits the definition of a "low-end disruption"—an innovation that challenges and displaces more established and more expensive market-leading firms. Bandon Dunes was innovative, but I don't think we've stolen any business from Pebble Beach or any of the other legendary resorts. The real disruption in the golf market has come in the form of declining memberships at private clubs as golfers, both young and old, increasingly prefer to spend their golf dollars at resorts.

In any case, business at Bandon was booming. (I'll often refer to the resort conversationally as "Bandon," but always use "Bandon Dunes" for the original course.) Pacific Dunes won even more accolades than its predecessor, and we found ourselves needing more of everything—more accommodations, staff, caddies, office space, a bigger kitchen. Howard was in overdrive, working with architects on these new buildings, including a clubhouse at Pacific Dunes to replace the double-wide trailer, surmounted by a clock tower with a big Rolex, that had long served as the pro shop.

We also had enough demand to consider a third course. Ever since I'd seen their splendid results at Sand Hills, I'd wanted to work with Bill Coore and Ben Crenshaw. So I offered them a site that began in the dunes, meandered through a meadow, and crossed the highest ridge on the property. Instead of an oceanside course, the third layout at Bandon would be inland, showcasing a different attribute of this country.

As our land planner, Howard had mapped out what he considered a generous footprint. Yet after studying it, Bill Coore said politely and apologetically—but firmly, in his courteous North Carolina accent—that he just might possibly need some additional land, not a whole lot, because without it, he just didn't know if he and Ben could build a course that would meet the standards that had been set so high. He and Howard had a long, friendly back-and-forth that was settled only when Bill got most of what he wanted and promised Howard that he'd treat the land with utmost respect. Bandon Trails is now a layout that meanders over several hundred acres, larger by far than the area occupied by any of the other courses. As the name implies, Trails is a journey that leads through a richly varied landscape of spruce, pine, and cedar, with an understory of kinnikinnick, blueberry, wild iris, and rhododendron.

Bandon Trails opened in 2005. By this time, several new patterns had settled into place. First, we would expand the resort incrementally, letting the success of one course generate curiosity about the next one. Second, we'd ensure variety by turning to different architects. Pinehurst has its collection of Donald Ross courses, and Destination Kohler has four by Pete Dye. By 2005 Bandon had three courses designed by three different design teams, and each of them has its own distinct identity. Bandon Trails had an air of mystery that Ben Crenshaw can best articulate.

BEN CRENSHAW: On my first visit to Bandon Dunes, my eyes just danced around, trying to take it all in. The coastline is spectacular, with its dunes and cliffs overlooking an ocean defined by the strange, dark, haunting shapes of the sea stacks. Our site was so different but no less beautiful. For a Texan like me, the evergreen forests of the Pacific Northwest appear gigantic and mysterious, like the enchanted forests in fairy tales. The entire area seemed wild and pristine. When I try to find words for the feeling inspired by the environment of Bandon Dunes, I keep coming back to the same phrase—lonely beauty.

MK: One of Howard's last contributions to the resort was the Japanese-inspired clubhouse at Bandon Trails that sits just a few steps away from the 18th green. Since 1996 he'd been fighting colon cancer using every weapon there was, including chemotherapy and Vipassana meditation. Twice the disease had been forced into remission. In

*The elegant Bandon Trails clubhouse is one of my favorite buildings in Oregon.*

2007, though, Howard and his many friends knew that the end was approaching, and he died in December. True to his nature, Howard spent many of his last days designing his service, a final effort to share his wisdom and mark a life well lived. For Lindy and me, this was a heavy loss, and I tried to express my gratitude for our friendship in a farewell letter.

October 11, 2007

Dear Howard,

What a lot of fun we've had, Howard, as we built the Mecca of Golf, the best "pure golf resort in the world."

Do you remember the joy we felt and shouted when we came upon the beautiful sea view on the south side of the Crook Point property, after Bill Crook gave us permission to roam? It was pure, unadulterated boyish discovery! . . . Our karma. It must have been our karma, indeed, that allowed us to finish an aesthetic feast of a development, Bandon Dunes Golf Resort, in only nine years. Absolutely stunning, given our original chances of success. . . .

The best meeting of the kingdom of golf and the realm of Howard McKee was Bill Coore telling you of his "need for the meadow and the dune beyond." And his promise to keep the meadow sacrosanct, even improved. The compact that you and Bill reached, and the friendship that similar imaginations and sensibilities created, was one of the blessed events of all our time together out on the primeval South Coast of Oregon. Bill Coore reveres your vision of how our place must be, and he delivered on his promise to maintain the meadow, just as you did so many times to local regulators and commissioners. . . .

I loved our arguments, Howard. It was always understood to be friendly, creative and friendly conflict. There were so many times that you or I would interrupt a dead-serious debate over a relatively small matter with a chortle that always implied, "This is really small potatoes. All that matters, really, is that we've got the big picture right."

And that was because we had a great partnership, one based on total respect for the other's position.

What a great teacher you've been, Howard. Think of all whom you've guided, prodded, pushed, bullied (yes, maybe your best weapon), coaxed, teased and defiantly said, "Oh, come on!" Here's some of what I've learned, Howard, in our 25 years together.

1st and foremost—Value that which is precious. Your favorite word is "precious" and we should all do whatever is necessary to protect it. I will do my best to protect the South Coast for *us*.

Second—listen to the artists and the wizards. Don't dismiss them as expensive gadflies.

Third—"The world without us" is a valuable sociological benchmark. Let's minimize man's footprint or else. This was our biggest debate, Howard. I've grown to love your argument and the political elite are starting to follow your lead. Mankind's footprint is too big. We now know enough to lessen it. You've been saying that the entire time I've known you.

Fourth and finally—Gentle and powerful are a winning combination. Here's where I resonate most with you, Howard. That spiritual, gentle side of you is what best captures our attention, enabling you to deliver the powerful and rational to an accepting audience. You're a master, and I am following as best I can in those big but sensitively trodding footsteps.

Let me turn to my favorite poet who will help me to say Goodbye, since his words sound so very much like you.

> If I should be where I no more can hear
> Thy voice, nor catch from thy wild eyes those gleams
> Of past existence—wilt thou then forget
> That on the banks of this delightful stream
> We stood together, and that I, so long
> A worshipper of Nature, hither came
> Unwearied in that service: rather say
> With warmer love—oh! with far deeper zeal
> Of holier love. Nor wilt thou then forget,
> That after many wanderings, many years
> Of absence, these steep woods and lofty cliffs,
> And this green pastoral landscape were to me
> More dear, both for themselves and for thy sake!

Once the foundations were secure at Bandon, I began to consider other projects that came my way. In Tasmania, at the instigation of Tom Doak, I got involved with a resort development at Barnbougle Dunes, aka Bandon Down Under. And in Nova Scotia I was drawn into a project I thought of as Bandon East. Bandon was still the ancestral home, but these siblings were the start of a family of courses that shared the same DNA with remote, authentic links. Each of them had its own character, but they offered the same kind of golf and a similar experience. Temperamentally, I'm less an empire builder and more an explorer; I like starting things, and once they're up and running I start looking for the next thing.

I already had an idea for the next course at Bandon: to resurrect the Lido, the most lamented lost course in the game. Once a marvel that stood on a tiny island off New York's Long Island, the Lido was the first truly man-made course, constructed in 1913 on marshy ground that had to be entirely capped with sand—a herculean task that required dredging two million cubic yards of sand from a nearby channel. I'd long been fascinated by the builder, Charles Blair Macdonald, a pioneer of American golf design whose roster of superb Golden Age courses is too long to repeat here. In its day, the Lido was considered as magnificent as any of them, but after a troubled history it was abandoned in 1942.

The idea of re-creating the Lido had been planted by George Bahto's biography, *The Evangelist of Golf: The Story of Charles Blair Macdonald*. After reading the book, I picked up the phone and called the author, who wasn't certain at first whether he should trust me. We'd never met, and he can't be blamed for being taken aback by a call from a stranger wanting to know if it would be possible to replicate the Lido. Hesitantly, he acknowledged that it might be.

I invited George to come to Bandon to look at a potential site. Over the next few years, I asked all my golfing friends what they thought about the Lido project. The usual answer: ho-hum. The concept didn't excite anybody nearly as much as it excited me and George, and then Tom Doak took it in a different direction. What about a course that re-created some of Macdonald's best holes, not as factual replicas but as contemporary versions, adapting his celebrated "template holes" right here in Bandon? In *Scotland's Gift: Golf,* Macdonald had left a detailed record of how he'd chosen his ideal holes. Tom was arguing for a tribute course, and that's how we came to build Old Macdonald. Our brand was sometimes called "throwback" golf, and this course would be the grandaddy of throwback courses. Macdonald had reproduced the most famous holes of the classic Scottish links, and now Tom was going to do the same with his.

Then we got smacked by the Great Recession of 2008, which sent the golf industry reeling. At Bandon we had to lay people off, and some senior staffers had to do double duty, filling in as starters and marshals. I considered delaying construction on Old Mac, but I was fully invested in the idea and pressed on even as the Dow was falling hundreds of points every day.

George was part of an advisory group that included Brad Klein, the architecture editor of *Golfweek,* and Karl Olson, the longtime superintendent of National Golf Links. I also proposed that Jim Urbina, Tom Doak's trusted associate, get billing as a codesigner. As the project manager at Pacific Dunes, Jim had spent 165 days on-site, keeping the books, arranging the work schedules, coordinating with vendors, and trying to bring the course in under the budget of $3.5 million. I'd told him that any savings would come back to him as a bonus, and during the last weeks of construction, the crew's standing joke was that they were spending Jim's money. At Old Macdonald, Jim duplicated this massive undertaking, carrying his design bible in the cab of his dusty truck—a battered, dog-eared copy of *Scotland's Gift: Golf.*

JIM URBINA: I love National Golf Links because it's so unpredictable. It's a course you're never going to figure out, and I wanted to have that same feeling—that mystery—at Old Macdonald. I don't talk about this much, but I think there's mystery out here. Power spots. Different spots have different vibes. Most people who come to Bandon have their special spot here, the place where they always go to soak up the atmosphere. One of mine is the labyrinth that Mike had built in memory of Howard. Another is the hub on Pacific Dunes, where the greens on the 3rd and 12th and the tees of the 4th and 13th all converge right on the edge of the bluff.

When I look around at Bandon Dunes now, I almost don't believe it. I remember when this place was mostly covered with gorse, and now

the coastline is all golf, three miles of golf. I think, Wow, we did all that. Tom, and Ken [Nice, the superintendent], and the whole crew—we did that. We changed this place.

MK: The friendship between Jim Urbina and Ken Nice began in 2000, when Jim was working on Pacific Dunes and Ken, a resort employee, was supervising the grow-in. We always try to involve our maintenance staff with the design teams so they have a chance to study and learn the architect's intentions. As any greenskeeper can tell you, a golf course is a constantly evolving organism, and it can easily turn into something the designer never envisioned.

Though Ken grew up in Oregon and played recreational golf, the courses that had always fascinated him were the ones he saw on TV when he watched the British Open—those shaggy, rumpled, tawny, browned-out links courses. Watching players struggle through the winds and weather, marveling at the crazy rolls as the ball bounded across the turf, Ken decided that he wanted not only to work in golf but to work on that specific kind of course. When Bandon Dunes opened,

*Built as a memorial to Howard McKee, the labyrinth has the serenity and quietude of a chapel in the woods.*

he was knocking on the door and looking for a job. How serendipitous was that, a native Oregonian magnetized by links golf who didn't even have to leave the state? The links came to him.

Ken supervised the grow-in at Bandon Trails, Old Macdonald, and the Sheep Ranch. Now the resort's chief agronomist, he oversees all the golf courses and has become a leading member of the international "fescue community," made up of superintendents who've been influential in expanding the range of these traditional but temperamental grasses. I confess that I don't know much about grass and am not eager to learn more. What I do know is that minimalist courses with fescue turf are inherently more sustainable than engineered courses that require heavy watering and large doses of chemicals. The Bandon courses have won environmental accolades without any compromise of the conditions that matter to golfers—firm, fast playing surfaces and greens that roll true.

KEN NICE: We have the right climate for fescue. The turf at Bandon Trails is a blend of 95 percent fescue, and Old Mac is 100 percent fescue. Most places can't do that. It's just better all around—it needs less water and practically no herbicides or fungicides. Guys coming out of superintendent school have a hard time with fescue because all their training has been about doing things—more inputs. It goes against everything they've learned to leave turf alone. With fescue, you have to have a light touch. Our chemical budget on these courses is ridiculous, about 10 percent of what they spend at a course with conventional grasses and methods.

MK: For many guests, the usual schedule at Bandon is to play thirty-six holes a day, eighteen before lunch and eighteen in the afternoon. That's about twelve miles of walking. After noticing that some of the guests weren't up for a second round, I began contemplating how to solve this problem. What about a par-3 course? Short courses of any kind are often viewed as second-class tracks, the minor leagues, but I happen to prefer par-3s. They can be every bit as dramatic and beautiful as longer holes. This course would be a much easier walk and offer a different kind of experience—more relaxed and informal, pure fun. Families could play together, grandkids could tee it up with their grandparents. It would be the one course at Bandon where groups larger than four would be welcome as long as they didn't slow anybody down, and where caddies and guests could have their own matches.

Right away I knew where the course could be located. When Bill Coore was routing Bandon Trails, he and Ben Crenshaw kept trying to figure out how to use the thirty acres of dunes just west of the present 1st tee. The terrain was rugged and dramatic, tumbling all the way down to the ocean, but they couldn't route any holes through it without destroying the natural topography.

When I mentioned the par-3 idea to Bill, he immediately thought of the same parcel. It turned out that he and Ben had both grown up playing shorter courses, and they'd been looking for an opportunity to build one. You can find some of the resort's best holes at Bandon Preserve, a thirteen-hole par-3 course that opened in 2012. Small they may be, but every hole has a view of the mighty Pacific.

BILL COORE: As usual, Mike gave us specific instructions but also a lot of latitude. He wanted all the holes at the Preserve to be good enough that they'd be worthy of a place on the big courses. He asked us to find the best holes we could, and didn't care how many. He just didn't want the number to be nine or eighteen. When we came up with a routing of twelve holes, he approved it. Then, when we started clearing, we found another hole all the way down at the bottom of the slope. Mike looked at it and approved that one, too.

In every project we've done with Mike, he's been completely open-minded. If we come up with a good idea, he listens—and if it's good enough, he goes with it. He doesn't approach any project with a set of preconceptions. I think that's why Bandon Dunes has six adjacent courses that couldn't be more different from one another. I don't know of any other golf resort that has such great variety, and it didn't happen by accident.

MK: The Bandon Preserve logo features a silvery phacelia, a plant that nearly killed our plans for Bandon Trails. Classified as a "threatened" species, the silvery phacelia is found only in a few counties in southern Oregon and northern California; it grows best in open, partly stabilized dunes, and its primary enemies are non-native species, particularly European beachgrass. I'm delighted to report that the silvery phacelia has thrived on Bandon Trails and the Preserve, demonstrating what I've always believed: that golf can go hand in hand with environmental stewardship.

Much has been written in recent years about "stakeholder capitalism," the idea that everyone involved in a business—not just the owners or shareholders—should share in its success. Employees, suppliers, local communities and their environments—all of these should benefit. This theorizing seems to me to be aimed mostly at multinational corporations that don't have deep ties to the places where they're located. To save money, they might decide to pull up stakes and start over elsewhere, taking hundreds of jobs with them. For a small business like Bandon, that's not a possibility. While a large resort, Bandon is still a small business that is privately owned and fixed in place. I could sell it, but no one can move the golf courses to Mexico or China to reduce costs and improve the bottom line.

For us, stakeholder capitalism isn't a theory or concept, it's an everyday reality. It's about working conditions, personal relationships, and quality of life. I know the names and faces of hundreds of people who work at Bandon. I know how they live and where their kids go to school, where they shop and where they go for a beer. The relationship between the community and the resort is symbiotic. The more the town thrives, the more our employees thrive—and the more the resort thrives.

As the largest employer in Coos County, excepting only the hospital, Bandon has an obligation to the region. Local people doubted our original projections that the resort would create over a hundred jobs. As of 2020, we have over 610 employees, and more than 400 caddies work as independent contractors. We pay more property tax than any other business. On top of that, our 6 percent lodging tax goes directly to the county to help fund the sheriff's office and promote tourism. Our annual payroll is approximately $20 million.

KemperSports and my son Chris develop and monitor the resort's budget, and the on-site comptroller is Breanna Quattrocchi, who's held the job since 2008. As our housing maven, she also oversees the growth of the Staff Village, which currently has seventy-three beds and more coming, as well as the purchase of thirty trailers for additional staff housing. At Bandon, we've been squeezed by our own success; local rents and real estate prices have risen, and we've found ourselves in the business of providing affordable housing to our employees. It's the kind of task for which there are really no models and certainly no manual—but Breanna approaches chaotic situations with the ideal attitude: bring me your mess and I will fix it for you.

BREANNA QUATTROCCHI: I started at Bandon in the summer of 'ninety-nine and worked three straight summers in different positions while attending college at Oregon State. I grew up and went to school K–12 in Bandon, and I knew there was no way I'd ever spend my adult life here. When my husband, Vince, and I came back in 2007, with many doubts, we decided to give it six months and see how we liked it—and we're still here. For us, it's been a great place to raise a family, but it's not for everybody. Some people just can't live in this area—it's too remote, no places to shop, and not much nightlife if you're used to living in a big city.

A lot of us who work at Bandon have grown into our roles. The unofficial policy is to hire from within, and I think that's what makes the resort unique and special in so many ways. Many who have been recruited from outside haven't stayed, and turnover is expensive. It's been more effective to fill jobs with people who are already comfortable with living here. Props to the Keisers, who've been willing to give people a chance to build careers here.

MK: The Quattrocchis are one of several couples who've been instrumental in shaping the culture of Bandon Dunes. Since 2014, Vince has been the director of caddy services, one of the key jobs at the resort. Like Breanna, he grew up in Bandon and started working here the year we opened. He was one of the first loopers. We were scrambling to find caddies. Shoe Gaspar—an early employee who's become a fixture at the resort—knew everyone in town, and he worked the phones to round up as many able-bodied candidates as he could. At the community center, he and Josh Lesnik made a recruiting pitch to a room full of guys who'd been loggers, fishermen, farmhands, cranberry pickers. Having played on the Bandon High School golf team, Vince was one of the few who actually knew what a caddie was. For the next four

LINDY HAS ALWAYS BEEN MY PARTNER IN PHILANTHROPY, and education has long been a top priority. In Bandon, we look forward every year to working with Joseph Bain, a guidance counselor at the high school, to award scholarships to students who otherwise might not be able to go to college. Recently, we also funded preschool childcare at Bandon's elementary school and gave a significant grant to expand the Bay Area Hospital in Coos Bay, the region's medical center.

All these causes remain important to us, but in recent years we've been focusing on the Wild Rivers Coast Alliance, a grant-giving organization whose purpose is to fund projects that combine ecological initiatives and economic opportunities. WRCA is fully supported and staffed by the resort, with all the Preserve's profits—about $800,000 annually—devoted to its efforts to protect streambeds, promote healthy fish and species habitats, encourage sustainable tourism, and preserve working seascapes and landscapes. Often, several of these goals merge in a single project; for example, we've backed the ongoing effort to improve Port Orford's harbor, which would benefit commercial fishermen, recreational boaters, and ecotourism in one of this area's most scenic towns. I apply some of the same considerations to philanthropy as I do to my commercial businesses. I'd say I'm a conservationist, not a strict preservationist, and I fervently believe the south coast—that gorgeous stretch from Bandon to Brookings—is a national treasure. The WRCA's overarching goal is to make sure it stays this way for generations to come.

Of all the grantees, a personal favorite is Washed Ashore, a Bandon-based nonprofit whose mission is to remove plastic debris from beaches and use it to create extraordinary sculptures of marine animals like turtles, octopi, starfish, and sea urchins. Exhibitions of this art have traveled across the country and encouraged thousands of volunteers to clear this ruinous trash off seasides nationwide. Especially poignant to me is the six-foot-tall statue of a tufted puffin that overlooks the Bandon beachfront near Face Rock, where these brightly colored birds used to congregate. That's one of the reasons we selected this lovable, unforgettable bird as the logo for Bandon Dunes. Today, alas, tufted puffins have all but disappeared from this coastline, and the Washed Ashore sculpture serves as a stark reminder of the environmental challenges ahead.

*This six-foot sculpture of a tufted puffin stands watch over the public beach in the town of Bandon, near the cliffs where actual tufted puffins used to nest.*

summers, he kept looping and used his earnings to help put himself through Oregon State University.

Now he manages a caddie program that's much larger and well ordered than it was twenty years ago. Over the course of a year, he deals with as many as 400 caddies. Guests spend more time with their caddies than with anyone else at the resort; they're our ambassadors, and most guests consider playing with a caddie an essential part of the Bandon experience. Nobody's required to take a caddie. Golfers can carry their own bags or use a pull cart, provided free of charge. Nevertheless, in the peak months of August and September, almost 80 percent of them request a caddy. In winter the rate is lower, but still high enough to indicate that golfers value what the caddie brings to a round. Golf is the main course, but caddies are the wine that accompanies the meal, adding to its savor.

Our caddies purchase their own coveralls and rain gear (superb, by the way, and they get a big discount). They also pay $200 for a contract that spells out their responsibilities and perks, which include unlimited play on the courses, provided they go out half an hour after the paying guests; unlimited time on the practice range, where they hit Titleist ProV1s; a locker in the caddie center, where TVs and video games are handy while they're waiting for a loop; breakfast and lunch, both meals offered at cost; and the use of industrial dryers, a welcome amenity on wet days.

It's a sweet deal, as it should be. I want the caddies to know these courses like their own backyards, and to feel proud of and loyal to the resort. At Bandon our caddie events feature the annual Looper Cup, with representatives of three other clubs coming in for a tournament. They have to get here on their own; after that, we pick up the tab for their golf and accommodations. In 2019, caddies arrived from Pine Valley, Pebble Beach, and Cypress Point—having survived fierce qualifiers at their home venues. Playing in the Looper Cup is a highlight of their year, and they're *all* keen to compete here.

VINCE QUATTROCCHI: You can't compare us to anybody else. Bandon has the biggest and best caddie program in the country, and we prove it every day. Caddies from all over come here to find work, and once they get here they don't want to leave. They're career caddies, or

lifers. They're professionals, and we don't have to train them. You don't tell a plumber how to do his job. Quite a few are migratory, spending summers in Bandon and winters in sunnier places, but we have approximately a hundred caddies who are year-round residents of Bandon, raising families here and paying mortgages. Some of them are burnt-out refugees from office jobs where they had to spend all day at a desk. They took up caddying to bring in some income while they tried to figure out what to do next—and they're still here.

They're not as hard-partying as the caddies used to be. The Wild West days are over, but the caddies now are still staunch individualists who want to lead life on their own terms. They're independent contractors, not resort employees, and that's a big difference. They can make their own work schedules. They value flexibility, independence, and work-life balance, not to mention the opportunity to play some of the best courses in the country. About 75 percent of them are avid golfers, and a lot of them have handicaps of scratch or better.

Good caddies can make a decent living at Bandon. We've had assistant pros who decided to start looping so they could make more money. Caddies keep 100 percent of what they make on the course, fee plus gratuity. Since they're independent contractors, we can't set a fee but we do recommend one and guests are welcome to pay more. They often do. In our system, caddies remain paired with guests throughout their visit, and friendships develop, sometimes long-lasting friendships. Many returning guests look forward to having the same caddies year after year.

The caddies have their own annual tournament, the Ray B, named for Ray Bursey, a beloved looper here from 2002 until his death in 2017. But they play a course in town, Bandon Crossings, so they can ride in carts!

MK: Lindy says that Don Crowe, the general manager, has the smile and manner of a born innkeeper. He's guided the resort through the last four years—the busiest, most challenging years we've ever had. We were booked almost solid in 2021, and the pace shows no sign of slowing down. On the contrary, we continue to add lodging, and we expect to build at least one more course.

Three factors have converged to drive the spike in reservations. First, the pandemic. Since golf is a safe, outdoor pastime with built-in social distancing, courses everywhere have seen increased business. Second, the opening of the Sheep Ranch, which might be the most beautiful public course in the world. Third, the phones haven't stopped ringing since the 2020 U.S. Amateur was played at Bandon and televised nationally for several days.

The most important business lesson I ever got was from Pap. As a naval aviator, he always believed he had the best crew in the service because he treated them with respect and gratitude. Let the staff shine, and they will make you shine, too. Don Crowe understands this. I think I get almost as many compliments about the service at Bandon Dunes as I do about the golf.

DON CROWE: I can't tell you how often people ask me how we do it—how our staff projects such a welcoming, genuine warmth and

THE EVANS SCHOLARS FOUNDATION is named for Chick Evans, the amateur who in 1916 won the two top titles in American golf, the U.S. Amateur and the U.S. Open. These victories made him one of the most popular players of the era, and he earned several thousand dollars from the sale of recorded lessons and an instruction book. Accepting this personally would have violated his amateur status, so he followed his mother's advice and put the money to a different use: a scholarship fund for caddies.

The Western Golf Association began managing this program in 1929, and now over a thousand Evans Scholars are enrolled every year at twenty colleges across the nation. They get a full ride, and almost all of them live in chapter houses that are modeled on fraternities and sororities. While they choose their field of study, living in these houses reinforces their caddie values of hard work, respect for others, and service. Most of these are at public universities in the Midwest, but I'd proudly note that an Evans Scholarship house opened in 2016 at the University of Oregon—thanks in part to our caddie operations at Bandon, where I annually host a three-day event for donors to this important cause. The resort has produced sixty Evans Scholars over the last two decades and inspired other courses and clubs in the Northwest to follow in our footsteps by supporting these guardians of the game.

interest in our guests. I wish I did have the formula. I was part of the opening team twenty years ago, and the culture of Bandon Dunes starts there—it starts with Mr. Keiser and his sincerity, his humility, his hands-on approach to making everyone feel comfortable and at home. That attitude has been adopted and passed along, and new staff members learn it from those who've been here for years. The people who work here don't have to act a part. We train them but we don't give them a script. We want them to be themselves. The way guests respond to Bandon Dunes is something we take personally.

MK: Nearly everyone who comes to Bandon looks forward to being welcomed by Bob Gaspar, better known as Shoe. Stationed behind his podium in front of the lodge, he's the smiling face of the resort. Shoe was the first person hired here, joining the staff after a career that included a stint in the Coast Guard, a job with UPS, and a few seasons in the cranberry bogs. He seems to remember everyone he's met over the last twenty years, though he leaves nothing to chance. He rises early to go over the bookings and refresh his memory. Shoe dug bunkers on each of the golf courses (one of the peskiest is the bunker in the middle of the second fairway at Pacific Dunes), and he posts a daily weather report on his Twitter account, @GolfShoeBandon, often accompanied by a photo and a tongue-in-cheek observation. He's made such an art of welcoming people and making them feel at home that he's earned a unique title: director of outside happiness.

SHOE GASPAR: When I became the outside services manager, the director of golf told me to do what I do best. I had to develop my role. Gradually, that became interacting and being interested in our guests and figuring out who they are. People think I'm nuts when I tell them what time I get to Bandon each day, so I just tell them "early." That could be 2 a.m. if it's really busy and I need time to go through the tee sheet. It also depends on how much time I'm spending on Google or LinkedIn. I'm really careful not to be too intrusive with our guests. The people we get here are the movers and shakers of industry in this country. No matter how big an oak desk they sit behind, or how many people are in their company, once they get here the ground is all level. And to a person, when they get here they are almost giddy to be here.

They are golfers. It amazes me. They don't just like this place—they love it.

MK: We have a few homegrown legends whose talents have added to the Bandon mystique, and nobody represents the genius loci more fully than Grant Rogers, the director of instruction. A lifelong aficionado of links golf, he'd made twenty trips to Scotland before he started working here, and it's been rumored that he went out one dark night and played St. Andrews backward. In addition to his official title, Grant's been called many other things: guru, wizard, links ninja, a real-life Shivas Irons. At last count, he had thirteen holes-in-one at Bandon, including a few where he used his putter for the tee shot. Whenever I can, I play a round with Grant, whose teaching method is a cross between Harvey Penick and a Zen master, a combination of parables and riddles.

GRANT ROGERS: When I first saw Bandon Dunes, I imagined that I was over in Scotland. It is a deep links experience—the turf and the ocean. The only difference is that we don't have skylarks in Oregon. And as soon as people play here they feel the same way. They get it. It's about tight lies and hard fairways, and you have to learn how to deal with the wind. And if it rains, you still go out and do your best. The people who come to Bandon are serious about the game.

*For Shoe Gaspar, the director of outside happiness, the day begins before sunrise.*

MK: I never imagined that Bandon would become such a meaningful place for so many, but people really do make pilgrimages—some have driven for days to get here, or saved for years to pay for their trip. It's important to me that the resort is accessible, and during the winter budget-conscious golfers can play here for $105. Rooms cost about the same, and the winters here are mild because Bandon happens to be in a banana belt. Our so-called off-season is now almost as busy as the high season. In the twenty years we've been in business, there've been very few days when the weather was so lousy that nobody teed it up. It's a badge of honor to play Bandon when the wind's howling and the flagsticks are bent double.

Many people have gotten married here, though we aren't in the events business. And even though it's illegal, I know that some Bandonistas have had friends scatter their ashes on their favorite holes.

Bandon attracts a true cross section of golfers, and it's famous as a buddy trip destination, perfect for groups that want to play two different courses every day, sit down to a hearty meal, tell tales by the firepit, fall into bed, then get up a few hours later and do it all over again. The Pied Piper of the buddy trip, Matt Ginella, has been here twenty-five times, and he usually brings a busload of friends. Matt describes himself as having been "born at *Sports Illustrated,* raised at *Golf Digest,* had a fun run at Golf Channel." At heart, he's an irrepressible storyteller who's taken all of golf as his subject matter.

MATT GINELLA: Every year I go to Bandon with a group of twenty-eight guys to play in the Uncle Tony, a tournament that I organized in memory of my uncle, Tony Kielhofer, who loved Bandon. Most of the guys who play in the Uncle Tony return year after year, but I try to have two or three new players. It's like showing a friend a favorite movie for the first time: you get to watch them discover it, and that gets you fired up again. No matter what they've heard about Bandon, people are still blown away by the wildness, the solitude, the beauty, the fantastic golf, the caddies, the walking, the camaraderie, the whole deal. Every detail is just the way you want it to be. A typical reaction is to want to thank Mike Keiser. It feels as if he built this place for you, just so that you could have this kind of experience.

I named my son Bandon. When my wife and I were thinking of names I suggested Bandon, not really expecting her to consider it. But she liked it, and when Bandon was eight months old we took him out to Oregon. Later, we took him to Ireland to visit his namesake town in County Cork. At the Bandon Golf Club, they treated him like royalty. For me, Bandon is something like a club, but it's obviously more than that—it's the spiritual center of my golf life. On a podcast, I asked David Kidd and Josh Lesnik if they could imagine their lives without Bandon Dunes and Mike Keiser. They couldn't do it, and neither can I.

MK: Competitive golf is played at Bandon almost every day of the year. High school and college tournaments, charity events, golf society retreats, private groups of every description—they all come here to take full advantage of an unrivaled venue. They find not only five full courses but also excellent practice facilities and on-site accommodations. The Preserve and Punchbowl provide a setting for friendly, informal competition after the main event is over. And the day ends over a hearty meal or maybe in front of the wood fire that crackles outside McKee's Pub.

Jeff Simonds, the director of golf, oversees a staff that arranges hundreds of events a year, including three competitions staged by the resort: the Bandon Dunes Cup, the Links Championship, and the Fall Match Play. Another fixture on the calendar, the Solstice Event, is played every summer on the longest day of the year, but it isn't really a competition; it's an experience. More than a hundred participants play seventy-two holes in a day, beginning at daybreak and walking more than twenty-five miles, averaging just over three hours per round. Last time I checked, there were over five hundred people on the waitlist.

The crown events on the tournament calendar are the national championships staged by the United States Golf Association. Right from the start, I envisioned Bandon as a showcase for amateur golf, and that meant hosting the top events. Before the first course opened, I was talking to the USGA about bringing tournaments to Bandon, and Mike Davis, who served a long and distinguished term as its executive director, immediately saw the unique potential of the resort. As a public facility, with walking golf on a links course, Bandon Dunes had a living connection to the history and traditions of the game. Mike's only concern was that the courses might not be long enough; on Bandon Dunes, there are a few Mike Davis tees located far behind the regular tees—and we've used them for USGA events.

*The Havemeyer Trophy, one of the oldest trophies in American golf, is awarded to the winner of the Amateur Championship. Here it stands in the heather outside the Lodge at Bandon Dunes.*

For a time early in the resort's history, there were discussions about formalizing a relationship with the USGA. One board member advocated making Bandon Dunes the western home of the organization, which is based in New Jersey. Another possibility, briefly floated, was that the USGA would purchase and operate Bandon Dunes. I didn't immediately rule it out, though I've always been satisfied with our unofficial relationship and proud that the USGA entrusted Bandon with so many of its competitions.

As Mike Davis said in 2019, "What is astounding is the fact that there are four championship-caliber courses here, all of which have been played for various USGA championships. Bandon Dunes has no rival in these regards." Now we have a fifth course, the Sheep Ranch, and we've welcomed seven of their events: the 2006 Curtis Cup, 2007 U.S. Mid-Amateur, 2011 Men's and Women's Amateur Public Links, 2015 Women's Amateur Four-Ball, 2019 U.S. Amateur Four-Ball, and 2020 U.S. Amateur Championship.

The U.S. Amateur, the nation's oldest tournament, was the culmination of long-held hopes, but it doesn't mark the end of the relationship. In an unprecedented announcement in July 2021, the USGA made public its decision to award Bandon Dunes thirteen championships over the next twenty-four years, including the 2029 Walker Cup, the most coveted of all amateur events. Had I been asked if Bandon Dunes would ever host a Walker Cup, I would have said, Not in my lifetime. The most venerable clubs in America are on the waiting list to host this biennial team competition that pits the United States against Great Britain and Ireland, and in this decade Bandon Dunes will follow St. Andrews and Cypress Point in hosting it.

Just as exciting to me is the opportunity to host the U. S. Amateur and the U.S. Women's Amateur in the same year—twice, in 2032 and 2041. The idea is to present the women on the same stage as the men, underscoring their skill and inspiring more women to take up the game—as they are already doing in increasing numbers.

USGA officials often heard me say how willing I was to support amateur golf, and they decided to take me up on it. I'm glad they did. This is something else that the golf experts once warned me about— they didn't see the value of linking the resort to amateur golf. I knew they were wrong, but I didn't know how wrong; our reputation as a capital of amateur golf has been a priceless asset. It separates Bandon from nearly all other resorts and builds loyalty in those who've competed here. The amateurs are the keepers of the game, and I'm glad that so many of them keep returning to the place where they were inspired to summon their best golf.

# 4

# The Bandon School of Golf Architecture

*Bandon Dunes has made an impact much greater than might be expected from a property only twenty years old. The irony is that it did all of that by returning to golf's roots, core tenets that were hidden in plain sight. If you're looking for the future of golf resorts—and maybe golf overall—look no further than Bandon Dunes and Mike Keiser. Wherever they go, the golf world is sure to follow.*

—GRAYLYN LOOMIS, *Links Magazine*

*From left to right: Tom Doak, Bill Coore, Ben Crenshaw, Mike Keiser, David Kidd*

THE SINGLE MOST IMPORTANT INVESTMENT I made in my golf education was a check I sent to Dick Youngscap, a man I'd never met. He sent me a letter describing a plan for a private club in a place I'd never been, a remote area of Nebraska known as the Sandhills. The nearest town was Mullen, population six hundred. Way out there in the middle of nowhere, with a five-month golf season at best, Dick thought he could build a club that would attract a national membership. He'd hired the team of Bill Coore and Ben Crenshaw to design his course, and his projected construction budget of $1 million was less than most developers spent on cart paths. I thought he was at least mildly deranged.

By return mail I sent him $50,000 to become a founding member.

Today, every golfer has seen pictures of Sand Hills, but I have to wheel out the cliché: the camera can't do it justice. Except by actually being there, you can't get anything close to the full effect of the big sky and the vast, unbroken landscape, a prairie rolling and undulating in every direction. Though often dismissed as flyover country, the prairie has a story to tell that evokes a mythic America of buffalo herds and Native Americans, endless prairies, homesteaders, and cowboys. At Sand Hills, it feels as though you've slipped through some time-space warp, and you wouldn't be surprised to see a wagon train trundling over the ridge. From the day it opened, this place has offered one of the incomparable experiences of the game.

Sand Hills shook the foundations of golf course architecture. Ron Whitten called it the "most natural" course ever built in America, a masterpiece of minimalist design. (Ron, by the way, had arranged my introduction to Youngscap.) At a preview round in 1994, I met Dick in person for the first time, along with several others who became friends and colleagues. Bill Coore, Ben Crenshaw, and Tom Doak were all at Sand Hills that day, and my conversations with them, still ongoing, have been tutorials in the art of golf course design.

I consider Bill, Ben, and Tom charter members of the Bandon School of Golf Architecture. With apologies to Dick, I am going to call it the Bandon School because all these architects have built courses at Bandon Dunes. Even though Sand Hills was the breakthrough course for minimalism, it has

OVERLEAF
*Sand Hills blends so naturally into the landscape that you have to look closely to distinguish between fairways and greens.*

always been a single, private course. With six courses open to public play, Bandon has been the most prominent showcase for a movement that's been variously described as links golf, throwback golf, minimalist golf, lay-of-the-land golf, and neoclassical golf. By any name, it is a radical break from those "championship courses" and lush, private venues that had for decades set the standard for American golf.

The Bandon School is best understood not as a particular style or rigid doctrine but as a collection of individual talents, akin to the Philadelphia School, a group of people brimming over with imaginative and intellectual energy. Some of them have been sharing ideas for years. All of them believe in golf architecture much as young actors believe in theater or young writers believe in literature: this is their calling, their art, the thing that matters above all else. They have studied it, obsessed about it, written about it, honed their craft, and sharpened their tools to become better at it. They regard it as a noble profession.

Why not call it the minimalist school? All these designers are routinely described as minimalists, but as Tom Doak has pointed out, a great many architects started calling themselves minimalists once the term became a buzzword—even though they kept right on doing what they'd always done. Furthermore, minimalism is not in itself an aesthetic philosophy; it's an approach to construction, a discipline, a means to an end. By imposing restraint, minimalism encourages a designer to take careful note of what the land offers and fashion it, via art and craft, into a distinctive golf course that seems to emerge naturally from the terrain.

As a developer, I consider myself an honorary member of the Bandon School. Dick Youngscap belongs, too, since both of us not only gave architects the ground on which to express their talent but also played a role as active collaborators. Sand Hills and Bandon Dunes were the catalysts of a widespread movement that has transformed course architecture at virtually every level—these lay-of-the-land designs look and play differently, and golfers have embraced them.

The success of the first course at Bandon led to a second, and a third, and a fourth, and before a decade had passed, it was clear that the appetite for these new/old layouts was general. It goes without saying that many other developers and designers were working along the same lines; even if they weren't directly influenced by Bandon, their work reflected a shift toward more traditional, natural, minimalist golf. If the pace of new course construction hadn't slowed down dramatically after the boom years of the early 2000s, I have no doubt that many more young architects would have had a chance to make their own mark as lay-of-the-land artists. As the field contracted, however, the Bandon architects were among the few who were steadily employed. On superb sites not just in this country but all over the world, from China to Australia to Scotland, they built extraordinary courses that quickly showed up on the Top 100 lists.

Since 2000, all the major rankings have been shaken up and rearranged, as older layouts are pushed aside to make room for recently built courses. Are we in a second Golden Age? I'm not the only one who thinks so. Scan the rankings and you find courses by the Bandon architects well represented. For golfers, they've become must-play courses; for architects who want to keep up with changes in their profession, these courses have to be seen and studied. They are, to borrow Michael's term, the new canon.

The return to classic design principles also reshaped the approach to course renovation. Historically, this had been the province of green committees, and they often had agendas that didn't match up with the original design intent. With the growing appreciation for traditional design, clubs took a more thoughtful look at their courses, hiring skilled, knowledgeable architects to carry out the work of renovation or restoration. Doak's firm, Renaissance Design, was employed by dozens of famous clubs, from San Francisco GC to Yeamans Hall, to recapture the vitality of their courses.

Symbolic of this movement to breathe new life into a hallowed layout is the restoration of Pinehurst No. 2 prior to the 2014 U.S. Open. Bill Coore and Ben Crenshaw took a studious approach, examining drawings and photographs from the 1930s when Donald Ross, Pinehurst's resident architect, was lavishing his attention on the course he considered his masterpiece. To re-create what Ross had intended, they decided that radical steps were needed. Coore and Crenshaw tore out acres of turf, getting rid of the grass that had taken over from tree line to tree line; they installed large, sandy wastes that were hand-planted with wire grass; they got rid of thousands of sprinkler heads to create a drier, firmer, faster playing surface, especially where the grass browned toward the fairway edges. Beforehand, Pinehurst No. 2 had gradually evolved to look and play like a standard-issue parkland course, groomed and manicured; afterward, it was rugged and natural, wilder and gnarlier, with the holes blending seamlessly into the Carolina landscape of pines and sand.

Although the renovation received high praise from the galleries and most players at the Open, not everyone thought it was an improvement. One

developer and resort owner, Donald Trump, tweeted, "I'd bet the horrible look at Pinehurst translates into poor television ratings. That's not what golf is all about." (Interestingly, Trump has acquired highly regarded links courses in both Scotland and Ireland.) For Pinehurst, the renovation led to the desired results—a higher course rating and increased bookings.

Tastes had changed, and I'd say that the change went deeper than taste. When remodeled with the lay-of-the-land approach, a golf course undergoes a fundamental transition. At Pinehurst No. 2, the holes are now more of a piece with the landscape of the Carolina sandhills. The game has been brought closer to nature.

At Bandon, we never intended to tame the landscape; we always aimed for the natural, unspoiled quality of the links. There wasn't much appeal if golf was a stroll in the park; I was more drawn to the idea of golf as an invigorating outdoor adventure. It's clear in hindsight that this notion was shared by the architects, and each of the first three courses was a little more rugged and wild than its predecessor. The following par-3s illustrate the progression.

*After the redo, Pinehurst No. 2 no longer looked like a manicured suburban lawn.*

*The first is the 12th at Bandon Dunes (1999), designed by David Kidd.*

*Here's the 11th on Tom Doak's Pacific Dunes (2001).*

*And this is the 17th at Bandon Trails (2005), designed by Coore-Crenshaw.*

"BANDON DUNES has always seemed like the right course at the right time. The four subsequent courses built at the resort directly inspired Chambers Bay, Streamsong, Erin Hills, Barnbougle Dunes, and others to seek out naturally rolling golf ground and choose traditional cool-season golf grasses. Bandon Dunes changed course architecture in America by reminding the industry of the beauty of coastal golf, and that not only can old school, hands-on, minimalistic design still produce the best results, it can also produce the best profits."

—DARIUS OLIVER, "Golf Architecture's Most Important Courses," *Links Magazine*

Much has been written about the originality and impact of Sand Hills, but I want to touch on the patterns in design before that course opened in 1995. After World War II, when bulldozers and excavators transformed the nature of course construction, it didn't matter nearly as much what kind of land had been chosen. Designers could remake any landscape. "Rape-and-shape" was the order of the day, and artificial features—waterfalls, bunkers shaped like shark's jaws, island greens—were in vogue. The crowning achievement of this trend was Shadow Creek, in the Nevada desert, where golf got the full Las Vegas treatment. For a reported $60 million, Tom Fazio, in league with casino mogul Steve Wynn, created a facsimile of the North Carolina highlands, planting a forest of twenty-one thousand trees and routing a bubbling, cascading stream that circulated throughout the property.

Yet in *The Architects of Golf,* which I mentioned above, Ron Whitten peered into his crystal ball and saw golf moving away from opulent, engineered courses that were hugely expensive to build. "The trend, if it could be called that, seemed to be an attempt to create something different. . . . Less well known architects, young and old, were rediscovering low profile architecture, the kind practiced eighty years before when courses were designed to fit the lay of the land with as little earth movement as possible. . . . If that is the future of golf course architecture, it looks very much like the past."

Among the practitioners of this new/old style, Whitten singled out Tom Doak and Coore-Crenshaw. As the architecture editor of *Golf Digest,* he had a great pulpit from which to praise and promote their work. When Dick Youngscap mentioned that he was looking for a designer, Whitten floated the idea of hiring Coore-Crenshaw. To a few aficionados, the Nebraska Sandhills had long been a temptation: a huge prairie that looked like an ocean of grass, with sandy blowout bunkers serving as the foam on the waves. It was perfect for golf, miles from any population. Whitten thought that these men would know what to do with this American version of linksland.

Already, the threads of a revolution in design were starting to weave together. Let's unravel a few of them.

In 1992 the Coore-Crenshaw firm was only seven years old. Despite having demonstrated their talents at Kapalua and Barton Creek, they didn't find themselves swamped with new commissions. Crenshaw, the 1984 Masters champion and a star on the PGA Tour, was a marquee name, yet success as a player hadn't led automatically to design contracts. Bill Coore had spent years toiling at his craft, many of them working for Pete Dye, the uber-architect of the 1970s and 1980s.

Though Coore became a very different kind of designer from his mentor, he shared Dye's ravenous curiosity about the game and became friends with Pete and his wife, Alice. When the Dyes traveled, they asked him to look after their dogs, and Bill spent many evenings reading the architecture books in their library. He was so enthralled by Robert Hunter's *The Links* (1926) that Dye told him to keep the copy. When he first met Crenshaw, Coore discovered that both regarded *The Links* as a design bible. It's impossible to say precisely how Hunter's—or Dye's—ideas informed their own understanding of design. But it's obvious that Coore and Crenshaw were immersed in the subject, reading and studying and conversing in ways that were preparing them for the opportunity that eventually came at Sand Hills.

Of course, they both talked about golf architecture with many other people, especially with a few like-minded peers. For Bill Coore, an essential companion was Rod Whitman, whom he met in Huntsville, Texas, in 1976 when he was superintendent of a course called Waterwood National. Whitman was enrolled at Sam Houston State, where he played on the golf team. To make a few bucks, he took a job on Bill's crew, and they spent many evenings together, eating pizza and watching TV, trading ideas and dreaming about careers they might find in the game. When they had the time and money, they visited famous courses like Pinehurst, Southern Hills, and Prairie Dunes.

Bill particularly admired Perry Maxwell. On the golf team at Wake Forest, where he got his BA in classical Greek, he played at the Old Town Club, a Maxwell design. An Oklahoma native who'd made a pilgrimage to Scotland, Maxwell described the site of Prairie Dunes, in Kansas, as American linksland. After drawing his routing plan, he famously said, "I've found 118 holes. The problem is to eliminate 100 of them." At Sand Hills half a century later, Bill and Ben walked the site repeatedly and had the same problem as Maxwell—getting rid of extraneous holes to find the eighteen that worked best together. Bill recorded 130 holes, with notations, on a drawing that became known as the Constellation Map. Now carefully framed, it hangs in the clubhouse at Sand Hills, one of the most treasured documents of modern golf design.

Crenshaw had encountered celebrated courses throughout his playing career. As a top amateur, he played many classic American layouts; as a pro, he'd not only played the famous courses that make up the rota for the Open Championship but also traveled widely in Scotland and Ireland to see other notable layouts. In love with golf and its traditions, he was enchanted by the ancient links. When asked how he felt after playing Royal Dornoch, he said, "Let me put it this way. I nearly didn't come back." (That's exactly how I felt, too!)

In 1981, when a student from Cornell asked him to support an application for a postgrad fellowship in the British Isles to study historic courses, Crenshaw wrote a four-page, single-spaced letter of recommendation. The student, Tom Doak, won the fellowship. Over the next decade, he and Crenshaw became "blood brothers" and got together regularly at tournaments, where Crenshaw would invite the aspiring young designer to come inside the ropes and walk with him during practice rounds.

One of their visits became a footnote to Crenshaw's victory at the 1985 Buick Open, played at Warwick Hills, in a suburb of Flint, Michigan. In the second round, Crenshaw had a morning tee time and that afternoon, at Doak's invitation, he flew up to northern Michigan to play Crystal Downs, an Alister MacKenzie design that Doak revered—and where MacKenzie's design partner was Perry Maxwell. On that day trip, Crenshaw played a friendly match with the club's head pro, Fred Muller, a short-game wizard and terror in regional tournaments. Muller remembers the day vividly. "Ben was leading the tournament, but Crystal Downs isn't a pushover. You need to know the course. On the first hole, Ben putted off the green. That afternoon I cut him a new one." Nevertheless, energized by his visit to Crystal Downs, Crenshaw won the Buick Open, and in the post-event interviews raved about Crystal Downs and the lift it had given him. (Little known back then, the course was ranked at No. 13 on *Golf Digest*'s 2019 Top 100 in America.)

To say these young designers ascribed near-magical powers to classic courses is not an overstatement. Their frame of reference included original links and their first-generation offspring, American courses that showed how links concepts could be adapted to inland landscapes. For Tom Doak, who also spent a few years working for Pete Dye, the trajectory of a career in design was always clear: to learn the trade so he could work for himself, building courses that were informed by the principles and values he'd discovered in Scotland. On Dye's crew, he was taken under the wing of Jim Urbina, a cheery, robust, ex-football player from Colorado, who taught him how to run a bulldozer. They were an odd couple, the earthy Urbina and the brainy Cornell grad, but together they were a good team with practical skills and intellectual chops.

About Pete Dye: four of the core members of the Bandon School—Coore, Whitman, Doak, and Urbina—got their start in the business by working for him. Much as they liked and admired him, their design philosophy seems to bear little or no resemblance to his. If they are minimalists, Dye was a full-out maximalist, the creator of several high-profile tournament courses that were marvels of engineering and damn near impossible for ordinary golfers to play. Features that Dye used frequently and prominently—island greens, bulkheads, water hazards—are almost entirely absent from the designs of Coore and the others.

In several respects, however, Dye served as a model. Most importantly, the man was an artist in every fiber of his being, and his layouts made people realize that a golf architect was a force to be reckoned with. Whatever else he might have done, Dye certainly proved that the playing fields of golf did not have to conform to any mechanical formula; on the contrary, they became more intriguing and exciting when shaped by an artist's vision. Furthermore, Dye didn't mind getting his boots muddy; he was definitely not in the tradition of tweedy, office-bound architects. He never worked on more than one or two courses at a time, spent a lot of time driving a machine, shaped features by feel and by eye. He expected hard work to yield inspiration. The members of the Bandon School have followed this example, and they credit Dye with teaching them the importance of *building* a course, making sure that concepts are accurately translated into the features on the ground.

Dye also built a team—or teams, since his shapers came and went on various projects and in various combinations. Every member of the crew was invited to contribute ideas. This precedent, too, has been adopted by the Bandon architects, who've gathered teams of associates and kept them intact for years, giving them more and more latitude to develop their skills, eventually helping many of them find commissions and establish their own independent design practice. Now, twenty years since the opening of Bandon Dunes, this ongoing collaboration continues to shape a younger generation versed in principles that have been thoroughly field-tested.

David Kidd is the outlier in what I'm calling the Bandon School. When I hired him to build Bandon Dunes, he hadn't yet completed a single eighteen-hole project. He was the in-house architect for Gleneagles Golf Development; his father, Jimmy, was the superintendent at Gleneagles, a renowned inland resort in Scotland. Having grown up there, David had an entirely different sense of the game's culture and only a sketchy idea of American golf. The courses that were his birthright and stomping grounds were those at Gleneagles and Machrihanish, a fabled links at the southern end of the Kintyre peninsula. In the summer, the Kidd family parked its camper there, and David roamed around a dunes course laid out by old Tom Morris himself. To get to know David, I visited several links with him and Jimmy, who showed me how to look at a course through the eyes of a greenskeeper. I came away convinced that David's understanding of the links was bred in the bone, and I hired him thinking that, being young, he would listen to me. Also, I figured I could fire him if he didn't.

He wrote me a detailed, six-page letter laying out his plans. No carts, therefore no cart paths. No real estate. No prime oceanfront squandered on a clubhouse. No forced carries. To be frank, I sometimes questioned his ideas, but David had the fire in his belly and knew instinctively what a links course should be. As he's said, "If Bandon Dunes was on the west coast of Scotland, it would fit right in as one of many links courses. No one would have told me that I couldn't do this, or that. On the west coast of the United States, it's the only one. But when I got pushback, Mike always took my side."

Once construction was under way, we spent less time talking about links qualities—that battle had been resolved in David's favor—than about making the course enjoyable for the retail golfer. The most basic test: Can you hit your ball, find it, and hit it again? Looking for lost balls interrupts the pace of play and ruins the mood. It's possible to lose a ball at Bandon Dunes, but

David laid out oversized fairways and greens; he knew that golfers would use every available inch of space when the coastal winds were blowing.

And he gave them plenty of different shots to consider. In addition to the bump-and-run and the classic, low-trajectory full shots suited to the links, David fashioned a course that presents a different look and temptation on almost every tee. Bandon Dunes is a course where you're invited to take a rip with your driver on the par-4s and -5s—but the obvious line isn't always the best, and on many holes there are seemingly random bunkers or mounds to take into account. These tee shots present a fascinating challenge that, after twenty years, I'm still trying to figure out.

David's work at Bandon Dunes had a direct if somewhat perverse influence on Tom Doak. That Tom and David mix like oil and water is well known, and I'm sure Tom felt competitive, but I never thought his motive was to outdo David. He had his own hard-won ideas of authenticity, and he saw Pacific Dunes as his chance to express them. Instead of large greens like David's, he built small ones; instead of removing most of the trees and shrubs, he kept the gorse and shore pines; instead of revetted bunkers, he used natural blowouts; instead of a symmetrical routing of two nine-hole loops, he designed a labyrinth with an irregular mix of holes as to length and par.

In very broad terms, Bandon Dunes features full shots, while Pacific Dunes emphasizes precision and finesse. Yet both courses require imaginative, honest shot-making from tee to green, and both are prime exhibits of the Bandon School of Golf Architecture. So what do they have in common? What are the main characteristics of this new architecture I'm attempting to describe? Here's how I see it.

- *The golf course should be a links.* Links courses have sandy soils, fescue turf, and firm, fast playing conditions. True links also have seaside locations, but some landlocked courses meet the standards (notably, Sand Hills).
- *The golf course should be playable.* This means that all golfers can rely on their own game—whatever it might be—to make their way around the course. The course should not dictate the strategy or the kind of shot that must be played.
- *The golf course should be fun, not a punishment.* A course is fun if you want to keep on playing after you've putted out on 18. It's fun

when you get to play shots at the outer edge of your ability—and have a decent chance of pulling them off.

- *The golf course should be beautiful.* It would be hard to build a Plain Jane course at Bandon. The beauty I have in mind goes beyond the pretty or picturesque. It stirs both the senses and the soul.
- *The golf course should have a distinct sense of place.* This is a matter of respecting natural landforms and incorporating them into the design, building holes that appear to emerge organically from the ground. The golfer feels that the course, embedded in the landscape, could not be anywhere else on earth.
- *The golf course should be made for walking.* The oldest, truest form of the game, walking encourages interaction with both your playing companions and the natural environment. All the Bandon courses (except Trails) move from an inland first tee toward the sea, touch it at several points, and return inland to finish. This is the pattern of the ancient links—away from the town, out to the sea, and back again. It's golf's primal journey.

These are the design principles I've consistently tried to apply. Naturally, readers familiar with the resorts at Bandon, Cabot, and Sand Valley will be able to point out some variations. My goal here isn't to pin down a certain style or to establish a hard-and-fast category into which all the courses can be neatly fit. More than anything, I'd say that the Bandon School was a mindset, an ethos, a shared philosophy that attracted a group of exceptionally talented architects and spurred them to work at the top of their powers.

To this day, I believe that the excitement we felt when building the resort resonates with visitors to Bandon. In those early years, the energy was flowing and palpable. We knew we were doing something disruptive, as David Kidd would say gleefully. We were going to shake things up. David and his motley gang of shapers took to wearing wraparound sunglasses and strutting around like rock stars who knew they had a hit song. During the heady genesis of Pacific Dunes, someone on Tom Doak's crew put up a sign in the construction trailer: *The Moons Are in Alignment.* They kept telling each other, "This is our Sand Hills. Let's not screw it up."

We're all older now, of course, but I don't think the enthusiasm has waned. Here at Bandon and wherever else these architects have traveled to build new courses, they've kept right on pushing back the expectations and boundaries of their profession. They've shown golfers a new way to look at courses and a new way to play—which, I repeat, is very much in keeping with the old way.

Is it useful to see them as belonging to a single school? I leave it to golf historians to decide. But for me, it's inescapable. I know these men as friends and partners, and I can't think of them apart from the hundreds of hours we've spent together on construction sites. Even when the ground was muddy and the wind was roaring, I was happy to be out in the field with them, a witness and participant in the flowering of the art of golf design.

Howard McKee was wise when he said, "Listen to the artists and wizards."

## 5

# The Sheep Ranch

*Five Mile Point is one of the most dramatic pieces of real estate along the majestic Oregon coast. . . . Standing on the tip of the promontory, it is a steep, 40-foot drop to the untouched sand and roiling surf below. What imbues the land with an otherworldly quality is its sheer desolation. . . . Yet on this pristine land lies the most tantalizing secret in golf.*

—CHRIS LEWIS, *Sports Illustrated*

I N NOVEMBER 2018, construction began on the Sheep Ranch, the fifth eighteen-hole course at Bandon. To be accurate, I should say that we began a makeover of the Sheep Ranch, the thirteen-hole course that was originally built in 2001 on a site shown on maps as Five Mile Point, just north of the resort.

The new course was designed by Bill Coore and Ben Crenshaw. Nine of the eighteen holes are seaside, and I mean that literally: one step off the edge of the green or tee takes you dangerously near the rim of the cliff. The Pacific Ocean is in play. On one hole, the 9th, the view from the tee is a phantasmagoric optical illusion: the fairway tumbles down to the Pacific, and the surface of the green, in a wide saddle between dunes, isn't visible at all. All the golfer sees is a flagstick on the horizon, and it looks as though the cup has been cut in the shimmering sea.

The Sheep Ranch has a complicated history, much of it myth that was amplified and embellished in caddie lore, but let's begin with the single most important fact: Five Mile Point is a spectacular section of the Oregon coastline, wild and isolated, a spot that has long been a favorite of kite surfers and beach combers. The surf starts building at least a quarter mile out, rolling shoreward in seven or eight parallel surges that break on the point, crashing against the jagged black rock formations—the sea stacks—that are home to sea lions and thousands of seabirds.

Five Mile Point abuts the northern end of the Bandon property, and the Sheep Ranch is often considered part of the resort. But it's not that simple. Phil Friedmann, my partner at Recycled Paper Greetings, and I bought the land fifty-fifty and named our company Bally Bandon—a play on Ballybunion, the jewel of Irish links courses.

By that point, the friendship begun at Amherst had led to three decades together at RPG. Our standing agreement there had been that we each had a veto, so if there was an idea that one of us didn't like, we wouldn't pursue it. Both of us might've grumbled about this on occasion, but the friendship always came first, ahead of any business plans.

This agreement hadn't yet been tested in golf. My fascination with course design had rubbed off on Phil, who took several golf trips with me. We'd also discussed the Bandon project in great detail. Twice, when I needed cash—

OPPOSITE
*The Sheep Ranch,
looking south over
the 1st green and the
snag-surrounded
17th*

the initial costs were five times greater than projected—Phil helped out with timely loans. But the opportunity to work with each other in golf hadn't presented itself until Five Mile Point came up for sale.

We bought it, then found we couldn't agree on what to do with it. While I looked at its potential as the owner of a resort that already had three golf courses and its own unique identity, Phil conceived of this as a place that could thrive as a satellite operation that stood somewhat apart.

When the Sheep Ranch finally opened in 2020, many golfers greeted it as the most exhilarating course at Bandon. Personally, I applaud it as the rewarding conclusion of a sometimes fractious process in a lifelong friendship.

To tell the story of the Sheep Ranch, I've pulled together statements from a number of different people and sources. Phil has always taken the lead in the development of the Sheep Ranch, but all golf courses are collaborative projects, part science and part art, that end up expressing the talent, imagination, and labor of many people. When the designers are Bill Coore and Ben Crenshaw, spending long days on-site, looking and listening in the way that artists do, the land itself becomes a collaborator. As it turned out, the Sheep Ranch had quite a tale to tell.

BOB JOHNSON, realtor: After working with Mike for years, I knew that he was interested in acquiring more coastal property, so I decided to see if Pacific Power and Light might consider selling the land at Five Mile Point. They owned about seven hundred acres out there, a parcel that straddled Whiskey Run Road just north of the resort. My timing was fortuitous. They had just had the land appraised, and it was valued at $2.2 million. When I heard that, I went to Mike, and within a week we were ready to make a cash offer for the full price.

CHRIS HOOD, land-use planner: PP&L had tried to develop a wind farm at Five Mile Point. There's plenty of wind out there, but it blows hard and the wind direction is constantly changing. The turbines they erected couldn't swivel fast enough. They were huge things. They looked like school buses up on top of a big pole with a massive propeller attached to the front bumper. The problem was that they had to be turned by a motor, and it took forever to get them lined up correctly with the wind direction.

*Before golf,*
*Five Mile Point*
*was a wind farm.*

BOB: By the time I made our offer, PP&L had received another bid from a lumber company. There was valuable timber on the east side of the property, and they outbid us. As soon as they harvested the timber, the land was back on the market—and now it was twice as expensive since they knew the resort was interested. At the time, Pacific Dunes was about to be built—this was in 2000—and Mike felt that the course could be improved if he bought the land just north of what he already owned. But he didn't want all seven hundred acres. I was able to get the timber company to agree to sell in two parcels. It was bisected by Whiskey Run Road, with three hundred acres on the south side of the road and four hundred acres to the north.

MK: I coveted the piece of land that PP&L owned south of Whiskey Run Road. Tom Doak had routed Pacific Dunes, and there was a fantastic green site just beyond the north boundary of the property. Tom and I argue about who discovered it first. Eventually, that green would get built—it is No. 13 at Pacific Dunes, one of the most photographed spots at the resort. But until I bought that extra land, we were stymied. Those three-hundred-plus acres I bought from PP&L gave us the 13th and 14th holes at Pacific Dunes, and the rest of the tract eventually became Old Macdonald.

PHIL FRIEDMANN: The other larger parcel of four hundred acres north of the road was still available. Mike didn't have any immediate plans for it and he was feeling strapped for cash. The resort was taking off and he was trying to keep up with the demand for lodging. Those four hundred acres included a full mile of coastline with Five Mile Point, the sea stacks, and the cliffs. Even after the lumber company jacked up the price, that land was still a steal. Without any definite plans, we decided to buy it together and figure out what to do with it later.

MK: Even if we weren't sure how to develop it, a northward expansion of the Bandon property made sense. The chance to own a three-mile stretch of unspoiled Pacific coastline doesn't come along very often.

TOM DOAK: Phil had come out to Oregon regularly while we were building Pacific Dunes, and he loved it. We played dirt golf together and then the preview holes. It was pretty clear that he wanted to be more involved.

PHIL: After we bought the land, Tom and his crew were finishing up at Pacific Dunes. I looked at that masterpiece of a golf course and thought, *Let's do something like that at Five Mile Point.* So I talked to Tom and we walked the land. We chose what we thought were exceptional green sites, and Tom came up with the idea of a thirteen-hole course that could be played in several different ways, approaching the greens from different directions. In effect, the course would have over fifty solid, playable holes.

TOM: Phil understood the limitations of the site, and he tried to buy additional land to the north of the Sheep Ranch so that we could build a full eighteen holes. The cliff formations up there weren't as steep, and there were potential green sites lower and closer to the beach. But the owners refused to sell.

MK: We were apprehensive about getting permits for another course. We'd just been through a long, complicated, expensive process to get the resort approved, and we tossed around different ideas that might make it easier. One was to bring in some sheep to keep the grass trimmed, and have a few rustic golf holes. We were in a hurry to start playing golf out there, and we didn't want to go through such a drawn-out ordeal again.

CHRIS: Not long after they bought it, they applied for a permit to build a stand-alone golf course. There was almost no discussion when the application came before the planning commission, which was odd. The application was minimal, to say the least, with very little detail about the routing of the golf course or about anything else—erosion control, environmental impact, infrastructure, and so on. Maybe the commission thought this was an afterthought, and they'd just been through a complicated battle that ended up with the approval of the resort. Anyway, the application sailed right through.

PHIL: I wanted a place that had the character of an ancient Scottish links, and what could be more classic than having a flock of grazing sheep to keep the grass short? Even after we were properly permitted, I wanted to see sheep on the fairways. Some people warned me that they wouldn't last long. There were coyotes out there.

ERIC WYATT, waiter at Bandon Dunes: My family was involved in a sheep operation, and I was known as a fast shearer. My personal best was shearing 305 sheep in eight hours. When Mr. Friedmann asked if I could run a few sheep out at Five Mile Point, I said yes—there was plenty of grass. I kept a small flock out there for several months, through lambing season in the early winter. We didn't see any coyotes.

TOM, on the *Renaissance Golf* website: "The furthest outside the box design of anything we've done, this 105 acre oceanfront property is designed so players can play cross-country, choosing their own routing on the fly. The task of designing holes, which could be played forward, backwards, and sideways was one of the most complicated projects we've taken on, yet the result is simple fun in a magnificent setting." [The approval actually encompassed 150 acres, but almost a third of that area was either topographically or visually unsuitable for golf.]

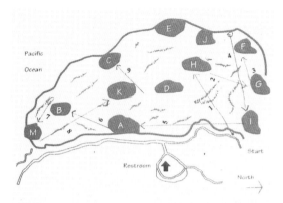

**The Sheep Ranch**
63 Likely Golf Holes - 30 Best Highlighted
* = Holes Comprising 18 Hole Loop

| FROM | | | | | | |
|---|---|---|---|---|---|---|
| St. | *A = 530 | D = 460 | H = 375 | J = 565 | K = 540 | |
| A | *B = 410 | D = 250 | H = 530 | N = 550 | | |
| B | A = 410 | *C = 500 | *K = 420 | M = 150 | N = 220 | |
| C | *B = 500 | *D = 215 | *E = 425 | J = 350 | K = 190 | |
| D | A = 250 | C = 215 | *E = 340 | *I = 450 | L = 440 | |
| E | *C = 425 | *F = 410 | *L = 450 | | | |
| F | E = 410 | *G = 230 | H = 250 | L = 365 | | |
| G | D = 630 | F = 230 | *H = 310 | J = 515 | L = 275 | |
| H | C = 515 | *D = 325 | E = 350 | G = 310 | | |
| I | A = 550 | D = 450 | F = 450 | H = 260 | *J = 485 | |
| J | C = 350 | D = 230 | *E = 130 | F = 340 | G = 515 | L = 420 |
| K | B = 420 | *C = 190 | I = 590 | | | |
| L | A = 590 | D = 440 | F = 350 | H = 170 | J = 420 | |
| M | N = 180 | | | | | |
| N | B = 220 | K = 530 | M = 180 | | | |

October, 2000
Renaissance Golf Design, Inc.
Traverse City, Michigan

| Hole | H | G | F | I | A | B | M | K | C | |
|---|---|---|---|---|---|---|---|---|---|---|
| Yards | 427 | 390 | 205 | 461 | 531 | 384 | 154 | 562 | 162 | 3276 |
| Par | 4 | 4 | 3 | 4 | 5 | 4 | 3 | 5 | 3 | 35 |

| Hole | E | F | G | J | E | D | B | A | I | |
|---|---|---|---|---|---|---|---|---|---|---|
| Yards | 327 | 401 | 205 | 465 | 135 | 230 | 541 | 384 | 535 | 3223 |
| Par | 4 | 4 | 3 | 4 | 3 | 3 | 5 | 4 | 5 | 35 |

**JIM URBINA:** I was building a mound on the south side of the huge green out on Five Mile Point. When Tony Russell [a local contractor] saw it, I told him I was building the Himalayas. "You mean the Jimalayas," he said, and the name stuck. The Jimalayas are still there.

**ERIC:** There were all kinds of rumors about the Sheep Ranch. I was up there often enough to know they were just rumors, but the caddie lore just kept adding new twists. One rumor was that there was a private club at the Sheep Ranch, and Tiger Woods was a member. The word came down that those of us on staff shouldn't talk to guests about it.

**MK:** The rumors got out of hand. When people heard these juicy tales about the Sheep Ranch, they wanted to see it. They wanted to know how they could play there. But it wasn't part of the resort. Phil was operating the Sheep Ranch, and it became a confusing distraction. Our people at the resort didn't know how to answer all the questions they got. They were in an awkward position. The easiest thing was just to put a moratorium on the subject. Which, of course, made people more curious than ever.

*At the original Sheep Ranch, the holes were lettered, not numbered, and designed to be playable from several different angles. Tom Doak once calculated that the course offered sixty-three "likely" holes, and identified the best thirty.*

**JIM:** We built thirteen greens. We also built a few tees, and Tom came up with a suggested routing. The greens were lettered, not numbered, and there was a rudimentary scorecard showing how you could put together eighteen holes with a par of 71. I don't think many people followed the routing. Part of the fun of playing at the Sheep Ranch was that you could go in any direction you felt like. One of the local traditions was that the winner of a hole got to choose the next one.

MK: There was some discussion about building a small lodge on the property and creating a private club. Members would be able to play the resort courses, and then they'd come back here and play the thirteen holes. The Sheep Ranch would be a kind of private playground for them. But that idea never went anywhere. One principle of the resort was a commitment to public play. We offered different levels of accommodation, but apart from that, all guests were treated equally. They got the same kind of service and enjoyed the same facilities. It went against the ethos of Bandon to create a special category of guest, with special privileges.

PHIL: I hired a superintendent to manage the property, a crew of one. Some areas were mowed as fairways, and we kept the greens cut so you could putt on them. To water the greens, we brought in an old fire truck filled with water and hooked it up to used sprinkler heads we got from a Coos Bay golf course. We could water two or three greens a day, depending on the wind.

MK: The Sheep Ranch developed a mystique. People started calling it Area 51—the forbidden zone where some spooky experience awaited. Its reputation was enshrined when a *Sports Illustrated* writer came out in 2003 to write about our new course, Bandon Trails, and basically ignored it. Instead, he gave the Sheep Ranch its first national publicity. He wrote a kind of exposé, suggesting that the resort was hatching a new plan. His headline was "Bandon Dunes Project X," and he claimed that we were "secretly" adding a course that would fundamentally change the character of the resort. Well, we weren't advertising the Sheep Ranch, but after that article it certainly wasn't a secret.

BLAINE NEWNHAM, former sports editor of the *Eugene Register-Guard:* "Easily, romantically, playing the Sheep Ranch earned it a spot among my greatest golf experiences. Up there with playing Royal

County Down in Ireland, or two of America's great places, Merion and Cypress Point, or winning a spot in the lottery to play Augusta National the day after the Masters ended."

PHIL: The experience wasn't just being able to go wherever you wanted. The experience was having the day change three or four times while you were out there, having the fog roll in, seeing the coast, seeing the water, seeing the rocks, being part of what I would call almost a mystical experience on that land.

JIM: When they came to Bandon to film the movie *Golf in the Kingdom,* they scouted around for sites that would evoke the same mood as the book—wild, haunted, beautiful. Of course, they ended up shooting the golf scenes at the Sheep Ranch. If you see the movie, check out the starter—that's me.

TOM: Mike told me years ago, when he hired us to design Old Macdonald, that whenever he finally got around to turning the Sheep Ranch into eighteen holes, he'd have to hire someone else for that, because I would already have done two courses at Bandon. I don't think I would have had the heart to tear up the course myself, anyway.

MK: I know some people were dead set against turning the Sheep Ranch into an eighteen-hole course. They saw it as something unique, and it was. But the fact is that despite the notoriety of the Sheep Ranch, not that many people went up there. That was partly a matter of safety—you couldn't have many groups out there, playing in different directions. For the most part, it was a private playground for Phil. Even though the maintenance was minimal, it still cost money to keep it playable. The business model, if you could even call it that, was not sustainable.

PHIL: To keep expenses to a minimum, I sometimes borrowed equipment from the resort. They had a complete maintenance department and at first Mike had no objection to occasional loans.

MK: This is where our different perspectives came into conflict. I was trying to run a profitable resort. We'd had previous issues when maintenance equipment and resources were provided, unauthorized, to non-resort projects, and the Sheep Ranch was its own thing—it wasn't a resort project. I was coming to see it as Phil's project. The notoriety that it was receiving made it seem like a competitor that could take rounds away from the resort. I told Phil he'd have to supply his own equipment.

PHIL: That's what we argued about—a bloody rake. And the occasional backhoe.

MK: We'd reached our first impasse in business, and it coincided with our selling RPG.

PHIL: Even though we continued to share an office and to see each other there most days, and also to see each other socially, there was a bit of chill in the air.

*With Phil in our office during Sheep Ranch construction. He's the one with the walking staff.*

MK: Phil kept the Sheep Ranch operating, and it remained one of those opportunities that we knew we had to fulfill. Eventually, we were able to renew our discussion. We were both getting older, and we realized

that if we were ever going to turn the Sheep Ranch into the kind of golf course we'd both imagined, we'd better not wait too much longer.

CHRIS HOOD: For zoning purposes, this wasn't a new course. It was a renovation of the existing course, which had already been permitted. This meant that once the decision to proceed was made, the work could begin immediately.

MK: Phil and I were considering both Gil Hanse and Coore-Crenshaw. Gil had been patient while working through the issues for the Bandon Muni, a project that we tried for years to get approved and then finally abandoned. In the end, though, we decided to go with Bill and Ben. I'd always felt their work at Bandon Trails was underappreciated since the course doesn't have the same exposure to the ocean as the others. And then Bill came up with a brilliant routing for the Sheep Ranch, with nine greens on the edge of the cliff. To have nine greens right on the ocean—that's off the charts.

BILL COORE: Before getting too deep into the project, I wanted to get to know Phil and make sure that he was prepared to give up what had been a kind of sanctuary for him. I knew he was serious about this course. Phil has an old rugby injury, and it's not easy for him to walk. But the first day he came out to visit the site with me—the rain was coming down sideways and the wind just about blew us over—Phil stayed out there for eight hours.

PHIL: It happened that Bill and I were often at Bandon in the middle of the week, and we had dinner together—our Wednesday-night dates. He understood that I had an emotional attachment to the place, and he wanted to make sure that I was prepared to let go. Once the golf course was built, if it was equal to the site, people were going to come, a lot of people. I knew that. I believed this site was the most spectacular at Bandon Dunes. I wanted to share the Sheep Ranch with others who could have something like the experience that I'd had.

CHRIS: Since the project was technically a remodeling, the holes were going to have to remain within the area that had been permitted for

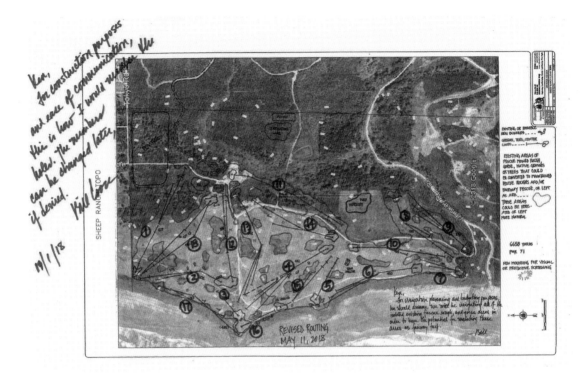

golf, and that was about 150 acres. Several acres were in the cutover section of the property, distant from the ocean, and unsuitable for golf. Those eighteen holes were going to have to be shoehorned into the site.

BILL: Over a period of months, I spent many days roaming the land, trying to find a way to route the holes. Before that, I'd only been there once, on a foggy day, and I don't think I even got out of the truck. The land looked flat. But one of my first discoveries was that the property has beautiful, natural contours for golf. Flat it is not. The prime real estate was along the edge of the cliff, that was obvious, and I wanted to use that land to full advantage.

MK: From a design perspective, the Sheep Ranch offered possibilities that weren't available at the other Bandon courses. Both Bandon Dunes and Pacific Dunes play parallel to the ocean, but the coastline is straight as a ruler. With Five Mile Point jutting out so dramatically, it was easy to imagine shots that had heroic carries like the 8th and 18th

*Bill Coore's routing plan for the Sheep Ranch, with notes for Ken Nice, the chief agronomist at Bandon*

at Pebble Beach, or the 16th at Cypress Point. These are legendary, inspiring holes, the subject of paintings and photographs that golfers hang on their walls so they can see them every day. Bill's routing for the Sheep Ranch showed several holes converging on Five Mile Point, using the Pacific not just as a backdrop but a hazard. Anyone who played the course was going to have a chance to send his ball soaring over the ocean.

JIM: The first thing I wanted to ask Bill was "How'd you get all the holes to fit?"

BILL: When I started, there were still a few people playing Tom's holes, and I wanted to get rid of the flags. They stood out like beacons. I wanted to concentrate on the landforms. When Phil finally closed the course, I took the flags down right away.

BEN CRENSHAW: Tom had already used some of the best features of the land to build his greens. We wanted to use his work wherever we could, not just ignore it to put our own stamp on the property. Five of his green sites are incorporated into the routing.

BILL: The key to the puzzle was to increase the size of the teeing areas, to make them serve more than one hole. The tees for No. 2 and No. 18, for example, are virtually side by side, but the line of play radiates out in different directions. There are three places where the tees are together like that, and it makes much more efficient use of the ground.

MK: Phil and I had often talked about design, but we had never collaborated on a project like this one. We had some fundamental differences of opinion. I wanted to get rid of all the gorse, and Phil liked it. He also liked blind shots, and I didn't. He wanted to save all the dead tree snags along the cliff's edge, and I thought they should go. I thought it would be more appropriate to have a clean, pure edge.

PHIL: Part of Bill's job was to balance our opinions. He spends a lot of time on every site, and his method is to work carefully, so there was time to make small changes and adjustments, to test different ideas and mull them over. Without compromising his own views, he manages to be a great diplomat. He lets Mike and me state our case, and then he steps in, courteously but firmly. Bill holds the gavel.

BILL: There are no sand bunkers on the course. It worries me a little that some people will think it's some kind of gimmick—a course with no sand bunkers. But that's not the reason we did it. The place is completely exposed to the wind, and if we had sand bunkers on this course, the maintenance would be next to impossible. Bunkers would need constant rebuilding. To get Phil and Mike to accept the lack of bunkers, I sent them a picture and quote from the Robert Hunter book, *The Links*. The gist of the quote is that someday there will be a piece of land so perfect for golf that sand bunkers will not be necessary. Ben and I had actually talked about this over the years, wondering if we would ever find that perfect site.

BEN: There are some scooped-out areas that look like they might have been bunkers—abandoned bunkers. They fit right in with the rugged landforms.

BILL: We also use plants—patches of gorse and some wispy fescue, some heather—to give the site definition and texture. Other native plants will fill in, too, as they have at Bandon Trails.

KEN NICE, superintendent: For now, the bunker floors are fescue turf. We thought about letting them grow and get more gnarly, but with the wind conditions, it doesn't make sense to make the course more difficult. The grass in the bunkers will be a little higher than on the fairway so golfers can easily get a club on the ball. We want them to have a good chance to recover.

BEN: Everything on the course has to be oversized because of the wind. We have some double fairways and gigantic greens to make it easier to keep the ball in play.

BILL: The first hole is a par-5 that takes the golfer out of the trees at the back of the property and tumbles all the way down to the ocean.

It does what Ben and I believe a first hole ought to do—it tells you what to expect from the course. Here at the Sheep Ranch, it does more than that—it shows you what's waiting for you out there. Some people think the first hole should be a handshake, but this first hole is a plunge. It doesn't tease you with a distant view of the ocean. It carries you right out to the edge. The ocean's right there in front of you on the first hole, and that's pretty much where it will stay throughout the round.

PHIL: I wanted a player not only to have a constant sense of the Pacific but to be able to see the ocean from every hole on the course.

TONY RUSSELL, construction contractor: They decided to keep the snags, but Bill wanted them placed in better positions to frame the holes. There are several of them down near that 1st green, and one was standing right in the middle of the 17th green. I dug them up with the excavator, then lifted them with a cable and kind of walked them to their new location. It was like rearranging the furniture.

PHIL: I couldn't picture this site without the snags. They're eerie, but for me they are an essential part of this landscape, having been there all along.

MK: I yielded on the snags. I'll try to get used to them.

BILL: The routing goes to the edge and back, to the edge and back. I wanted to approach the cliff edge from different directions, to get you to look at the ocean and the sea stacks from a different angle, to play a variety of shots into the oceanside greens.

MK: The town of Bandon is famous for its sea stacks, the big rock formations that are found all along the south coast. But Five Mile Point is the only place on the resort where you see them and the sea lions close up.

JIM CRAIG, shaper who worked on the huge double green for the 3rd and 16th holes: A writer came out here and said that when you stand at the edge and look back at the green, it's like looking at the back of a big wave that's just about to break. Right there, that's the power of suggestion—the whole time I was working on this green, that's what I saw every time I looked up, row after row of waves rolling in.

**BILL:** This was one green where we wanted to keep what we could of Tom's design. After Jim did some initial work, though, a big storm came through and just blew everything away. It left a trough through the middle of the green. Maybe that was an omen.

**PHIL:** I like this green, and the next tee even more. [The back tee for the 17th is at the far end of this green; the golfer will look over the beach back toward the fairway on the mainland, a tee shot that calls for heroics.] You'll have to bite off a big chunk of the Pacific when the tee is out here.

**MK:** These are four strong finishing holes, with 15, 16, and 17 on the ocean, and 18 a short par-5. It's tough to design an inland finishing hole after a sequence of dramatic oceanside holes. That's always been the knock on Cypress Point, that the 18th is a letdown—but what do you do after those glorious ocean holes?

**BILL:** Late in the construction process, we were still uncertain about the numbering of the holes. I liked the overall pattern, but we had differences of opinion about the sequence. Initially, the numbering was mostly a matter of convenience—you have to have numbers to com-

TER WIND

OCEAN

SUMMER WIND

CLIFF

TEE

REAR PORTION OF GREEN IS SUNKEN TROUGH

WISPY GRASS

ABANDONED BUNKERS

UPPER SHELF ON GREEN

#5 Sheep Ranch

DIRECTION OF PLAY

*Bill often says he can't draw, but this sketch of the 5th hole is typical of the renderings he shares with his team. Note especially the intricate detail of the putting surface and green surrounds.*

*This rolling, tumultuous double green looks as if the surf climbed right up the cliff and turned to grass.*

municate to the guys who are out there working. You can't say, "Oh, Jim, you need to work on that fairway with the squirrelly little bush on the left."

MK: There are two, maybe three sequences that could have worked.

PHIL: Maybe we should've decided to play it that way, with different eighteen-hole routings on different days. That would be in keeping with the spirit of the Sheep Ranch.

BILL: Some days we'd go back and forth on which sequence made the most sense, and I'd threaten to do what Perry Maxwell did at Southern Hills. When he finished building the course, he gave the club his routing plan—but the holes weren't numbered. They came back to him and asked which hole was supposed to be which. He said, "I built the holes. Now you can number them."

MK: One green that everyone is going to remember is the 11th, the hole we've been calling the Volcano Hole. The green is on the highest point of the property where there used to be a sand mine, and it's been hollowed out like a crater, with sides that look like the walls of a quarry.

PHIL: From the fairway, before any shaping, you were looking at the wall of the crater. It was a doozy of a blind shot, and I wanted to leave it like that.

MK: I didn't.

BILL: We compromised. At first, we made a narrow opening in the wall and we were going to have something rugged, a kind of lava flow coming down from the crater. But it was so steep that I wasn't sure people would be able to get up the slope. After taking away a little bit at a time and raising the fairway, we ended up with a wider opening and gentler grade. It's still a blind shot if you don't put your second shot in the correct position, and if you miss left, you might be on short grass but you are in a world of trouble.

PHIL: This green is going to blow people away. It's one-of-a-kind, with these walls that look chiseled out of sandstone, and all the odd, irregular shapes.

MK: Bill looks at it as if he's composing a picture. He talks about cutting away a little more in the opening, to give it a "quarry cut" that would resemble the walls inside the crater.

BILL: I kid Mike and Phil about how differently they view things. At the front edge of that 11th green, there's a little ridge just a couple of feet high that will be a problem for the golfer who's short and left. One morning after the green and the surrounds had been seeded, Mike came and looked at the ridge and asked, "If we find that this doesn't work after people start playing, can you lower that by about ten inches?" I told him that yes, we could remove the turf and then take away some of the dirt, replace the turf, and lose ten inches. That seemed to satisfy him. Less than an hour later, I was still there at the 11th green when Phil came by and pointed at that ridge. He said, "Bill, how hard would it be to raise that by about ten inches?" So I explained the process to him, as I had to Mike. That night at dinner I made a toast to Len Levine, their financial guy for decades, because that's the kind of difference he's reconciled throughout his career. They single out the same ridge, and they come up with exactly the same number for making an adjustment—but in diametrically opposite directions.

LEN LEVINE: I told Bill he missed his calling as a diplomat. The great thing about Mike and Phil's partnership is that they recognized their differences and accepted them as part of the dynamic, using them often as a source of strength.

CHRIS: The golf course has transformed this land. When PP&L owned it, it was an industrial site with high-voltage wires running all over the place, concrete pads for the windmills, roads for heavy equipment that weren't much more than deep ruts. The gorse was out of control. Now the whole place will be cleaned up and stabilized. It will have a chance to heal.

BILL: I've told Phil and Mike that the Sheep Ranch has one of the best clubhouse sites I've ever seen anywhere. There can't be many places in the country that have such an unobstructed view of the ocean and such privacy. I don't usually think much about the buildings on a property— that's for someone else. But to be up here on this spot, where the entire golf course is spread out in front of you, and beyond that the Pacific Ocean fills the entire horizon . . . it's magnificent.

PHIL: It was all worth waiting for. By waiting I got to meet Bill Coore, and he was the perfect guy to make this happen. Maybe the Sheep Ranch is a good example of the journey being more important than the destination.

MK: On a bluebird day in September 2019, Phil and I played the first preview holes at the Sheep Ranch. Bill joined us for a couple of holes, and so did Bob Johnson and Len Levine. It took two decades to get to that experience, five decades if you count all the years of our partnership. Is the Sheep Ranch the grand finale, the crown jewel of our partnership? If so, we finished in style.

PHIL: The chill has ended. The balmy breezes of a fifty-five-year friendship continue, and the love child is the Sheep Ranch.

## Barnbougle Dunes

Bridport, Tasmania, Australia

───────────

2004 **BARNBOUGLE DUNES**, 6,724 yards, par 71
Tom Doak and Michael Clayton
#11 on *Golf Digest*'s 100 Greatest Golf Courses 2020
#5 in Australia, *Planet Golf*

2010 **LOST FARM**, 6,849 yards, par 72
Bill Coore and Ben Crenshaw
#47 on *Golf Digest*'s 100 Greatest Golf Courses, 2020
#4 in Australia, *Planet Golf*

2021 **BOUGLE RUN**, 14-hole short course
Bill Coore and Ben Crenshaw

# 6

# Barnbougle Dunes

*Though the gorgeous island state of Tasmania has long been a popular tourist destination . . . it was not until the 2004 opening of Barnbougle Dunes, in the sleepy seaside village of Bridport, that the entire golfing landscape in this most southerly corner of Australia changed forever. Tasmania is now a major international golf tourism player.*

*—Planet Golf*

N 2000, BEFORE PACIFIC DUNES OPENED, Tom Doak and I were standing on the high ground that is now the 10th tee, a scenic exclamation point where you crest a ridge and see the jaw-dropping holes strung along the rim of the cliff. "Have you ever seen a more beautiful spot for golf?" I asked him.

Any other architect would've agreed with me. But Tom answered very much in character: "I know of one in Australia that might be just as good. Or even better."

Tom Doak cannot tell a lie, not even a white lie to please a proud property owner.

The place Tom had in mind was a farm called Barnbougle, on the Bass Strait in the town of Bridport, Tasmania, and our conversation that day was the beginning of Bandon Down Under. I didn't actually get to Barnbougle until December 2001, when I went to Australia with my oldest son, Michael Jr., then a freshman at Santa Clara. We made the trip to visit friends in Sydney, play some golf, and see what Tom was talking about.

I wanted to spend one-on-one time with Michael and, frankly, to make sure he did something over the Christmas vacation besides drink beer with his friends back home in Chicago. As a student, he reminded me of myself: intellectually curious, drawn to big ideas, not motivated by grades, restless in and out of the classroom. When he was in the eighth grade, he decided he wanted to be an ice climber, an obsession that alarmed Lindy and me. He used to rappel down the walls from our twelfth-floor apartment in Chicago. With the confidence of a teenager, he didn't see how dangerous this was. I didn't want to stifle his boldness, but I did want to temper it.

Tom had put me in touch with Mike Clayton, a central figure in Australian golf, a touring pro who was also an architect with an encyclopedic knowledge and forceful opinions—Doak's Australian counterpart, in other words. Many of Mike's opinions, I came to learn, had been influenced by Tom before they'd ever met. An Australian columnist published excerpts from an early mimeographed copy of what was later released as *Confidential Guide to Golf Courses*—prompting the author to ask if he understood the meaning of "confidential"—and Clayton read them avidly. Then, in England for the British Open, Mike found Doak's *Anatomy of a Golf Course* in a book-store and was excited to see many of his own ideas articulated and solidified. And when Tom, who was entranced by the courses in the Australian Sand-belt, started exploring opportunities in Oz, he teamed up with Mike Clayton in a loose partnership that soon benefited both of them.

Together they'd staked out a routing at Barnbougle. The concept was Tom's, but it was Mike who guided us through the property. So here I was again, scouting out a potential golf course at the end of the earth—this time on a cattle ranch/potato farm that seemed even more remote than Bandon. At least Oregon was on the mainland. Tasmania was an island, a distant part of an already distant continent. Ironically, I was now in the position of those experts who'd warned me off Bandon because people would never go so far away to play golf.

One difference in this scenario was that the landowner, Richard Sattler, was in no hurry to develop any part of the fifteen thousand acres he'd bought to fulfill a lifelong dream of running a big spread. About golf he was cheer-fully ignorant. "I have a healthy relationship with golf," he likes to say. "I've swung a club, but I've never filled in a scorecard." Unlike me, he didn't need to be discouraged from getting into the golf business. On the contrary, he had to be persuaded into considering any such thing.

The notion of golf at Barnbougle had originated with a young Tasma-nian named Greg Ramsay. When he first presented the idea, Sattler thought he was a madman. Ramsay did have a relevant pedigree; his family owned Ratho Farm, site of Australia's oldest course. After a stint in Scotland, where he tended bar, caddied at Kingsbarns, and became absolutely smit-ten with links golf, he'd secured a contract with the Tasmanian government to assess the sport's potential to spur tourism. The officials never acted on any of Ramsay's recommendations, but Ramsay wasn't deterred. Convinced that Barnbougle was the best property in Tasmania, he decided to develop it himself and kept pestering Sattler. By general consensus, Greg Ramsay is a super-salesman who never takes no for an answer, and he finally was granted an option.

From Richard's point of view, he wasn't giving up anything valuable, just a strip of sandy dunesland that wasn't much good for grazing or planting. Ramsay, a dreamer on a large scale and another avid reader of Tom Doak's writing, was able to lure him and Mike Clayton to visit the site. When I met Greg, it didn't take me long to understand why the press has sometimes referred to him as a golf "tragic"—Aussie slang for people so obsessed with a subject that they lose all perspective, along with an awareness of how their single-mindedness is perceived by others. Greg believed utterly in Barnbougle's perfection, but he was less sure of how to realize his dream.

The Barnbougle dunes were indeed gorgeous, and Richard Sattler was a good bloke. Around my age, with ruddy cheeks, a fringe of white hair, a ready smile, and a supply of one-liners and homespun wisdom, he seemed to me to possess all the virtues of the Australian archetype: affable, hospitable, optimistic, direct, down-to-earth, brimming over with good humor and a can-do spirit. A poor boy whose first real job was shearing sheep, he'd started with nothing, and now he was running a herd of 2,700 grass-fed cattle and sold more potatoes to McDonald's than anybody else in Australia. In between, he'd made his first real money as a hotel owner in Hobart, Tasmania's major city. But farming was in his blood. He

*Richard Sattler*

took a big plunge when he bought Barnbougle and moved his family back to the land. Herding his stock from his pickup truck, with his dogs as his companions, Richard seemed completely in his element.

A Tasmanian farmer had to be perplexed by visits from golf architects and American businessmen. By temperament and upbringing, Richard wanted to do business with people he knew and trusted. When Mike Clayton brought him a standard architectural contract of ten pages to sign, Richard got halfway through it, asked if it was really necessary, crumpled it up, threw it in the trash, and closed the deal the old-fashioned way, with a handshake. Within the man of the soil, however, there lurked a shrewd entrepreneur, and his antenna went up when I talked about Bandon Dunes as a business. I've heard him say, "Don't underestimate the farmer. He has a lot of time to think as he goes about his chores. He's always working out a strategy."

After a single visit I wanted the Barnbougle project to work, partly because I liked so many things about the place—its remoteness, its population of marsupials, its magnificent dunes. Even the strictest purist agrees that it meets all the criteria of true linksland. I also wanted the project to work for Tom, Mike Clayton, and Richard, who was quickly becoming a friend.

To give him an idea of what he might be able to accomplish at Barnbougle, I invited him to visit Bandon Dunes, where we opened our books to him. He spent a week studying them, and as an experienced hotel manager he was impressed by our numbers. My pitch was that a golf course would be less trouble than farming. Every ten minutes, four strangers would show up and pay $100 or more to walk around the property for a few hours. While Richard asked questions, I could tell that a plan was forming.

So, how to put the deal together? Greg Ramsay was trying to find investors, but his chances of succeeding were, in my view, between slim and none. The best way forward was to allow his option to expire and to encourage Richard to finance the operation himself—which is exactly what happened. Ramsay brought a few of his investors to the final deal and was rewarded for his efforts with a small equity share in a company called Links Golf Tasmania. Richard put up a substantial sum of his own money to buy a 60 percent stake in LGT. The Tasmanian government provided additional funds. When it came to the crunch, I put up the last million he needed—as a loan, with an interest rate that increased annually to encourage a quick payback (the loan has now been retired). Being able to promote the resort as Bandon Down Under, with an oceanfront course designed by Tom Doak and Mike Clayton, meant that Barnbougle Dunes would attract worldwide media attention when it opened in 2004. The American model was being transplanted to Australia.

It's a long way to Tasmania, and Tom and I didn't spend nearly as much time together there as we had at Pacific Dunes. He is, I had learned, a whiz at working with topo maps; with his three-dimensional imagination, he can look at the contour lines and visualize the actual topography with amazing accuracy. Yet he is not infallible. I'd warned Richard not to let Tom talk him out of running the finishing holes along the beach, but Tom didn't figure out a coast-hugging route until he discovered a perfect, natural site for the 17th green. This happened only after we'd walked up to the high ground that became the 16th tee—a place he refers to, I'm happy to say, as "Mike Keiser's dune." The downhill 16th, a par-3, is now part of a sequence of marvelous seaside finishing holes.

Mind you, I still think Pacific Dunes is just as beautiful.

For Michael and me, the trip to Tasmania became an annual event, our way of starting the Christmas holidays. Business discussions took place around Richard's dinner table, where I got to know his wife, Sally, and their four children. It was familiar territory for me: another remote location, another start-up, another links course. Then on the mainland, with Mike Clayton as our guide and tutor, Michael and I played the great courses of the Australian Sandbelt—an experience that opened Michael's eyes to the fascination of classic design. When he graduated from Santa Clara, the Sattlers welcomed him into the family, and he got his first taste of the golf business as an intern at Barnbougle.

*Mike Keiser's memo to Tom Doak re Barnbougle*

From 1999 to 2010, I was continuously involved in projects with Tom Doak. In those eleven years, we built three courses together: Pacific Dunes, Barnbougle Dunes, and Old Macdonald. Four, if you count the Sheep Ranch. To be clear, Tom wasn't working exclusively for me, and I had other projects going myself. But for both of us, Pacific Dunes was a threshold to new opportunities.

For Tom, the golden doors swung open immediately. Pacific Dunes had been open for exactly one day when Julian Robertson, founder of Tiger Management and a hedge fund legend, visited Bandon. After a round on David Kidd's course, he wanted a replay and was annoyed that no tee times were available. Would he mind playing the new course? Yes, he would, but four hours later he walked off the 18th green at Pacific Dune a full-fledged Doak fan. Robertson was getting ready to build a golf course on Hawkes Bay, in New Zealand, and he'd been looking for an architect. Tom got the job. When the first photographs of Cape Kidnappers began to appear in 2004, most people, including me, went weak in the knees. Built on headlands that are separated like the fingers of a hand, Cape Kidnappers sits five hundred feet above the sea, majestic to behold, a work of design on a scale that invites comparisons to places like Machu Pichu. Am I gushing? Yes, but so does everyone else who sees the place. It is one of the wonders of the golf world.

Tom was well and truly launched. Pacific Dunes, Barnbougle Dunes, Cape Kidnappers—in a span of less than five years, he designed three seaside courses that landed instantly on Top 100 lists. He added others in the open spaces of the American West, Ballyneal and the Rock Creek Cattle Company, that have won the same honor. Moreover, his Renaissance Golf Club was built in the heart of Scottish golf, tucked between Muirfield and North Berwick. Finally, in one of the most hallowed American golf locations adjoining Shinnecock Hills and National Golf Links on Long Island, he teamed up with Jack Nicklaus to codesign Sebonack. He was being hailed as the global superstar of golf design.

Later, I'll have more to say about Tom, but my point here is that we came to Barnbougle Dunes during a surge of international development that's easier to define in retrospect than it was at the time. After 2000, when American courses were opening at the rate of one a day, construction in the United States slowed to a trickle—and the rest of the world took up the slack. Many designers found work in China, where statistically none of the population plays golf. Dozens of courses were built in a style best described as American Sunbelt on super-steroids. Big-name architects, manufactured layouts, luxury real estate, and mega-clubhouses whose epitome might be found in Shenzhen, where Mission Hills clubhouse is 300,000 square feet.

Extravagance has been the norm for golf developments in Asia and the

Mideast. I've seen pictures of the Jumeirah Golf Estates in Dubai, where luxury housing surrounds "eco-signature courses" named for the four elements. The one called "Earth" was designed by former tour star Greg Norman; despite being built smack in the middle of the desert, it's described on the website as "inspired by the great parklands of Europe and North America . . . a magnificent pastiche of flora, rolling terrain, and rushing water."

I'm in no hurry to book a tee time.

By comparison, Barnbougle was a modest, even humble venture. Basically, we were doing what Dick Youngscap had done in Nebraska and I'd done in Oregon. Instead of fretting about the market, we'd found great pieces of ground, built great courses there, and let the market come to us. In this age of air travel, the world had grown smaller, and for a growing number of travelers, and golfers, "remote" was a positive term. Faraway resorts promised an experience in a place that had remained unspoiled and pristine, an escape from Freud's "civilization and its discontents." By 2020, the number of beautiful, remote, seaside courses had increased significantly. In Tasmania alone, aside from Barnbougle, links had also opened at Cape Wickham and Ocean Dunes.

To my mind, Barnbougle Dunes belongs to a generation of global enterprises whose owners and architects shared the same goal: to create courses that were worth a journey because they displayed the game's architecture as an art form that can complement—and help reveal—the finest landscapes.

Such courses are also reminders that the twenty-first century could foster a sense of global citizenship. Julian Robertson was a prime example of this. Though he grew up in North Carolina, he'd based his hedge fund in Australia, and his whole family was head over heels about New Zealand, where they vacationed. One of the most insatiable golfers I've ever known, Julian had played all over the world. On the headlands at Cape Kidnappers, he wanted to build a marvel of a golf course—and a place that could help sustain the unique ecology of the area. On his six thousand acres at Cape Kidnappers, Julian created not only a magnificent golf course but a preserve for its unique ecosystem, which is home to the world's largest colony of gannets and many other rare and endangered bird species. I know exactly what Julian meant when he said, "My greatest success with these places would be to have them serve as a model for development, the kind that enhances—or at least doesn't detract from—nature and the natural beauty of the place."

Yet another American who's become a figure in global development is

Ric Kayne, who selected Tom Doak to design his ultraexclusive course in New Zealand. It pains me to admit that Tara Iti might be the most beautiful course in the world. On *Golf Digest*'s 2018 list of the World's 100 Greatest Golf Courses, Tara Iti debuted at No. 6—the highest rating ever awarded to a new course.

I'm aware that owners like Julian or Ric (or me) are sometimes seen as engaging in a "sport of kings," plundering the globe for trophy courses. But Ric's next two courses, near Tara Iti, will be public, and I applaud the care, decency, time, and effort with which he has secured land leases from the Maori owners. We've been in frequent contact during the process, and the first course, designed by Bill Coore, is scheduled to open in 2023. Tom Doak will design the second course. Both are being developed in a manner fully attuned to the tribe's long-term commercial, cultural, and environmental goals. I would also submit that this part of New Zealand will be seen and enjoyed by more people because of these courses, that its natural resources will benefit from Ric's stewardship, and that the Maori will value him as a tenant.

In December 2004, a who's who of international golf writers had gathered in Bridport, Tasmania, for the opening, and since many of them were also course raters, Barnbougle Dunes got off to a fast start, with glowing reviews soon followed by high rankings. The course shot to the top of the lists as the best modern course in Australia.

By now its major rival for the No. 1 ranking is Lost Farm, the second course at Barnbougle, a Coore-Crenshaw layout that opened in 2010. Another course had always been part of the plan, and Richard and I both wanted to move ahead quickly on a timeline similar to Bandon Dunes'.

This sounded simple enough, but one snag after another led to a mind-boggling "legal stoush." In essence, control and ownership of this new entity was being contested by Greg Ramsay, Links Golf Tasmania, and Richard Sattler. At issue was Richard's legal right to create a second company. Alleging that they'd been assured that they could invest in any future development, the shareholders of LGT sued Richard, who owned the majority interest— which meant that Richard was suing himself! The leader of the plaintiffs was Greg Ramsay, who'd been offered what I considered a fair, even generous, ownership position in return for his role in launching the project. When he rejected the offer, I felt almost as if I was being sued personally.

The trial lasted forty-five days, eight of which Richard spent on the witness stand. I flew to Australia, appeared in court, and flew home the next day. I was proud to state my support for Richard, and I cited my formula—1 + 1 = 3—to suggest that all parties would profit from Lost Farm.

After years of filings and depositions, arguing and haggling, the judge finally ruled that "the future of Lost Farm was a question for Sattler to determine, as landowner." For Richard, who'd felt that his integrity and good name had been called into question, this verdict was sweet vindication, but he did not emerge unscathed. In a last twist of the bizarre legal situation, he ended up paying over $6.5 million in legal fees—including some of the fees for Links Golf Tasmania.

He now owns 100 percent of the golf operation at Barnbougle, and thrives on it. For many visitors there, an encounter with Richard is a special part of the experience. He lives on the farm and stops by the club for coffee or a drink at the bar and often dines in the spectacular Lost Farm restaurant, perched atop a high dune with a wall of windows overlooking the coastline. His daughter Penny is the resort's general manager. His son Steven runs the farming operations and has also become an avid golfer; since he grew up on these links, he finds it strange and disorienting to play a course with trees. Another daughter, Lisbeth, lives in Melbourne and handles all Barnbougle's marketing, while her younger sister, Olivia, works in media and communications, the only sibling who is not employed in the family business. Their mother, Sally, prefers to stay behind the scenes, keeping a watchful eye on everything from housekeeping to menus.

As an already experienced innkeeper, Richard fashioned the amenities and lodging to his own specifications, aiming to "Australianize" the model of Bandon Dunes. Despite being relatively small, the resort caters to a broad range of golfers, offering accommodations from basic and comfortable to stylish and sophisticated, and Barnbougle Dunes has quickly become a fixture in the Down Under golf scene.

For someone who knew nothing about the game starting out, Richard has settled with ease into his role as a godfather of accessible, authentic links golf. Mike Clayton considers him one of the most important figures in Australian golf. Richard has learned, as I did, that the game's community is large and varied, and his friendships within it have opened new worlds for a man who spent many years without straying far from his ranch. Top Australian pros have paid their respects at Barnbougle, and Adam Scott invited Richard and Sally to Augusta National in 2013, when he became the first Aussie to win the Masters. He called Richard his good-luck charm.

*Lost Farm in the foreground, Barnbougle Dunes on the other side of the estuary. Though it looks like Fife, this classic linksland is in Tasmania.*

Richard has also learned enough about golf architecture to put his own stamp on the layout at Lost Farm, designed by Bill Coore on land with dunes taller than those on the first course. The best golf terrain also reached farther inland and encompassed a central meadow, where in rough weather farmers would often find their cattle sheltering from the elements—hence the name Lost Farm.

With room to spread out, Bill fashioned a layout that could be played in the heavy coastal winds: broad fairways, large greens, holes that played to all points of the compass. He spent weeks in Tasmania, giving Lost Farm the kind of finish that is a hallmark of Coore-Crenshaw designs. Like me, Richard wasn't wedded to a nine- or eighteen-hole formula, and when it was finished, Lost Farm had twenty holes. I am partially responsible for one of the extras; I didn't like Bill's uphill 17th, and when I proposed an alternative, Richard insisted on building both. Then Richard himself, flexing his rights as the owner, suggested adding a par-3 bye hole that could be played after the 18th to settle any outstanding bets. When Bill initially winced at the notion, Richard won him over with an argument based on historical precedent. He'd read that St. Andrews had once had twenty holes, so why couldn't Lost Farm?

Recently, Richard called on Bill to design a third course—Bougle Run, a fourteen-hole short course consisting of twelve par-3s and a pair of drivable par-4s. Bill laid out the course during a three-day visit in the fall of 2019 and then left the construction to an associate who used drone photography to keep him up to speed with the progress.

For now, Barnbougle is fully built out, and in peak season the resort is booked solid. No one has to explain to Richard that he's competing for a share of a small market. Barnbougle Dunes has succeeded for the same reason that Bandon Dunes succeeded: visitors don't just like the place, they love it. They go home and tell their friends about it, and they return year after year. Barnbougle, only an hour's flight from Melbourne, has become a second club for many golfers—or the first, the epicenter of their playing life.

Calling himself an opportunist, Richard has made his resort an anchor for Tasmania's growing tourism industry. It pleases him that visitors are stunned to arrive at an honest-to-God working farm that combines a glimpse into the mythic Australian past with contemporary luxuries and exhilarating golf. In semiretirement, he's stepped back from running the business day to day, and there's one final twist in this Australian rags-to-riches story. In a long-term, multimillion-dollar project, sand will be extracted from the huge, rolling dune on the Barnbougle property, loaded onto ships, and transported to Sydney. Richard Sattler's farm has made him a rich man, but in ways he could never have imagined.

Barnbougle is the second golf destination where courses designed by Tom Doak and Coore-Crenshaw are side by side. The first was Bandon Dunes, and the third was Streamsong, in Florida. Bill Coore is now at work on the second course at Tara Iti, and if all the projects on the drawing board are completed, the Coore-Crenshaw/Doak pairing will occur at two more destinations of mine: Sand Valley and Cabot Cape Breton.

In the annals of golf architecture, there is no precedent for this. As the owner who first made this pairing and knows how much these designers respect each other, I see their relationship as a friendly but serious competition that brings out the best in everybody. They're at the top of their game when aligned like this, just as Tom Watson and Jack Nicklaus made each other shine when competing against each other.

Golfers who play their courses one after the other can't resist comparing them. How does Bandon Trails stack up against Pacific Dunes? Is Barnbougle Dunes better than Lost Farm? How does Streamsong Blue rate against Streamsong Red? I'm not foolish enough to try answering these questions, so I'll let Tom have the last word on the matter: "Honestly, the difference between my style and Bill Coore's is about the same as the difference between MacKenzie's and Maxwell's."

Despite that caveat, I can't resist describing a couple of holes that I know like the back of my hand and might reveal something of this architectural and artistic competition. For a representative Doak hole, I've chosen the 2nd hole at Pacific Dunes. For Coore-Crenshaw, the 15th at Bandon Trails.

*Pacific Dunes, No. 2, par-4, 368/345 yards (yardage is for back tees and regular tees)*

My first reaction on the tee: What the heck is going on here? Tom builds holes that bristle with activity. He comes at you like a magic man, a circus performer who keeps a dozen plates spinning in the air on little sticks. This hole has so many shapes, slopes, edges, ridges, textures, and dangers that it's hard to get your bearings. The sandy expanse shouldn't be a problem, but how are you supposed to navigate the humped fairway with a bunker placed exactly where you want your drive to land? All sorts of things are going on up at the green—grassy sideboards, bunkers, swales, a dune shouldering in from the right and hiding part of the putting surface. Hovering over the whole composition of sand, fairway, marram grass, shore pines, and bunkers is the horizon of the Pacific. If you're jolted into a state of high alert and unable to decide on a wise strategy for playing the hole, then Tom has succeeded. No. 2 at Pacific Dunes is a reflection of Tom's personality—puzzle-loving, slightly confrontational, always several steps ahead of you.

Now look at this hole designed by Bill Coore. My first reaction on the tee: how elegant this is! The design doesn't call attention to the shots that will be required as much as to the richness and variety of the landscape. On either side of the fairway and up at the distant green, evergreen trees and native plants blend seamlessly with the golf. If there's such a thing as a polite cross-bunker, that ragged-edged one in the fairway surely qualifies; you don't have to carry it, just decide how close you want to get, left or right, long or short. Sitting in a perfect natural amphitheater, the green appears to be an extension of the fairway, innocent-looking despite the bunkers that merge into the native plants. Yet the green turns out to have a false front, and the slope is scary steep. The more you study this hole, the more you appreciate its charms, dangers, and intricacies. The 15th reflects the Coore-Crenshaw personality: restrained, graceful, complicated in ways that reveal themselves after close observation.

*Bandon Trails, No. 15, 406/367 yards*

# 7

# The Doak File

*The classic definition of engineering is the application of a system to a specific situation. In golf architecture, this would be the application of the game of golf, with all its complexities and varying appeals, to each individual piece of land.*

—TOM DOAK

WHEN I CALL MYSELF A DOAK DISCIPLE, I mean it. Before I met Tom, I was clipping his articles out of *Golf Magazine*, filing them for my own reference or copying them to send to friends. I wanted to spread the gospel. Everything Tom wrote—every magazine article, every course critique—was part of the same coherent design philosophy. I saw him first as someone who cut through the platitudes and skewered courses that deserved it, secondly as an evangelist for minimalism. He was able to articulate things that I was just beginning to realize. He taught me how to think about golf courses—how to appreciate them, evaluate them, and tell the good from the bad. Along with Ron Whitten, the other writer whom I've long regarded as a tutor, Tom directed my education in golf architecture.

What follows is my undeniably biased evaluation of the man who, right before my eyes, evolved from golf's arrogant whiz kid into the eminent architect whose courses are ranked among the best in the world. I've learned and profited from his work. I've ticked him off by criticizing his greens. I've also ticked him off by choosing other designers for projects that he wanted to do. He's ticked me off with remarks about my business model. Still, I'll soon be working with him again, at Sand Valley and Bandon, and I look forward to it. My son Michael is dealing with him most directly at Sand Valley, and I always can tell when he's been talking to Tom because he's fired up with ideas.

This is my own Doak dossier, and I have to begin with some personal observations.

First, Tom is confident. He is a complete stranger to self-doubt. When working with him, you start out knowing that he knows more than you—and he knows you know it. He has a clear, logical reason for every decision he makes. If you're going to question or challenge him, you'd better have solid reasons of your own. Even so, he might bristle. He might not answer you right away. He might just look at you, or through you, or far past you with a thousand-yard stare. The expression on his face seems to say, Do I really have to answer this person? I know several developers who've worked with him, and we've all gotten that stare. It took me a while to realize Tom's actually *listening*, and if any suggestion or idea will improve the golf course, he'll use it.

*Tom hitting the first shot in the dirt on the 5th at Pacific Dunes, with Jim Urbina looking on*

Second, Tom isn't universally liked in the golf business. Of course not. He's always been a lightning rod. Being scandalously honest, he's punctured more than a few big egos. I think he'd rather be understood than liked. That said, I've played golf with Tom, traveled with him, and count myself among his extensive network of loyal colleagues and supporters. Owners who've worked with him don't hesitate to recommend him to others. For the last twenty-seven years, his Renaissance Cup—hosted at one of his courses—has been attended by clients, writers, photographers, fellow architects, and avid golfers who consider themselves members of Club Doak.

Third, I've heard people say that Tom has been lucky. His best courses, their argument goes, are on idiot-proof landscapes, so beautiful that anyone could have built a great course there. I don't think so, and neither does Bill Coore. After walking Pacific Dunes for the first time, Bill told me, "I don't know that I could have done such a good job with that site."

Fourth, now that I've mentioned Bill, I have to add a suspicion about Tom. Maybe, since I myself envy what Dick Youngscap pulled off in Nebraska, I'm just projecting, but I think Tom must wish that he'd built Sand Hills, which is always identified as a breakthrough course for lay-of-the-land architecture. On the timeline of minimalism, Tom follows Coore-Crenshaw. Everything I know about Tom tells me that he likes to go first. He wants to blaze the trail.

Fifth, he has trouble sharing credit. Jim Urbina was his friend, associate, and right-hand man until Old Macdonald, where I proposed that Jim deserved codesigner credit. For reasons I don't expect to ever understand, this shared billing upset the chemistry of their relationship. No doubt there was more to it, and only the two of them will ever know the full story. But they went their separate ways at the end of that project, and I've regretted that I intervened. I've tried to get them back together, and they do share design credit for the Punchbowl, the two-acre putting course at Bandon. But the frost has never thawed.

Sixth, in contradiction to what I've just written, Tom makes sure to praise his design associates, several of whom have figured prominently in courses built by Renaissance Golf Design—Don Placek, Brian Schneider, Eric Iverson, Brian Slawnik, and Bruce Hepner. On every project, one of them is designated the lead associate. Since Tom's preferred method is to visit sites at intervals, the day-to-day management is entrusted to the lead associates, who play a crucial role in translating ideas to the ground and crafting the details. The understanding on his team is that Tom has the last word and all Renaissance designs are Doak designs—a traditional practice in golf architecture. (I've lately learned that Tom has reorganized his business, and Renaissance is now a separate company from Doak Golf, a move intended to bring the associates more commissions and greater individual recognition.)

Seventh, Tom did it his way. When he founded his own firm in 1992 and named it Renaissance, Tom was proclaiming a mission that at the time seemed like pie-in-the-sky. Who was this untested, ballsy twentysomething setting himself up as the Leonardo da Vinci of golf? Did he really expect to launch a successful career by scoffing at the reigning titans of his profession, by telling them they'd been doing everything wrong, by coming on as if he could sweep away decades of flawed design and replace it with some kind of throwback golf that, he alleged, was true to the timeless spirit of the game and far superior to the contrivances and claptrap of modern design? As a maverick developer, I admired the maverick designer and wanted him to succeed. I saw a lot of myself in Tom.

## HIS WRITING

No golf course architect has been as prolific a writer as Tom. None even come close. Writing has always come easily to him—more easily than talking, I suspect. For an undergraduate assignment at Cornell, he submitted an article to *Golf Magazine,* and George Peper, the editor, accepted it. Tom got an A for the course, and Peper, describing him as an "idiot savant," continued to give him space in the magazine. Though never officially a staffer, Tom became their authority on architecture and eventually took over their course ratings when he was still in his twenties. Long before he made his mark as a designer, Tom was building a following of readers who admired his seriousness, knowledge, sharpness, and honesty.

In the late 1980s, *Golf Magazine*'s ratings weren't much more than a glorified editorial caucus, and the entire practice was vulnerable to all kinds of gaming. Quite a few people benefited in one way or another from this arrangement. Course owners could cultivate raters, and raters could parley their role into complimentary golf and free trips. Tom put a stop to this fine boondoggle. Young whippersnapper though he was, he immediately reorganized the ratings, established a system, laid down ground rules, and knocked some integrity into the process. When his own courses later become eligible for consideration and there was some muttering about a conflict of interest, Tom was indignant and promptly resigned his position. During his tenure, the magazine's ratings—previously considered inferior—came to be regarded by many as the most informed and reliable. (Disclosure: I've worked as a rater myself.)

*The Confidential Guide to Golf Courses* (1996). The first edition of the *Guide* is one of the few cult books in the game's literature. Initially self-published, the *Guide* was a mimeographed collection of course reviews that Tom had circulated to a small group of friends, who passed it on to other friends, who passed it on to their friends, until owning a copy was a sign of one's insider status.

Courses were ranked on the 1–10 Doak scale, with no punches pulled. Naturally, his most scathing remarks attracted the most attention. He wrote that without seeing a Nicklaus-designed course, he was confident in giving it a 5—a grade slightly better than mediocre. He was describing the work of a golf legend and dismissing it with the back of his hand. About another well-known designer he wrote, "He [architect X] might not be the worst architect ever, but if you were going to make the case, you'd start with [course by architect X]." He knew how to wield a poison pen.

After its underground notoriety, the *Guide* was published commercially in 1996 and set the tenor of Tom's career, branding him as an iconoclast in his chosen field. He's never completely shaken off this reputation and is still incapable of speaking in empty, mealymouthed niceties. Members of the American Society of Golf Course Architects are prohibited in the bylaws from disparaging one another. Tom Doak has never backed off his criticisms and never joined the organization. Come to think of it, one of the few things I know about the ASCGA is that he isn't a member.

*The Anatomy of a Golf Course: The Art of Golf Architecture* (1992). Written before Tom had designed a notable course, this was the first book in decades written by a golf architect about his profession. This minimalist manifesto remains required reading today, and my edition is crowded with pencil notations. Tom's discussion of shot values, strategic routing, aesthetics, and other fundamental considerations are explicated by quotes drawn mostly from the builders of classic Scottish and American courses—making a strong case that the principles of sound architecture have never changed. Tom has been demonstrating this ever since, and on his website he sums up the minimalist's objective: "to route as many holes as possible whose main features already exist in the landscape, and accent their strategies." The beauty of this philosophy is that since every site's unique, a course that truly respects it will have its own character.

*The Life and Work of Dr. Alister MacKenzie* (2001, with James S. Scott and Raymund H. Haddock). Of course Tom would be drawn to the curmudgeon who designed some of the world's most iconic courses, including Augusta National, Kingston Heath, and Cypress Point. As a writer, MacKenzie had many of the same attributes as Doak: he was logical, assertive, independent, strong-willed, and didn't mind offending people. In MacKenzie, intellect and imagination were balanced like a pair of fine-tuned Rolls-Royce engines. There are many astute critics of design, but very few MacKenzies. Or Doaks.

*The Confidential Guide to Golf Courses* (2014). Taking a leaf from Tom, who's reviewed a few courses he didn't visit, I'm going to comment on a book that I have read only in part—because I don't know who could possibly read the whole damn thing. With five projected volumes, this new edition of the *Guide* is organized by continent and will include write-ups of 2,500 courses, a task so ambitious that Tom has enlisted three coauthors: Ran Morrissett, Masa Nishijima, and Darius Oliver. Each course is graded on the Doak scale by each author who's seen it.

At first glance, this reeks of megalomania. Why should any sane person need to plant his flag everywhere on planet golf, when no one else is ever going to see more than a tiny fraction of the courses he describes? The game has always had its list-chasers aiming to play the world's Top 100 courses, but here Tom makes them look like underachievers.

This new edition of the *Guide* obviously offers a wealth of information about lesser-known, ever-obscure tracks, not just marquee courses. With its lists of best clubs, favorite holes, dream eighteens, and so on, this is a frankly opinionated guide, as any Doak project is bound to be. No matter where you open it, the book makes you feel like you're dropping in on a smart, informed conversation that won't end anytime soon. There's an irony here: loaded down with those lists and numerical ratings, the book becomes more interesting and useful once you can get past the numbers and pay attention to the stories.

*The Little Red Book* (2017). This is a collection of observations initially posted to the *Golf Club Atlas* website. This is Tom's most informal, personally revealing book. As always, the observations have bite and lucidity, and a sly sense of humor is threaded through many entries, along with affectionate portraits of some of his favorite people in golf and fond references to his family. Is Tom mellowing?

*Getting to 18* (2020). The Tara Iti of golf books, it is lavishly produced in a limited edition of 1,500 that's stunningly beautiful. At $350, it's the same price as a round of golf at a top course, and worth it. The photos are superb, and the maps, memos, and scorecards give you the sense that you're sitting at Tom's drawing table. The text is fascinating and surprising; armchair architects who think of course design only in artistic terms will be schooled by these detailed accounts of how he arrived at the routings for his first eighteen courses. These real-world stories delve into the many complicating factors: money, committee politics, owner directives, land constraints, drainage issues, wind direction, to name only a few. Though Tom is sometimes thought of as an artist in his ivory tower, here you see him as the head of a firm who has to pay the bills, stick to a budget, meet a payroll, and deal with clients. His practicality made me recall something Tom said long ago, back at the start of his career. Asked what he'd consider success as an architect, he replied, "I want to be the guy who keeps getting hired."

## HIS COURSES

Tom's books wouldn't have the same authority if he hadn't built such extraordinary courses. When we first met, he was better known as a writer than an architect, and I wasn't sure his design talents would live up to the expecta-

# THE DOAK SCALE

## 0 JUST AWFUL
A course so contrived and unnatural that it may poison your mind, one I cannot recommend under any circumstances. Reserved for courses that waste ridiculous sums of money in their construction, and probably shouldn't have been built in the first place.

## 1 BASIC
A very basic golf course, with clear architectural malpractice and/or poor maintenance. Avoid even if you're desperate for a game.

## 2 MEDIOCRE
A mediocre golf course with little or no architectural interest, but nothing really horrible. As my friend Dave Richards summed up: "Play it in a scramble, and drink a lot of beer."

## 3 AVERAGE
About the level of the average golf course in the world. (Since I don't go out of my way to see average courses, my scale is deliberately skewed to split hairs among the good, the better and the best.)

## 4 MILDLY INTERESTING
A modestly interesting course, with a couple of distinctive holes among the 18, or at least some scenic interest and decent golf. Also reserved for some very good courses that are much too short and narrow to provide sufficient challenge for accomplished golfers.

## 5 ABOVE AVERAGE
Well above the average golf course, but the middle of my scale. A good course to choose if you're in the vicinity and looking for a game, but don't spend another day away from home to see it, unless your home is in Alaska.

## 6 VERY GOOD
A very good course, definitely worth a game if you're in town, but not necessarily worth a special trip to see. It shouldn't disappoint you.

## 7 EXCELLENT
An excellent course, worth checking out if you get anywhere within 100 miles. You can expect to find soundly designed, interesting holes, good course conditioning, and a pretty setting, if not necessarily anything unique to the world of golf.

## 8 BEST IN REGION
One of the very best courses in its region (although there are more 8s in some places and none in others), and worth a special trip to see. Could have some drawbacks, but these will clearly be spelled out, and it will make up for them with something really special in addition to the generally excellent layout.

## 9 OUTSTANDING
An outstanding course, certainly one of the best in the world, with no weaknesses in regard to condition, length, or poor holes. You should see this course sometime in your life.

## 10 NEARLY PERFECT
Nearly perfect; if you skipped even one hole, you would miss something worth seeing. If you haven't seen all the courses in this category, you don't know how good golf architecture can get. Call your travel agent immediately.

tions he'd created in print. Now, twenty-five years later, all doubt has been removed.

Here's a quick inventory of his work:

- Thirty-nine original designs.
- Four courses with codesigners: Sebonack, with Jack Nicklaus; Old Macdonald, with Jim Urbina; Barnbougle Dunes and St. Andrews Bay, in Australia, with Mike Clayton.
- Four courses in *Golf Digest*'s 2020 World Top 100: No. 2 Tara Iti; No. 16 Barnbougle Dunes; No. 22 Cape Kidnappers; No. 91 St. Andrews Beach in Australia.
- Four courses in *Golf Digest*'s list of U.S. Top 100: No. 17 Pacific Dunes; No. 34 Sebonack; No. 46 Ballyneal; No. 50 Old Macdonald.
- Six courses on *Golf Magazine*'s Top 100 World: No. 24 Pacific Dunes; No. 27 Tara Iti; No. 35 Barnbougle Dunes; No. 44 Cape Kidnappers; No. 57 Ballyneal; No. 99 Rock Creek Cattle Company. With six courses, Tom has more than any other contemporary designer. Coore-Crenshaw is next, with five.
- Three courses have hosted significant professional competitions: Sebonack, 2013 U.S. Women's Open; The Renaissance Club, North Berwick, Scotland, Scottish Open and Ladies Scottish Open; Memorial Park GC in Houston, Vivant Houston Open.
- Twenty-one restorations, including San Francisco GC, Yeamans Hall, Mid-Ocean, and both courses at Royal Melbourne. At least seven of these have appeared on various Top 100 lists.
- Thirty-seven consultancies (clubs where Renaissance provides a master plan to maintain the integrity of course design by other architects).

I've cited three top categories to underscore the uniformly high quality of Tom's courses. I'd also note that raters don't always agree on which are the best. Tom himself usually avoids mention of any specific list and simply observes that nine of his courses have been rated in the Top 100. This total doesn't include some courses for which he has high personal regard, such as Streamsong Blue, in Florida, and Dismal River, in Nebraska. Tom has not been especially prolific; like his mentor, Pete Dye, he prefers to concentrate on a course or two at a time. His body of work is more impressive for its quality than for its quantity.

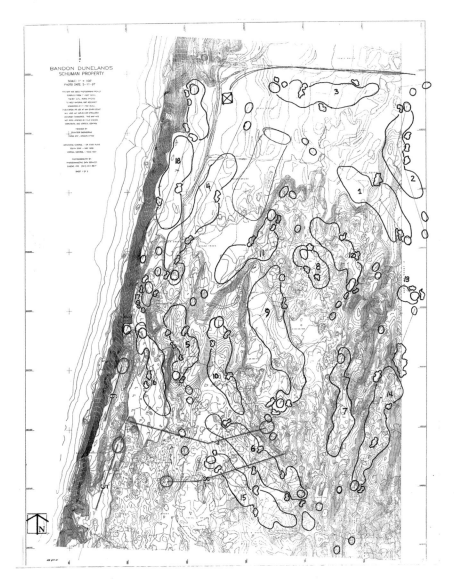

BANDON DUNELANDS
SCHUMAN PROPERTY

*Tom's initial routing for Pacific Dunes was never built. David Kidd had claimed the southern end of the property for several holes—his centerlines are noted in red—and I hadn't yet acquired the land to the north, now the location of the superb 13th at Pacific Dunes. The takeaway: great courses aren't always routed on the first try.*

The conspicuous gap in his résumé is that he's never designed a course specifically for high-level professional competition, as Pete Dye did at TPC Sawgrass, the Ocean Course, and Whistling Straits. However, the owners of the Renaissance Club, an exclusive private club, wanted a course that could host the pros, and the European Tour deemed it a fit venue for the Scottish Open. Also, Tom has just renovated Memorial Park GC in Houston, working with PGA Tour pro Brooks Koepka to make the popular muni into the permanent home of the Houston Open. Personally, I am more interested in Memorial Park as a muni than as a playground for the pros, but I understand why Tom wants to check every box.

He's become known as an architect whose daring and flair enhance spectacular properties, and there's not much argument that his aesthetic instinct ranks up there with the greats of this profession. Proof of this can be given in two words: Tara Iti.

If Tom heard this, he might give me the stare. He'd certainly insist that strategic design and shot values take precedence over aesthetics. He might be right, but if you asked me what I remember about, say, the shot values of the 13th hole at Pacific Dunes, I'd have a hard time answering. I'd be thinking of the way the green sits between the Pacific on one side and an Everest of sand on the other—just an unforgettable image. I remember its beauty.

Another of his strengths: routings. For someone who's cerebral, Tom is finely attuned to the psychological aspects of the game, and articulate about how and why a routing shapes the experience of a round. Back in 1994, I invited him on a trip to Northern Ireland. In a group of eight older golfers, he took on the role of tour guide and did his best to educate us about the courses we visited. At Royal Portrush we all had a blast, and I asked Tom what made that course so much fun. He answered by explaining in detail how the routing led the golfer to the sea in the middle of both nines. It's hard to talk about the game's mental effect on a player, but it was clear to me that he understood the rhythm of a round, the building of anticipation at Portrush, and the way its sequence of holes influenced our mood.

Architects often describe routing as an exercise akin to solving a puzzle. While I don't disagree, I would respectfully add that the process is more mysterious, a matter of art and inspiration as well as spatial reasoning. And I do know and *feel* that Tom has the gift of engaging you throughout a round, creating surprise and intrigue, catching you up in the course's twists and turns to hold you in a state of heightened interest. The experience is like watching a good movie, gladly lost in a world that's like the real world but far more exciting, and you're in no hurry for it to end. If Tom's courses didn't have this special quality, I don't believe they'd sink their hooks into you so deeply.

Among his other strengths:

*He's versatile.* He's built excellent courses in many different landscapes. He's probably right in thinking that his inland and mountain courses are underappreciated. His take: "Almost all of my most highly ranked courses are oceanfront. Really? Does this mean that all my best work is on a major body of water?"

*He's a master of the short par-4.* Neither the first nor the only architect to relish them, Tom looks for opportunities to build them when routing a course. On both his own and others' designs, he frequently singles out the short par-4s as favorites. His advocacy is one reason they've become more popular than ever.

*He's just as good with short par-3s.* What he calls his "little devils" seem particularly inspiring to him. Golfers love tiny holes like the 7th at Pebble Beach and the Postage Stamp at Troon. But it really takes guts to build a hole that can be played with a wedge.

*Those greens of his.* Jim Urbina speaks of Tom's "wild green self," almost as if a Mr. Hyde takes over Tom's better-behaved normal self. He and I have had plenty of conversations about greens, and my role has always been to represent the golfer who doesn't want to four-putt. Tom maintains that while circus greens make it tough for a good player to get close to the pin, they don't make that much difference to the weaker player, who'll never get that close anyway. He believes that the short shot—the chip, pitch, or lag putt—will be more interesting if the green is strongly contoured. I don't buy that argument, not for a public resort course. More "interesting" can just as easily mean more frustrating and discouraging.

I should add that Tom has respected my misgiving when we've worked together. For him, the greens at Pacific Dunes and Barnbougle Dunes are almost sedate by comparison to those on some of his other courses. His wild green self was checked at the door.

*His innovation.* In northern Michigan, Tom recently built the Loop at Forest Dunes, a fully reversible eighteen-hole layout that can be played in either direction (and hearkens back to St. Andrews, no less). His design for the original Sheep Ranch, using all the teeing areas and multiple angles of approach to the thirteen greens, created the possibility of playing sixty-three different holes. The back nine at Pacific Dunes has one of the most unorthodox scorecards in golf—four par-3s, two of them back-to-back, three par-5s, and only two par-4s. He's never short of new ideas, or afraid to try them.

OVERLEAF
*Barnbougle Dunes, No. 7. This one is actually called "Tom's Little Devil."*

## HIS INFLUENCE

Tom has devoted a big chunk of his career to making golf course architecture a field of serious intellectual endeavor. Many others have shared in this work, including Ron Whitten, at *Golf Digest;* Brad Klein, the architecture editor of *Golfweek;* Geoff Shackelford, author of several books on classic design and a media savant who regularly discusses architecture and course set-up; and Ran Morrissett, the founder of *Golf Club Atlas,* the website that's become the digital meeting place for hard-core aficionados. Andy Johnson, founder of the online *Fried Egg,* has used a number of media platforms to provide a younger generation with news about golf architecture. As someone who grew up blithely unaware of the role of the architect in the evolution of golf, I can testify personally to the impact of these chroniclers.

Tom's career has been a road map for young people who want to work in this field. For him, no such map existed. At Cornell, he cobbled together his own curriculum, got a degree in landscape architecture, and then went to Great Britain on a fellowship, caddying at St. Andrews for three months and spending the rest of the year visiting over two hundred courses, taking careful notes all the while. Ron Whitten told me, "When I got into this business, I thought I'd talk to architects about the great courses and the old masters of the craft. I didn't—except when I talked to Tom Doak." Having educated himself about theory and history, Tom decided that he also needed to learn what actually happened in the field, so he went to work for Pete Dye and served an apprenticeship on a bulldozer. Then he hung out his own shingle and basically built his first course with his own two hands, doing everything from the drawing board to the shaping.

He's resuscitated the reputation of many overlooked gems. The best example is his home course, Crystal Downs, in Michigan. Before 1985, when Tom arrived, it was a small, quiet, out-of-the-way place on Lake Michigan that wasn't on anybody's radar. On the most recent *Golf Digest* Top 100 in the United States, it's ranked thirteenth and has become a mythical, bucket-list course.

He's been a leader in the movement to restore historic courses. His former partner, Gil Hanse, has done more restorations, and many other architects have been engaged in an historic effort to reclaim forgotten treasures of American golf. Instead of the slapdash approach that prevailed for decades, when new owners or ambitious green committees left behind random, mismatched "improvements," designers now use whatever they can find—old photographs, renderings, correspondence—in order to understand the original design before undertaking any remodeling or restoration. Tom has consulted with sixty golf facilities on these projects, in the process educating club members and maintenance staff about how to care for their properties.

He's proved that great courses don't have to cost a fortune. When he was starting out in the era of design overkill, the price tags were astronomical. One of the biggest line items in a construction budget is earthmoving, and designers boasted about moving mountains of dirt. The minimalists took a different approach, and Tom inherently is thrifty. He doesn't like to spend money unnecessarily, even when working for billionaires.

He's set a model for sustainability, not least because minimalist courses are innately more eco-friendly. In any discussion of golf's environmental impact, most people think first of chemical use, water supply, and maintenance practices; but the real starting point is with design and construction. At his first course, High Pointe, Tom worked with an experienced superintendent, Tom Mead, who stressed a fundamental truth about sustainability: the less the ground is disturbed, the healthier it will remain.

He plays the long game. No one can spend time with Tom Doak without acquiring a deeper sense of the history, artistry, and lasting value of golf's architecture. My own thoughts about legacy are affirmed when I work with him. As much as Tom craves present success, his real competition is with the historically great designers whose work has endured.

He is, most of all, an original. I've already mentioned his innovation and his routing talent, and originality includes those traits as well as a great many others. It's what makes the familiar elements of a golf course seem new again. It's the ancient game reimagined, a traditional art reinvented. In golf architecture as in all arts, originality is the difference between nearly and truly great.

# 8

## On Beauty

*I have not the slightest hesitation in saying that beauty means a great deal on the golf course; even the man who emphatically states that he does not care a hang for beauty is subconsciously influenced by his surroundings. . . . There are few first rate holes which are not at the same time, either in the grandeur of their undulations and hazards, or the character of their surroundings, things of beauty in themselves.*

—ALISTER MACKENZIE, *The Spirit of St. Andrews*

MAYBE WE SHOULD CALL IT THE B-WORD. Many golfers tiptoe around the subject since the greatest players and role models have been warriors—fierce competitors who went out to do battle with the golf course. Ben Hogan, aka the Hawk, was the embodiment of the warrior-champion who said, after winning the 1951 U.S. Open at Oak Hills, "I brought this course, this monster, to its knees." To him, the layout was his adversary and the goal was conquest. If anyone ever asked Hogan after a round if the course was beautiful, his famous gaze would've been his scorching answer.

Hogan, Nicklaus, Woods—they all exhibited that intense single-mindedness. When I played on my college team (as an also-ran), I psyched myself up to play well. I wanted to win. I wanted to score. Much of the culture of golf has been based on the idea that the scorecard is the real measure of success and "there are no pictures on the scorecard." And that playing this game presents such devilish difficulties that trying to overcome them takes years of lessons and practice, and presumably that satisfaction comes as a result of doing so successfully.

I wonder. Golf does offer a lifelong opportunity for improvement, and I can't deny that the days when I've scored well still glow in memory. But is this the only way to measure success on the course? Does every round have to be a contest? What about those days when we hack and chunk and flail? What about the player who shoots 90 or 100? As I become that player, I'm less interested in Ben Hogan than in another great champion, Walter Hagen, whose best-known advice has nothing to do with the swing but everything to do with life: "You're only here for a short while. Don't hurry, don't worry. And stop and smell the flowers along the way."

Alister MacKenzie understood this, too. Known for his gruffness, the architect did have his soft spots. He once said he wanted to live where he could practice golf in his pajamas—and achieved this goal when living beside the 6th fairway at Pasatiempo. In his writing and his designs, it's clear he placed a high premium on beauty as an element of the golf experience. When hired to build Cypress Point, MacKenzie realized that he'd been entrusted with a site of such incomparable beauty that the usual expectations didn't apply. Nothing less than a masterpiece would do, and when Cypress Point was completed in 1928, he felt that he'd created something that rivaled his beloved St. Andrews. His own verdict: "There is [at Cypress Point] a natural beauty found only on British seaside courses. . . . It is unsurpassed, having awaited for centuries only to have the architect's molding hand to sculpture a course without peer."

He might also have compared Cypress to the course just a few miles up the Pacific coast, Pebble Beach. Originally laid out in 1919 by a pair of inexperienced architects, Douglas Grant and Jack Neville, Pebble Beach set a standard of thrilling beauty in American golf. From the start, Neville's concept was to capture the coastal Pacific landscape in his design, and his account of building the course places him squarely in the camp of the minimalists: "It was all there in plain sight. Very little clearing was necessary. All we did was cut away a few trees, install a few sprinklers, and sow a little seed."

The prime mover behind both Cypress Point and Pebble Beach was one of my heroes, Samuel Morse. Known as the Duke of del Monte, Morse developed not only the golf courses but the entire Monterey Peninsula, including the lodge and the private homes; he also set aside the greenbelts that have protected and preserved the coastline, the Del Monte Forest, and the native flora and fauna. At the outset, Morse overruled a plan to allow residences along the oceanfront, reserving this astounding landscape for golf instead of exploiting it as real estate. Though a sportsman (and captain of the undefeated Yale football team of 1906), he didn't know much about golf. But he certainly knew the future of his resort depended on the beauty of a jagged coastline where the blue waters of the Pacific Ocean surged against the shining dark cliffs. He was selling beauty first, golf second.

My chief takeaway: the beauty of a golf course begins with the site. True, some courses in ordinary settings are considered beautiful, and I don't want to offend anyone by naming them. Since I'm not as systematic as Tom Doak, I'll just say that in my opinion most suburban, parkland courses would fall right in the middle of his scale: above average. They're leafy and pleasant, but like the neighborhoods in which they're located, they tend to blur together. The impulse to control the natural environment is the basis of suburban planning, and it leads inevitably to blandness and predictability—traits that also show up in golf design. I like a nice green lawn, but I don't like courses where you can't tell the fairway from some guy's backyard.

For me, a developer, the heart of the job description is finding a glorious property. This takes nothing away from the designer's genius; as MacKenzie realized, this challenge can inspire their best work. Tom Doak acknowledged as much in some notes he made about the evolution of Pacific Dunes: "Mike already knew what no architect's ego will allow him to admit—that a great golf course is often more a matter of what nature provided than what the architect did. If he wanted to build one of the best golf courses in the world, it wasn't a question of whom he hired, so much as where he chose to build it."

I still get goosebumps at Pebble Beach. The architects might have been untested, but with the encouragement of Samuel Morse, they created one of golf's mythic playing fields. They also created a legacy—nearly a century old now—that belongs in spirit to all golfers, even the ones who never get there, just as a cathedral belongs to all believers.

Sometimes my friends in the golf business who have MBAs or degrees in accounting or marketing raise an eyebrow when they find out that I was an English major in college. Maybe I should remind them that Bobby Jones's degree from Harvard was also in English literature. Among my favorite writers, then and now, are the Romantic poets, especially William Wordsworth, who often took natural beauty as his subject. A prodigious walker who composed many poems while hiking through the English countryside, he estimated that he had logged, on foot, some 180,000 miles. Wordsworth would have loved the Summer Solstice event at Bandon, when golfers play four courses and walk twenty-six miles in a single day. He had, at the very least, the makings of a fine caddy.

Beauty was the topic of a Wordsworth-inspired essay that I wrote for the first volume of *Golf Architecture: A Worldwide Perspective* (2002), edited by Paul Daley. Here I argued that playing a round on a beautiful course, far from spoiling a walk, would actually make this walk far more enjoyable and not necessarily just for a golfer. I think Lindy would second me on this point. As a non-playing companion, she walked countless courses with me, and responded to them as she would to a park or garden. Her appreciation of the beauty found on the game's landscapes surely helped motivate her to become such an enthusiastic player herself.

My thesis was that a beautiful golf course was a form of "nature perfected," a concept that guided the English landscape designers of the late eighteenth and early nineteenth centuries. Like the Romantic poets, they were highly attuned to the pastoral charms of England's countryside, which they saw as threatened by the Industrial Revolution. On aristocratic estates, landscape architects created elaborate parks that were imitations—or, some would say, idealizations—of nature. Sometimes covering hundreds of acres, these private parks included immense lawns, artfully sited groves of trees and blossoming plants, man-made or manipulated lakes and streams. These elements were arranged to create scenic vistas and deliberately framed perspectives, much like real-life paintings of rural beauty. Despite the elaborate artifice, the architects sought to make their pictures entirely convincing—so much so that the designer's hand was completely invisible and the composition didn't seem at all contrived. It was supposed to look like pure, God-given Nature.

Sounds like a golf course, doesn't it?

The exact opposite of the English approach was provided by the French, whose landscape ideas were on display at Versailles and Fontainebleau: formal gardens, symmetrical plantings, geometrical shapes and patterns in the walks and *allées,* rigorously pruned trees and shrubs, and so on. Contrivance wasn't concealed but proudly displayed. American landscape designers of the nineteenth century followed the English style, and some of the most ambitious parks here were public—notably Central Park, in New York, designed by Frederick Law Olmsted and built in the 1850s. With its lawns, groves, lakes, and famous sinuous walk, the Ramble, Central Park was (and remains) an example of a landscape that made every effort to appear pastoral, picturesque, and natural.

By now you see the connection: that golf architects were headed in the same general direction when the game had its first boom between 1910 and 1930. A remarkable number of courses were built all over the country, many of them modest layouts that had a "natural" look because it held down construction costs. But the best of them—now considered classic courses—were based on the principle that they had to imitate nature.

As Robert Hunter, a colleague of MacKenzie's who directed the construction at Cypress Point, wrote in *The Links* (1926): "When we build golf courses, we are remodeling the face of nature, and it should be remembered that the greatest and fairest things are done by nature and the lesser by art."

C. B. Macdonald had vigorous opinions about everything, including obviously artificial features: "Viewing the monstrosities created on many modern golf courses which are a travesty on Nature, no one can but shudder for the soul of golf."

A. W. Tillinghast, whose ideal course was "rugged and natural," lamented the difficulty of achieving this appearance: "And while we do succeed in approaching nature by artificial means so frequently we are in utter despair . . . in my eyes there seems always to be lacking an indefinable something as the artificial work proclaims that it was made by man."

A century later, contemporary designers express similar views: "We don't want our holes to look like golf holes. They should look like landscapes which just happen to include a golf hole. . . . I can't compete with nature and it would only showcase my futility if I tried. So I try to cooperate." The speaker? Bill Coore, describing what he and Ben Crenshaw have aimed for at all their courses.

Call it naturalism or lay-of-the-land design—this approach has regained its place as the dominant aesthetic in golf design. And we shouldn't forget that the game was invented in entirely natural landscapes, home to the shepherds and flocks that had used them for centuries with only wind and sand and sea for company.

> And I have felt
> A presence that disturbs me with the joy
> Of elevated thoughts; a sense sublime
> Of something far more deeply interfused,
> Whose dwelling is the light of setting suns,
> And the round ocean and the living air,
> And the blue sky. . . .
>
> —WILLIAM WORDSWORTH,
> "Lines Composed a Few Miles Above Tintern Abbey"

Though most golfers have a hard time talking about it, they *do* respond to beauty. They'll avoid artsy, poetic language and talk instead about "eye candy" or the "wow factor" or express their response in physical terms: jaw-dropping, eye-popping, spine-tingling.

Now, I don't go around a course quoting Wordsworth, but the "sense

Among the Sierra
Nevada, California,
*by Albert Bierstadt*
*(1868)*

sublime" he invokes in "Tintern Abbey" could serve as a description of an evening round at Bandon Dunes that's perfect in every detail. You can check them off one by one, and they express feelings toward a place that go far beyond recognizing a scene as pretty or picturesque.

The idea of the sublime also informed the visual art of the nineteenth century, with its abundance of mountains, precipices, cataracts, snowcapped mountains, storms at sea—images of the power and grandeur of nature. In America, poets and political leaders found evidence of the sublime in the wonders of this young country. Thomas Jefferson and Theodore Roosevelt used the word to describe a continent that was still being explored.

Eyes would roll if a golf writer described a course as sublime, and your eyes might be rolling now. But I can't help thinking that the feelings inspired by the sublime are an essential part of the experience of golf at Bandon.

The 6th at Bandon Dunes embodies my idea of the sublime. As you emerge from the dune-enclosed 5th green, the view opens and keeps expanding as you walk toward the tee. The hole itself is a medium-length par-3, framed by beach grass and gorse, but it seems to jut out into space, occupying the last sliver of solid ground at the edge of the cliff. The green appears to levitate, magically perched above the beach and the Pacific. In the distance you

see Five Mile Point and surf breaking on the sea stacks. Eye candy, for sure, but since you're playing golf, you aren't just observing this landscape, you're participating in it. You breathe the champagne air. You hear the surge of the waves. With the flag fluttering in a fresh wind, you aren't thinking about a number on a scorecard but about hitting a shot equal to this majestic setting.

The camera on your phone might capture the basic elements of the scene but not one iota of the exhilaration of standing on that tee. The poets are right: this kind of beauty can inspire awe, wonder, and a sense of the eternal.

Some of the world's most spectacularly beautiful courses were built in the last twenty-five years, and to my eye several are as gorgeous as any ever built. Architects are more daring, and new and improved construction methods have enabled them to set holes in places that once would have been written off as impossible. Cape Kidnappers illustrates this point. I don't think such a course could have been conceived of, much less built, fifty years ago.

*Another hole that wasn't on David Kidd's original routing, the 6th at Bandon Dunes offers a sublime view of the Oregon coast.*

*What can anyone say about Cape Kidnappers? It takes the breath away.*

The fervent pursuit of beauty seems to me a natural consequence of living at a time when visual images are so omnipresent and so hardwired into our judgments. Our expectations have risen accordingly. I'm old enough to remember when TV was black-and-white, and when color photographs of golf courses—as striking as they looked then—were in fact bland and fuzzy. When I first got into the business, there was one fellow specializing in golf photography who'd lug a stepladder around with him so he could shoot elevated views. That was the state of technology. Now there are dozens of talented photographers, their vans filled with expensive equipment including drones, lenses that can capture amazing depth of field and the full spectrum of changing light, making these artists capable of lifting every feature into high definition.

Today, to be successful a course had better be photogenic, and it also needs to live up to the glamor shots that most customers have seen before arriving there. It needs to be ready for its close-up. Inevitably, rating systems began to pay more attention to beauty—or to "aesthetics," a term that the magazines generally prefer, I guess because it sounds more scientific and objective.

Not that long ago, in the course rankings pioneered by *Golf Digest,* beauty wasn't a consideration. Toughness was all that mattered. Published in 1965, the first list was called "America's 200 Toughest Courses," and four years later was revised to "America's 100 Most Testing Courses." In 1975, when additional criteria were added, the list was rechristened "America's 100 Greatest Courses." Despite such modifications, the most important criterion remained this one: "A great course should test the skills of a championship player from the scratch tees, challenging him to play all types of shots." In short, the rating system placed a premium on difficulty, and the courses selected in 1981 left no doubt as to what the panelists valued: "Scene of the highest scores on tour" (Butler National); "Small greens and severe rough" (Canterbury); "Hilly and demanding layout" (Cascades). And so it goes, with one course after another being praised because it is so damn tough.

All three of those courses, by the way, have now fallen out of the Top 100. To be blunt, those old rankings not only were misguided but also spurred a generation of developers and architects to build penal, frustrating courses. In recent years, *Golf Digest* adopted new criteria for their panelists, who now assign points in seven different categories: Design Variety, Resistance to Scoring, Shot Values, Memorability, Aesthetics, Ambience, and Conditioning. Each category counts for 12.5 percent of the overall score, with double points—25 percent—awarded for Shot Values.

For me, the most important new category is Aesthetics. Raters are now asked to consider beauty, for which the magazine's euphemistic definition is "scenic values."

These revisions have spread through rival list-keeping systems, and some of their followers think the pendulum has swung too far. The most outspoken critics are often talented players or devoted students of golf architecture. The gist of their complaint is that the new emphasis on aesthetics encourages raters to evaluate the experience instead of the course itself. Mike Clayton, my Aussie friend from Barnbougle Dunes, feels these changes have turned the ratings into "beauty contests."

This he sees as a fault, albeit one that stems from human weakness: "Who is not swayed by beautiful surroundings, a course they play well, or one where there is a real emotional connection?" When it comes to evaluating courses, however, he wants to eliminate emotion. In his view, rankings should be based almost entirely on the merits of the design and how well the course expresses "the principles of strategic golf."

Mike rightly speaks like a proud architect, whereas I can only respond as a proud owner. Given a choice between (a) beautiful surroundings with emotional impact and (b) the principles of strategic golf, which one is the retail golfer going to choose?

The correct answer is (a).

I'll probably never convince Mike that beauty is as important to most golfers as strategy or shot-making. But very few indeed make the long journey to the south coast of Oregon—or Tasmania—in order to hit a pure five-iron to a well-defended green. They can find that opportunity anywhere. No, they make this journey so they can hit their five-iron in a setting of incomparable beauty that's given an exclamation point by the flight of the ball. One of the game's deep mysteries is how a small white ball, hanging in the air, has the power to bring a whole landscape to life. Ask yourself, would you rather hit that five-iron into the backdrop of a wall of condos?

I could put that question to Mike Clayton, who might say that I'm exaggerating to make my point. But this isn't really an either-or proposition: a course can be beautiful and also brilliantly designed. Mike already knows that, not least because Barnbougle Dunes has a double-barreled appeal—beauty and strategic integrity.

That is the goal for every course, and I stand by my position that both qualities are essential. Still, if I were the ratings czar, I'd be tempted to double the points given for beauty. For twenty years I've been listening to golfers who've just played Bandon or Barnbougle or Cabot or Sand Valley, and I can't remember very many who wanted to tell me about the shots they played. Instead, they want to tell me how they felt. They want me to know that they found the courses to be beautiful, thrilling, soulful. And I understand, because even after hundreds of rounds, that is still exactly how I find them.

# CABOT

## Cabot Cape Breton

Inverness, Nova Scotia, Canada

———————

2012 **CABOT LINKS**, 6,854 yards, par 70
designed by Rod Whitman
#35 on *Golf Magazine*'s 2020 Top 100 in the World
#5 in Canada, *Golf Digest* 2017

2016 **CABOT CLIFFS**, 6,765 yards, par 72
Bill Coore and Ben Crenshaw
#11 on *Golf Magazine*'s 2020 Top 100 in the World
#1 in Canada, *Golf Digest* 2017

2020 **THE NEST**, 10-hole, par-3 course
Rod Whitman and Dave Axland

## 9

## Golf Comes to Inverness

*When I would come back up (from the mine), occasionally there would be a
tourist wanting a picture of this person so covered in black coal dust, only the
whites of my eyes showed. Now when I go back to that very same spot, people are
taking my picture next to a brand-new, picturesque golf course. Who dreams of
such a thing?*

—JOHN MACISSAC, Inverness town father,
quoted in *The New York Times*, June 30, 2012

WASN'T IN THE MARKET for another golf project when Ben Cowan-Dewar talked to me in 2005 about his ambition to build a links course in Nova Scotia. My plate was full. At Bandon, we were opening a third course, Bandon Trails, and we were still trying to build out the resort, adding more rooms, expanding restaurant capacity, and planning a new clubhouse at Pacific Dunes. On top of that, I'd been making trips to Tasmania to help get Barnbougle up and running.

Moreover, the future of Recycled Paper Greetings was weighing heavily on my mind. For a couple of years, Phil and I had been considering whether to put RPG up for sale. Every company has a natural life span, and our amazing growth had been slowing down. While it wasn't a choice between selecting greeting cards or building golf courses, if it were I would have chosen the latter without hesitation. Furthermore, it was obvious that all written communication was moving away from paper-and-ink and into digital forms, and I was worried that we might've held on to the company for too long. But then, in 2005, I was relieved and a little surprised when we agreed with a buyer on a selling price far north of our asking price.

Even so, I was unpersuaded when I first heard about Ben Cowan-Dewar, a twenty-five-year-old who wanted to build a course in Nova Scotia on a slag heap left behind by a defunct coal-mining operation. Rod Whitman, a Canadian golf architect, had urged me to meet with him, as had Ran Morrissett, the proprietor of *Golf Club Atlas;* Ben was cofounder of this popular website devoted to course design, so I knew he was a true believer. Ben was on track to become one of the youngest people ever to play all of *Golf Magazine*'s Top 100, and he also ran a company called Golf Travel Impresarios.

I soon learned that as an eight-year-old in his hometown in Ontario, he built a par-3 in his backyard with a shovel and a rototiller. By the age of fourteen, he was writing to developers and passing himself off as a prospective client so he could visit and play their courses. He was obviously golf-mad and entrepreneurial to his core. Of course I agreed to meet with him.

Our partnership started out slowly, and the Great Recession nearly closed us down. In truth, had it been solely up to me, the Cabot project would've been delayed or possibly abandoned. Ben's tenacity kept it alive.

BEN COWAN-DEWAR: This all started at a dinner in Toronto, where I was seated next to Rodney MacDonald, a representative of the district of Inverness in the Legislative Assembly of Nova Scotia. He was an unusual politician, a former schoolteacher who'd toured as a fiddler and was passionate about the region's Scottish-Gaelic cultural heritage. The minute he heard that I was in the golf business, he started telling me about this amazing site on land that had once been used for coal mining. I was skeptical. With respect, I said people told me about amazing sites everywhere I went, but he was so persuasive that I agreed to go to Inverness and have a look.

What I found was a little company town that had seen better days. The mining operations had once occupied a now-vacant stretch of land that sloped down to the beach and the Gulf of St. Lawrence. I thought immediately of such Scottish towns as St. Andrews and North Berwick, where the linksland starts on the edge of town and runs right to the sea. Though I hadn't developed a golf course yet, I recognized this as a once-in-a-lifetime opportunity. I doubt there's any other small town in North America like this, with a mile of ocean frontage and a piece of land that's exactly the right size for a golf course. Here I was in Nova Scotia, which means New Scotland, looking at a place that seemed destined to be a golf course so Inverness could fulfill its Scottish heritage. If I hadn't already been a believer in serendipity, I would have become one after seeing that land.

However, the banks didn't share my conviction that a course in Inverness was meant to be. I was able to get a meeting with the head of a big bank in Toronto. He said he didn't know anything about golf and gave me what I'd call a polite brush-off, passing me along to a colleague who was more familiar with this kind of project. That meeting didn't last long. Building a course almost four hours away from Halifax, he said, was "the worst fucking idea I've ever heard."

At that point, I realized that I needed an equity partner. With or without bank financing, I was already committed. I'd been able to secure a government loan from a fund that was created to promote tourism, but I knew I was going to have to find a source of equity.

MK: By the time Ben and I spoke in early 2005, he had immersed himself in the complex situation in Inverness. A local group, the Inverness

Development Association, had been proactive, and they had good leadership. They looked across Cape Breton island to Ingonish, where the Keltic Lodge and the Highland Links were big draws. The IDA wanted something similar in Inverness itself. Some of the principals had traveled to Scotland to look at St. Andrews and other courses.

They'd not only won political backing for their cause but had also convinced several architects and developers to visit Inverness. Dr. Michael Hurdzan, a highly respected American designer who'd done notable work in Canada, described it as one of the fifty best remaining golf sites in the world. Jack Nicklaus had done a routing for a course, and so had Graham Cooke, the Canadian golfer and designer. While these projects hadn't gotten past the preliminary stages, I was intrigued. And the strength of the community support was a huge plus. In this day and age, any golf development is likely to encounter fierce local opposition wherever it's located. I'd had a taste of it at Bandon, and never would have proceeded at Cabot if I'd anticipated serious resistance and a long, costly fight just to get started.

BEN: Mike heard me out, and he had a suggestion. He thought I should start trying to put together land for a second course. My head was spinning. I still had a long way to go to assemble all the pieces for the first one, I didn't have much money, and was already feeling that I'd taken on more than I could manage—and Mike was asking me to take on twice as much. He told me a resort with a single course wouldn't work. And if the first course was any good, the price of land for a second was going to rise sharply. It was good advice, but I thought I was getting another polite brush-off. He wasn't saying no, exactly, but he was setting the bar so high that I'd never get over it.

After that initial phone conversation, I continued to look for other sources of funding. Ran Morrissett had backed the project from the start, and we tried to find other investors within the *Golf Club Atlas* network. I had one substantial Canadian investor, but still only a fraction of what was needed. I had to find a major equity partner, and for a links course in a remote location, the obvious partner was Mike Keiser.

I had just enough money to see the project through the early stages. I got Rod Whitman to visit the site with me, and he came up with a routing plan. Rod is an architect's architect, but his courses had never received the recognition they deserved. Rod's also Canadian, and that was important because Cabot Links was a Canadian project, and one that would bring attention to the quality of the golf across the whole country as well as to Nova Scotia, one of our most picturesque and interesting regions.

My family was still in Toronto while I was spending time in Inverness, working with Rod and talking to the owners of the thirteen parcels of land on which we hoped to build the Links course. At the same time I was doing what Mike had suggested, looking at land to the north—the property that would eventually become the Cliffs.

MK: Once the Cabot project was on my radar, I was rooting for Ben to pull it off—without me, if possible. He reminded me of myself two decades earlier, when I was trying to get people interested in Bandon Dunes and the door kept slamming in my face. The difference was that I had enough money to push ahead, and he didn't. When he came back to me in 2006, I agreed to send Josh Lesnik out to Inverness to have a look—a hard look. I still wasn't eager to get involved in a new project that was on the opposite side of the continent from where I'd started. But when he returned, Josh said, "Mike, there's something there. You should go see it."

Josh was the bridge to Cabot. He stayed in touch with Ben and started putting together a deal memo. After his tenure at Bandon Dunes, Josh had recently moved back to Chicago and taken a position in-house at KemperSports. We still worked together closely and talked nearly every day. Josh knew how to get a resort up and running—how to budget it, how to stage the development, how to put together a staff, open a restaurant, do the marketing. He wanted to make the Cabot deal happen.

JOSH LESNIK: On Mike's first visit to Inverness in March 2007, the weather was miserable—cold, wet, windy. Several of us had flown out from Chicago, and we had one day to study both sites. Mike suggested that we split up into two groups. He'd walk the Links site in town, and he asked Ben to lead the other group around the Cliffs site. I could see that Ben was dying to accompany Mike, but I also understood why

Mike wanted to see the land with Rod. Ben could sell refrigerators to the Eskimos, but Rod was the architect, and Mike wanted his perspective. He knew he'd learn more about Rod if Ben wasn't there. It was vintage Mike.

*Inverness mines and railway, circa 1906*

RAN MORRISSETT: Bill Coore and I were in Mike's group that morning, and our tour started at a recycling center. The place was a mess— trash everywhere, dirty snow on the ground, mud. A rutted road ran down toward the beach where there was an old ice plant and fish processing center. Before we even got started, a plastic trash bag blew against Mike and he slowly peeled it off. I wouldn't have been surprised if the tour had ended right there.

BILL COORE: Rod Whitman is one of my oldest friends, but he's not very good at selling himself. My wife, Sue, refers to him as the Man Who Does Not Speak. When we got to where the second hole would be, Mike saw an industrial building of some kind and asked, "What's that?" Rod said, "The sewage plant. But it doesn't stink." After that I noticed that Josh, who'd started out with a lot of enthusiasm, got quieter and quieter. He'd been up front, walking beside Mike and Rod, and he slipped back with the rest of us. He was worried that Mike wasn't liking what he saw.

MK: For a links lover, the situation was almost too good to be true—the land was nestled between the small town of Inverness and the Gulf of St. Lawrence. But the property had once been a coal mine and a railroad yard, and some of it was just plain ugly. That day, the place looked like a wasteland.

RAN: We'd taken a gamble to have Mike come in March, but it was one of the only free dates on his calendar. There was still a lot of ice on the Gulf. Down at the beach, the wind had driven ice floes up against the shore. In the summer, the sound of the waves is part of the appeal—it's gentle, soothing. That day the big blocks of ice made a terrible grinding, groaning sound. But as the tour continued, I got the impression that Mike was starting to like what he saw. He's seen enough sites to be able to look past superficial flaws.

BEN: I went back to the Cliffs site that afternoon with Mike. Even though most of it was wooded, we were able to get to the promontory that juts out into the Gulf—the rocky point where the 16th green now sits, high above the beach and waves. It didn't matter that the day was gray and gloomy. No one can stand there without fantasizing about playing a hole that soars over the beach.

Mike and his whole group were staying that night in one of the nicest houses in Inverness, and I made lasagna and Caesar salad for everyone. I was the chef and the server. Despite the weather and a rough day in general, the conversation was positive, and I had a feeling that Mike was considering some kind of involvement. After dinner, the offer came. He said, "Ben, I want to do this project, but we should start with the second course. That's the better site."

I felt as though I'd been punched in the gut. I didn't have to think about my reply. After all the efforts I'd made to win over the townspeople, to convince them that a golf resort really was the way forward for Inverness, I knew I had to say no. The links course had to be built first. If we went a mile out of town and built a course at the end of a long entry road, it would be as if we'd turned our back on the community that had already worked so hard to get us this far.

"I can't," I told Mike. "We have to start with the town course."

I gave my reasons, and then . . . silence. It felt like it lasted ten minutes, though it was probably only ten seconds. Everyone in the room seemed to be holding his breath. Had this really happened? Had a twentysomething kid, a would-be developer with no experience and no money, just turned down an offer from the most successful developer in the business?

Mike said, "Okay, I like that answer."

I was elated. I remember cleaning up the kitchen and going into town, where I was staying at the motel. I think Ran and I were the only people there that night. The wind was howling, the rain was hammering on the roof, the windows were rattling, and I climbed in between the sheets feeling as though I had just won the lottery.

MK: That night confirmed many of my impressions about Ben. When he turned down my offer, I realized that he had a clear vision of what he wanted to accomplish at Inverness and how to go about it. He wasn't going to abandon that vision to please me. I'd been in Inverness all of six hours, and he'd been spending time there for more than two years. He knew the town. He'd earned people's trust, and he knew that this was his most important asset—as important as any investment that I could make.

At the time I respected his integrity, and in retrospect I see how absolutely right he was. The personality of Cabot Links, the feel of a place where the golf is right at the doorstep of the town—it all starts with Inverness. If we'd built Cliffs first, and put the lodging and clubhouse out there, it would've been a slap in the face to the many local supporters. The Links would anchor the resort in the community, and if Ben could secure both sites, Cabot would have two very different courses.

My decision to buy into the Cabot project had as much to do with Ben as it did with the project itself. When described as a "visionary," I don't flinch as I once did, but I do think the term implies a kind of solo mission that simply isn't accurate. It also suggests that vision is granted to a select few, and I don't believe that, either. My experience is that many people have good ideas but then, for one reason or another, don't follow up on them. Only a few have the persistence, discipline, and judgment to turn those ideas into realities. I was confident that

*Ben Cowan-Dewar*        Ben had those qualities, and I left Nova Scotia looking forward to our partnership.

   All along I've depended on my partners for knowledge, expertise, and talents that I lack, and most of all for the kind of deep friendship that develops when you share a passion and responsibility. This bond between business partners is underappreciated in my view, and often misunderstood. Some observers might note that partners have different personalities or skills, then speculate on how they complement each other. Much harder to recognize is the synergy, the creative conversation that isn't always about solving a specific problem or achieving a certain result. It's about batting ideas back and forth, trying to articulate them, figuring out how to work together and make the hundreds of small, daily decisions that ultimately shape the outcome. As partners who listened to each other and valued what the other brought to the equation, Ben and I were able to create something at Cabot Links that was better than either of us could have created on our own.

BEN: With Mike on board, the community was almost convinced. There'd been so many disappointments in the past, beginnings that just fizzled out. During the summer of 2007, I made a push to secure all the land for the Links. It was grueling, often frustrating work. I was dealing with thirteen different landowners who, though sympathetic to the project, still had lingering reservations.

MK: As it turned out, we couldn't have started with the Cliffs even if we'd wanted to. Georgie Gillis wouldn't have allowed it. She and her husband, Peter, owned much of the land up there, and Georgie wouldn't have agreed to any sale unless the "town course" was built first. For her, a native of Inverness who left at the age of eighteen, the Cabot project was valuable only if it was of benefit to her hometown. Like so many others of her generation, she'd had to leave Cape Breton to find work. After a teaching career in Alberta, she and Peter returned to Inverness and had just finished restoring their retirement house. For Georgie, retirement didn't mean sitting still. She'd started running marathons at the age of thirty-nine, and by now, in her seventies, she has completed over thirty of them, competing in New York, Boston, and Greece. At the 2016 Canada Senior Games, she carried the flag for Nova Scotia and won six gold medals. Georgie was one of the first female caddies at Cabot and set up a training program for young women interested in following her example.

That would come later. When we were getting started, Georgie stepped forward as a staunch representative of the community. To me, she embodies the complex pride of the Invernessers and their fierce attachment to their ancestral home. They might have lived much of their lives elsewhere, but their heart was always in Cape Breton.

BEN: We hit a major snag. In addition to Mike's support, I had governmental financing to help build the course. There was just one condition: they couldn't make the loan unless I owned all the land. When I told the various owners that the lease arrangement was off and they were going to have to sell their land to me, the initial reaction was that I'd been acting in bad faith. Basically, I was asking them to give me their land, and to trust that I could turn it into something of value. At a meeting in November of that year, I sat in the town hall showing them a slideshow of Bandon Dunes, trying to convince everyone that this miracle could happen in Inverness, too—and feeling inside that the whole dream was slipping away.

But everybody signed. There wasn't a single holdout. They had been burned so often that it was astonishing they could trust anybody. But I guess by this point I'd managed to convince them that I wanted this project to succeed every bit as much as they did.

MK: Once he'd sorted out the land, Ben went all in. He and his wife moved from Toronto to Inverness; Allie had given up a job in the financial industry, and she was thirty-five weeks pregnant with their first child. Just as they were getting settled, the Great Recession began to unfold. Later, when the resort opened, Allie was asked by *The New York Times* what it was like to live in Inverness, and she replied, "I feel like I'm in the witness protection program."

At Bandon Dunes, I'd decided to go ahead with the fourth course, Old Macdonald. Nearly every golf project in the world had stopped in its tracks, but I was determined to keep going. This meant trimming down the staff across the resort, and some key people were reassigned to new tasks. Grant Rogers—a PGA master professional—was reduced to working as a starter. Nobody knew how long this crisis would last, or how devastating it might become.

I had to call Ben and tell him that in these bleak conditions I couldn't justify putting money into Cabot Links.

BEN: The only good news in that call was that Mike said he'd do right by Allie and me. He understood how much we'd counted on his support when making the move to Inverness. But his top priority was to finish Old Macdonald, and he couldn't get it done unless he pulled the plug at Cabot.

That would've killed the project. My government financing was contingent on continued development of the course, and I couldn't do that without cash. Rod was already there doing preliminary field work. Over the next few months, we talked often, and in April 2009, Rod and I flew to Chicago to lay out a plan that cut costs to the bone. My pitch: "Give us $305,000, and Rod will move to Inverness to keep working on the course.

Mike said, "That's your plan? To come up with a budget so laughably low that we proceed with the project?"

But he agreed to the proposal. Rod moved here and did the rough shaping of the entire course with a bulldozer, an excavator, and one dump truck. I was out there with him nearly every day. When Mike came out in 2009 to see how we were doing, he flew commercial and rented a car to drive here from Halifax. I knew he meant it when he said he had to cut expenses.

MK: Within a year, the economy had stabilized and we were all breathing more easily. I think the experience of working within a tight budget helped bring us together as a team. Building a golf course is expensive, and I'm enough of a cheapskate to appreciate it when everybody else on a project is watching pennies too, not just throwing money around.

Ben might have deferred to me (slightly) on some questions relating to golf, but on the resort buildings I deferred to him—just as I'd deferred to Howard McKee at Bandon Dunes. Ben has style and a taste for fine things, and it shows in the buildings, rooms, and restaurants. He was working with the best architects and designers in Nova Scotia.

The low-slung, shingled Cabot Links lodge buildings are literally steps from the main street of Inverness. At first glance they might remind you of a breezeway motel—but one that is unmistakably sophisticated and elegant. In scale and form, the lodge fits in with the architecture along Central Avenue, but a second look reveals its understated contemporary flair, cedar siding, and outdoor sitting areas. Every guest room has a view of the golf and the sea, and one magazine has called them "the coolest rooms in golf."

In addition to seventy-two rooms in the Lodge, Cabot offers the alternative of nineteen privately owned villas so similar in style that they appear to be part of the Lodge. In deciding to build them, we were acknowledging that equity is a finite asset. Even with Ben's loans and grants from the provincial government, we had to guard our equity, and we decided not to use it for lodging. I won't go into all the calculations, but the most prudent way of expanding Cabot's accommodations was to build villas, sell them at cost, put them in our rental pool, take care of all the maintenance, and share revenues with the owners.

For them, this amounted to having a rental property on one of the best golf courses in Canada.

The nerve center of the resort is the busy area between the pro shop and the terrace outside the Cabot Bar. Golfers, caddies, and resort guests come and go throughout the day, on their way to the first tee, or to the bar, or to the Panorama restaurant on the top floor of the clubhouse. When you sit on the terrace outside the bar, the golfers on the 18th green are so close you can read their putts.

From his office above the pro shop, Andrew Alkenbrack keeps an eye on what's happening right below him. Since taking over as general manager in 2012, he's been our Johnny-on-the-spot, greeting arrivals, giving directions, connecting instantly with everyone, and setting the tone for the staff. A Canadian, he grew up in Ontario, not far from Ben Cowan-Dewar, and they stayed in touch as Andrew built an impressive career in the hospitality industry that led him through some of the world's most expensive and luxurious resorts. What attracted him to Cabot was the chance to go into business with an old acquaintance and get involved in creating a destination whose story hadn't already been scripted.

For Andrew and Ben and the rest of us, its theme was clear—and urgently so—from the very beginning. Since the mines began closing down in the 1950s, Inverness had been in steady decline, with someone from almost every family leaving to find work elsewhere. Many of them went to western Canada, where the oil economy was booming. When Cabot opened, we had hundreds of jobs to offer, especially for young people. Many were seasonal gigs, like most positions in Nova Scotia's tourism business. We also needed caddies, so we set up a clinic to train loopers, most of whom had never set foot on a golf course. In 2019, the resort had almost five hundred employees, and another 250 people worked as caddies. Even with a six-month season, there are nearly a hundred full-time positions in reservations, maintenance, human resources, management, and other departments. Create a hundred year-round jobs in Chicago, and it doesn't make much of an impact. In Inverness, a town of 1,387, it fundamentally alters the local economy.

The rejuvenation of Inverness is evident from the moment you drive into town. Flower baskets hang from the lampposts, and many of the buildings on the main street have been freshly painted in bright yellows and reds and blues. After years of neglect, the rows of company houses have been repaired and modernized. Cabot has been a major driver of change, just as the town's officials had hoped. One of my long-standing colleagues was quick to point out similarities between Bandon, Oregon, and Inverness, Canada, noting how golf—a business sometimes portrayed as marginal or even irrelevant—has given a pair of struggling communities a new lease on life.

One final note: Ben Cowan-Dewar has assumed the overall management of Cabot. During the planning and construction stages, KemperSports had been actively involved in all phases of the development and wanted the relationship to continue. But Ben dug in his heels. Having launched the project and shepherded it safely through the recession, he saw no reason to cede management responsibilities to anyone else.

When he said, "I don't think I'd make a very good employee for Kemper," I had to agree with him.

## 10

# Cabot Links

*It is a remarkable thing that though golf courses are often in lovely places it frequently so happens that the beauties of the landscape are to be seen from anywhere except the course. Who, for instance, ever heard of a self-respecting seaside course where one could get a view of the sea! One may hear it perhaps roaring or murmuring, according to its mood, beyond an interminable row of sandhills, but save with the artificial aid of a high tee one never dreams of seeing it.*

—BERNARD DARWIN, *The Golf Courses of the British Isles* (1910)

THE RELATIONSHIP between the developer and architect is a dance, and Rod Whitman and I got off on the wrong foot.

For years I'd been aware of his work, thanks mostly to Bill Coore. Rod had worked as the lead shaper on several Coore-Crenshaw projects in addition to designing several well-received courses of his own. I'd never seen or played any of them. On all previous occasions, I'd spent time with the architects before our collaboration began, playing golf with them, touring or playing their own courses, and gotten to know them well enough to feel confident that we'd have a solid working relationship.

The initial tour of the Links property had been awkward. Then, at dinner that night, we'd talked about the superiority of the Cliffs site. Though Cabot Links might be his breakthrough opportunity, Rod had to know that Cabot Cliffs was the headliner, waiting in the wings to steal the show. In fact, even before the course opened, we made sure that writers and other media visitors to the Links were also shown around Cliffs.

Nor did it help that I was the newcomer in this project. Rod and Ben had already forged a friendship as they worked out the routing. Ben had selected him for the commission, and Rod must have wondered if I would've made the same choice.

Sometimes Rod and I just didn't get one another. At first, on the raw land where the holes were little more than stakes in the ground, the greens, tees, and fairways might have been visible in Rod's mind, but I had a hard time seeing them. Rod is laconic, not at ease painting pictures in words. When asked a question, he often pauses to consider it before making a deliberate reply. His natural conversational pace is that of a tortoise, and mine is closer to a hare's.

Walking construction sites, I often give each hole a score between 1 and 10, and initially some holes at Cabot got low to middling marks, 4s and 5s. The architects with whom I've worked frequently understand this is a kind of shorthand, a starting point for a discussion, not a final grade. I'm not sure that Rod realized that.

After several visits in better weather, all my doubts about the property's potential had vanished. The Gulf of St. Lawrence has the warmest ocean water north of the Carolinas, and Inverness is a popular summer destina-

OPPOSITE
*Cabot Links, No. 14*

"When I work on a golf hole, I depend on what I call my sight. I see the way a hole should look. It's something I've always had, this kind of sight. I think some shapers aren't exactly sure what they want, and they push dirt around until they find something. I can't do that. I see clearly what I want to do, like someone drew a picture for me before I started."

—ROD WHITMAN

*Portrait of the artist, Rod Whitman, with his favorite implement*

tion. Beachcombers roam the coastline looking for sea glass, and fishing boats are moored in the harbor. Just inside the outermost dune ridge, the town had built a popular boardwalk that runs only a few steps away from the 8th tee and fairway. Even without golf, the place had a cheerful, relaxed, holiday atmosphere.

However, some sections of the course remained scruffy and problematic. The Inverness Railway and Coal Company had left behind a disturbed landscape when it closed down. In 2001, to prevent leaching from the ashes and tailings, the provincial government had cleaned this up, covering much of the contaminated area with a foot-thick layer of impermeable clay. Some of these areas were smooth and flat; here and there, the level surface was broken by blocky mounds where slag heaps had been capped. And dominating the grounds was a squarish, flat-topped aberration that jutted up like a mesa—the minehead where the miners had taken elevators thousands of feet underground to work in tunnels that reached for miles beneath the floor of the sea.

Could Rod Whitman—or anyone else, for that matter—transform a partially degraded industrial landscape into a links that could rival the best in the world? At either end of its rectangular shape, the land was wonderfully suited for golf, with the rumples and ridges of natural linksland. The large central area, though, looked as if someone had covered a parking lot and a big-box store with a layer of dirt and clay.

Ben Cowan-Dewar and his family were living in a house that overlooked the course, and he kept watch, with binoculars, on Rod's progress. He was going to *will* this dream into reality. Every morning Rod climbed into the cab of his dozer and kept pressing forward, a man and his machine, tenacious, ant-like, transforming this piece of Cape Breton one grain of sand at a time.

Rod Whitman was hired for his first job in golf by Bill Coore. Their careers have been intertwined since the late 1970s, when Bill was the superintendent at Waterwood National GC, in Huntsville, Texas, and Rod played on the golf team at nearby Sam Houston State. To make some pocket money, he started working for Bill on the grounds crew. He was soon fascinated by golf architecture, and he and Bill became close friends. Many evenings, in Bill's small apartment, they'd order pizza, watch TV, and spend hours talking about design.

Eventually, Bill found Rod a job with his former boss, Pete Dye. Rod worked for Dye for most of the 1980s, complementing his income as a shaper with independent commissions that began coming his way. And once Bill teamed up with Ben Crenshaw, they often called on Rod's services. His talent as a "dirt guy" was widely recognized; among those who build golf courses for a living, Rod was considered a Michelangelo on a bulldozer. At Friar's Head, a private Long Island club that's one of Coore-Crenshaw's most highly ranked courses, Rod's earthmoving tied together its disparate landscapes, blending hilly, wooded dunes with the expanse of flat potato fields, giving cohesion to a course that otherwise might have seemed disjointed. One of Rod's best solo designs, Golf du Médoc, is in France and is a companion course to a Coore layout.

Rod and Bill have never forgotten the lessons learned on the seat of a bulldozer. Like Pete Dye, they believe their art depends on the ability to translate concepts into features of the terrain. They log long hours in the field, walking and looking. To me, they're a pair of earth-whisperers who pick up messages from the ground that the rest of us can't hear. They're both perfectionists. If either of them builds a feature that doesn't harmonize with the natural landforms, he can't rest until he's got it right. I've seen Rod spend a full day working on the slope of a green only to come back the next morning, squint at it, knock it down, and start over from scratch.

During the construction of Cabot Links, Rod and his wife, Glynis, moved to Inverness. Both Canadian, they settled easily into the community. Out-

going and lively, she knew how to get her husband talking. I should probably add he doesn't look like some "dirt guy." Of medium height and build,
with a little paunch just starting to show, he wears glasses that give him a
thoughtful, reflective appearance. Away from a construction site, in neatly
pressed jeans, western belt, and a plaid shirt, he could easily be mistaken for
a rancher, albeit one with a strong independent streak; he projects an air of
self-possession and quiet individuality.

During the first year, I flew to Nova Scotia without the usual entourage
and spent days with Rod and Ben. The recession might've worked to our
advantage. My projects are never fast-tracked, but here, with limited funds,
the work moved even more slowly than usual, a pace that suited Rod just
fine. We had plenty of time to get to know each other and figure out how to
accomplish our goals.

As a developer, I fall in a middle range in terms of active engagement in
course design. At one end, there's the hands-off type, which includes most
real estate people; rather than getting involved in golf, they leave it to the
design team. At the opposite end, you'll find developer-architects such as my
late friend Mark Parsinen; during construction, he basically took up resi-
dence on the grounds, completely immersed and collaborating closely with
the architect he'd chosen.

My habit is to visit a site at intervals and to contribute ideas that I expect
to be seriously considered. I also expect, most of the time, to have them
batted down—or, if adopted, to be so transformed by the designer that they
fit seamlessly into his vision of the course. Though I'm the owner, I count
myself a part of the crew, and the architect is our boss. Admittedly, since I
can fire him, a certain tension always exists, but it's critical that it remain
beneath the surface.

Although we altered the sequence of holes at Cabot Links, and I bought
a few additional acres for a new 7th hole, Rod's initial routing remained
largely intact because it wove so wonderfully across the property. He first
identified several natural green sites, and then determined how to maximize
other strong features of the property. As I suggested above, some of the most
beautiful stretches are found at either end—marsh and harbor in the south,
gullies and dunes to the north. Like a pair of tent pegs, these areas bolted
down the entire routing.

The southernmost hole and one of my favorites is the 6th, a natural dogleg that bends around MacIsaac's Pond. An ideal spot for the green was just

sitting there, protected by a dune, only yards away from the fleet of lobster boats. A photo op, as the saying goes, and we call it the Harbor Hole.

On the north end, the 16th doesn't have a name, but the Sunset Hole would come close. The green sits on a clifftop at the end of a tumbling fairway, defended by a small ravine and surrounded by a weathered wood fence. Late in the afternoon, this is where golfers linger to watch the sun setting over Cape Breton, gaudy bands of pink and orange and yellow that make for a picture postcard.

Given the rectangular shape of the property, most of the holes run parallel to the beach, and Rod had very cleverly transformed the flat-top mesa over the old mineshaft into a kind of crossroads, with three tees, two greens, and even the mid-round snack shop. From this elevated, bird's-eye perch, players can orient themselves, seeing holes just played and those still to come. This spot also has its own energy; it's not every day that you stand above a shaft sunk deep into the bowels of the earth.

• • •

*The food stand just over the dune makes the freshest lobster rolls in town.*

OVERLEAF
*The 16th is the last infinity green on the Links, a place to linger and take in the Cape Breton sunset before heading for home.*

As the illustrious Bernard Darwin observed, the old links rarely offer a full-on view of the sea. Golfers might hear its murmur or catch a glimpse of sparkling waves beyond the dunes, but most early courses kept a safe, respectful distance. Today, with modern construction methods and grasses that withstand salt water, designers can build as close to the sea as they dare. At Kingsbarns (2000), Mark Parsinen and architect Kyle Phillips demonstrated how a contemporary links can make dramatic use of a seaside location; some holes look as if they are about to be swept away by the North Sea.

At Cabot Links, the ocean is visible from just about everywhere. Few courses in the world have this much ocean exposure, and I couldn't stop harping on the need to make the most of it. *Seaside golf, seaside golf, seaside golf.* In any complex design project, someone has to keep hammering away at the simplest objectives. I didn't mind being that somebody.

Rod routed six holes so close to the beach that you could easily hit a wild shot onto the sand or the cobbles. Others overlook a series of gentle terraces stepping down to the Gulf. Still, I wanted more emphasis on the marvelous view, and I asked Rod to build as many greens as he could with infinity edges (where the surface of the green cuts across the ocean or sky. To be exact, I asked for twelve of them). His answer was "Huh?"

It was Mark who first made me notice, and count, infinity greens. On a trip to Scotland in 2010, we'd played Castle Stuart, another of his stunningly beautiful courses. After the round, Mark wanted to know my opinion of his eleven infinity greens. Eleven what? I'd noticed several greens near the water but hadn't been keeping a tally. Mark urged me to play a second round, this time paying closer attention. According to his definition, an infinity green didn't have to create a bold, straight line, as an infinity pool does, in order to count; he included any that had a small segment bleeding into the horizon. Sure enough, there were eleven. To play a round checking them off, while noting how he and codesigner Gil Hanse had used them to frame the waters of the Moray Firth and the distant Highlands landscape, was a case study in the art of integrating a course into its scenic environment.

Even after describing this experience, Rod looked at me as if I'd lost my marbles. So I made a proposal. "Give me a dozen infinity greens," I said, "and I'll send you and Glynis to Hawaii for ten days."

That changed his expression. He'd at least try to humor me, since he did want to take that trip with his wife. We agreed that once Cabot Links was finished, Josh Lesnik and I would play his course and count the infinity greens. We would be the sole and final judges. If we found a dozen, then . . .

•  •  •

At Cabot Links, our purpose was embodied in the name: we were building a links course. Even though we were going to have to manufacture a few holes, the intent was to remain faithful to the true links aesthetic, and it came as a surprise to me that Rod had never been to Scotland. He'd read about those links, naturally, and his first solo design, Wolf Creek, was admired as an example of an inland links. But his direct experience of links golf was bound to be idiosyncratic because his mentor was Pete Dye. "I must have built hundreds of pot bunkers," he once told me, "and I installed thousands of railroad ties." Both have indeed been used on several Scottish links, but Dye was a restless innovator whose eclectic style overrode any textbook definitions. In his version of links golf, traditions were reimagined, reinvented, and repurposed to express his own personal aesthetic.

It was time for Rod to go to Scotland. From my own education in golf, I knew this pilgrimage could be life-changing. Rod went twice, with Ben as his guide and companion. After those trips, he and I often talked about specific courses and holes, and Rob fluently borrowed ideas for our own use. For example, the mounds on the left side of Cabot's 1st fairway? He'd seen something like that at Prestwick. With this frame of common reference, we meshed better as a team.

Obvious as it seems, an awareness of those traditional elements led to specific design decisions. For instance, the model we followed was that of simple, old-fashioned, low-profile links bunkers whose upper lips look like a breaking wave of turf and grass. They provide an important element of the course's visual signature and give it the appearance of having been there for a great many decades. Another links feature is the double green that serves the 8th and 13th holes. We didn't build it just so we could say that Cabot Links had one; Rob massaged this green for hours, tying together its fascinating contours. A different template is seen at the 2nd hole, where the swale dividing this par-3's green invites a classic, low-trajectory shot that can be run up to the flag.

During construction, it's a magic moment when you see a hole emerging clearly. For me, it's a little like one of those visual puzzles where you have to spot a hidden object—and once you do, it seems like it was obvious all along. You've found the desired image. To mention just a few instances:

**NO. 3, 330/290 YARDS.** This was what I call an architect's hole, one of those blank spots in the routing where the designer has to make something up. Rob turned this wetlands area into one of the most memorable holes on the course, a short par-4 that's drivable in some winds—the kind of hole that makes players ponder their plan of attack on the tee. First, the fairway needed to be created with countless truckloads of sandy soil. Then Rod and his project manager, Dave Axland, and the rest of the crew had intense discussions about all the other possibilities, including the exact tilt of the green and the curve of the crescent-shaped fairway. The mounds on the left side of the fairway are fair examples of Rod's artistry as a shaper; asymmetric and varied in size, they look like the remnants of an eroded dune ridge. Some designers build mounds that seem almost preassembled, but Rod's appear to have been sculpted by centuries of wind and weather.

**NO. 11, 620/490 YARDS.** The downhill drive has to skirt an expanse of native vegetation: pale green beach grass, dark-leafed bayberry and Labrador tea, purple wild iris and bird vetch, bright magenta beach rose. The fairway then heads uphill, where the green is perched next to a ravine. The shot I most enjoy is the approach. It figures that Rod would be a master of shaping the ground for running shots, and you can use the slope left of this green as a sideboard, letting the ball curl across it toward the hole. If you like playing the ground game, you'll love Cabot Links. I think Rod would agree that Scotland sharpened his sense of how to work with rumpled landscapes.

**NO. 14, 102/92 YARDS.** A 10 on the Keiser scale. The tee box sits atop the former minehead, and far below the green seems to hover over the ocean, a wedge shot away. The hole's been called a dropkick, and once even "dinky." Sure, on a calm day it might pass for a pushover, but its mood can change in a hurry. When the wind's up and the surf's pounding, the tee is so exposed that you feel you're trying to land a Ping-Pong ball on a distant postage stamp. For me, the 14th is a sassy little enigma, just the kind of hole I love: thrilling, beautiful, within the power of any retail golfer.

At Cabot Links I watched an almost–ugly duckling grow into a glorious swan. Inverness was now the only town in North America that had a true links a block away from main street, and I wasn't a bit surprised our course was immediately proclaimed one of the best in Canada. "I spent my whole life training to build this course," Rod Whitman said on opening night, when he was full of praise for Dave Axland and design associates Jeff Mingay and Keith Cutten, and included Ben and me on what he called an all-star team.

After the toasts and tributes, he slipped away from the clubhouse. When Bill Coore followed him outside to congratulate him, he saw that tears had welled up in his eyes.

This moment of recognition had been a long time coming. For Rod, Cabot Links is the course that has secured his place in the top rank of designers.

Links took almost three years to build. I can't imagine how we would've pulled through the Great Recession if Rod hadn't been willing to rely on a ridiculously tight budget. He was exactly the right man for a course that had to be built up layer by layer, adding intricacy and nuance so deftly that it appeared native to this ground. He also brought to the work the hallmarks of a true craftsman: humility, discipline, precision, patience, mastery, integrity. He built a golf course that is rooted rock-solidly in place.

By the end of a process that took many years, Rod and I had the bond of people who've weathered a rough journey together. We'd learned how to talk to each other, and how to needle each other, too. Asked by a journalist why the course had taken so long to build, Rod answered, "My plan was to go just as slow as I could and still have Mike keep me on the payroll."

As promised, when it was finished, Josh Lesnik and I played a round to count the infinity greens. Occasionally we had to try a few different vantage points before we could see the edges of one green or another cutting sharply against the waters of the Gulf of St. Lawrence, but we'd counted twelve by the time we got to the 16th hole. That was the winning number. Rod and Glynis earned their trip to Hawaii. First-class.

## 11

# The Hottest Destination in North America

*Midway through my maiden round at Cabot Cliffs, strung along ocean bluffs above the town of Inverness, Nova Scotia, I became overwhelmed by an emotion best described as giddy. I'd already played through four landscapes, from highlands to river valley to sand dunes to pine trees and was now standing on the ninth tee facing a short iron downhill to a cliff-edge green backdropped by the shimmering Gulf of St. Lawrence, which is the Atlantic Ocean as far as I'm concerned. My thought at that moment: This must be how it felt when golfers first played Cypress Point.*

—RON WHITTEN, *Golf Digest*, November 2019

WISH I HAD A DOLLAR for every time I've heard someone say, *If you build it, they will come.* In case you never saw the movie, that line comes from *Field of Dreams.* The actual words are *If you build it, he will come,* and they're spoken by a mysterious voice that only the character played by Kevin Costner can hear. Haunted by this instruction, he obediently builds a baseball diamond on his Iowa farm, and the ghosts of Shoeless Joe Jackson and many other big leaguers do indeed come striding out of the high cornrows. James Earl Jones gives a stirring speech about how people will pay to watch baseball on this magical field. "People will most definitely come," he says. "They'll pass over the money without even thinking about it, for it is money they have, and peace they lack."

It's a goose-bumps moment. Movies are in the business of happy endings. At Cabot Links, though, we were in the resort business, and the ending wouldn't be happy unless people handed over the money. Building the golf course was the first step, and in some respects easier than the second—to get retail golfers to come. This was a marketing task, and our efforts were dependent on the media. The story of any business is a narrative woven together by many tellers, and the owner can do only so much to shape the message and make it compelling. The world offers thousands of fabulous destinations, from mountain lodges to fairy tale castles to Aegean islands. We had to convince would-be travelers to fly to Halifax, rent a car, and drive almost four hours to a small town in order to play golf on a brand-new course.

Furthermore, we had to convince them to pay a premium price for a high-end golf experience in an area where tourism had traditionally meant family vacations, camping, mom-and-pop motels. To break even, we would need to sell 15,000 rounds and 5,000 room nights every year. (Spoiler: there is a happy ending. In 2019, Cabot sold 43,000 rounds and 15,487 room nights.)

In broad terms, the business challenge would be comparable to what I'd faced in Bandon, and before that, at Recycled Paper Greetings. Cabot Links would be a small, niche operation competing for a share of the upscale golf travel market with larger, established resorts. Many belonged to corporate chains, and this provided significant advantages. They could advertise pro-

OPPOSITE
*Cabot Cliffs, No.16.
This is the shot
everyone anticipates.*

lifically, their brands had been around for decades, they were easier to get to, and they had programs to reward loyal clients.

We couldn't compete head-on, not on their terms. To entice golfers to come to Cabot Links, we would have to offer something else—a superior product. While we had to capture only a small fraction of the market, we'd be starting small, with only forty-eight rooms and a single golf course, and our season was just six months long—seven months if we got lucky with the weather. During our peak season, from mid-June to mid-September, we'd have to stay close to fully booked.

To say we had a marketing "plan" for Cabot Links would be slightly misleading. Ben and I talked nearly every day, and the concept for the resort emerged naturally from our conversations. We were in agreement on the talking points. Since I was involved and we were building a links course in a remote location, from the start one of the main threads of the story was whether Cabot Links could repeat the miracle of Bandon Dunes. In this narrative my role was usually overstated, with my first outing always lurking in the background.

Our revised narrative, however, took place in a different context. Bandon Dunes debuted in the middle of a golf boom, and we had to scramble to get the golf media's attention because new courses were opening nearly every day. But now, the recession perversely worked to our advantage. Cabot Links was one of the few courses being built anywhere in the world. Every trade magazine wanted to run a piece about it. And Canadian writers—including those covering travel and business—were interested in what they saw as a national story.

The first component of any brand is its name, and Cabot Links was a winner. The words were straightforward, easy to say and remember, and they made you want to know more. John Cabot was an explorer who is believed to have made landfall at Nova Scotia in 1497. He's the namesake of the Cabot Trails, the scenic highway that loops around Cape Breton Island, chiseled into the slopes rising steeply from the sea. This is Canada's version of Highway One at Big Sur, California, an iconic route. So the name evoked history, scenery, adventure, escape—and links golf. (In 2020, a rebranding took place quietly, and the resort's now known as Cabot Cape Breton.)

Ben was our point of contact with writers and the media. Engaging, witty, articulate, a natural storyteller and phrasemaker, he has a full kit of language skills—something I value highly after decades of working with artists to craft messages on greeting cards. We decided not to hire a publicist because we not only wanted to save money but also believed that Ben could do a better job himself. A story's likely to be better if the writer gets it from the source.

Ben also has the right temperament for this work. He can graciously answer the same questions over and over, making it sound like he's never heard them before. He has the knack of praising without exaggerating. His marketing pitch doesn't come across as a pitch at all, just ordinary, informed conversation. It helped that he had a history with many of the writers, editors, bloggers, and tastemakers that he spoke to; he'd known them for years through his golf travel business or his tenure at *Golf Club Atlas,* and he'd already established his credibility as a discerning judge of resorts and courses.

His influential network continued to expand while Cabot Links was a work in progress. Because the project was so often in the news and he met so regularly with local individuals and organizations, Ben became something of a public figure, and was appointed as the chair of the board of directors of Tourism Nova Scotia from 2012 to 2017, and then to the same position at Destination Canada, a public-private organization that promotes international tourism. In short, he became a force in that industry, deeply familiar with its plans, trends, research, organizations, and also with business and media leaders.

Compared to Ben, I was a relic of the twentieth century. I don't tweet, text, or blog, and I still like to read things on paper, not screens. I've never given up my lifelong habit of clipping out magazine and newspaper articles and sending them to people who might be interested. That is, I slip the article into an envelope, stick on a stamp, and drop it in a mailbox. I have a cell phone but use it rarely. I prefer a landline. On any important matter, I'd much rather talk to someone on the phone than exchange emails. Those mail threads, with multiple addressees and exchanges, are the invention of the devil.

Nevertheless, when it came to getting the story of Cabot Links out, Ben and I were in complete accord and stuck to a few simple guidelines. We tried to spend time with everyone who wanted to do a story, interview, or media feature. It never hurts to show a writer around, tour the course with him, have a beer together. The two of us were partners in a start-up, not a billion-dollar corporate venture, and personal involvement was integral to this story. Since we both have an aversion to media jargon and MBA-speak, we wanted to set a tone that carried over into other aspects of this venture. We didn't have shareholders to please, but we certainly weren't the only people who had a stake in Cabot Links. The citizens of Inverness were counting on us to make something out of the land they'd entrusted to us, so we encouraged writers to seek them out and didn't try to micromanage their reporting.

That was another principle: let the place and product speak for themselves. Writers are more invested in their stories if they do their own research, I've found, and no decent writer likes to be coaxed, steered, pushed, or leaned on. Inevitably, we had our critics among the townspeople and the media, but most people who made the effort to understand our enterprise came away as supporters.

To what extent did our approach contribute to favorable coverage? There's no way of quantifying this exactly, but it seems to me that Cabot was a media sweetheart all along. On everything from Twitter to blogs to local papers and TV stations, from major golf monthlies to urban newspapers to travel magazines and state-of-the-art videos, Cabot Links was the beneficiary of extensive, detailed, varied, and imaginative coverage. It wasn't always what we expected, and that was fine with us. The media generated a multithemed story that started auspiciously and kept growing and broadening, encompassing a range of insights and perspectives that have helped give Cabot its own complex personality. So herewith a kind of media scrapbook:

- "The man who made rustic and remote seaside golf popular in the U. S. appears to be ready to leave his mark in Canada." That's from an early story by Robert Thompson, writing in *SCOREGolf,* Canada's leading golf magazine in the May 2007 issue, before I'd announced my partnership. A prolific writer about the architecture and business of the game, Thompson covered the Cabot development in various magazines, papers, and digital forms. He owned this story much as a beat writer owns a team's story.
- "The golf world is eagerly awaiting the debut of Cabot Links," George Peper and Malcom Campbell declared in *True Links.* As I noted above, this 2010 book offers a rigorous definition of the term and fixed the number of links courses worldwide at 246. Very precise, very select. Making this list made us feel that Cabot had been anointed. *True Links* enabled us to state clearly what made us different from nearly

every other contemporary golf course, giving us both an identity and a pedigree.

• "Cabot Links: The New Scotland?" That was the title of Adam Lawrence's January 2011 article in *Golf Course Architecture,* which noted that its low-profile dunes and in-town location gave Cabot Links a Scottish look and flavor that distinguished it from Bandon Dunes.

• "Canada's first links course is a golf purist's paradise." This story in the *Toronto Globe and Mail,* on July 23, 2011, showed how the links idea would also be taken up in general-circulation media. For Canadians, the *Globe and Mail* is the totem newspaper, *The Wall Street Journal* and *The New York Times* rolled into one. Several associated words—"pure," "authentic," "Scottish," "classic"—would figure prominently in descriptions of Cabot Links.

• "On this continent, seaside-links golf of Cabot's caliber is matched only by Bandon Dunes. Heading east, the next stop would be Ballybunion, in Ireland," wrote Thomas Dunne, a trusted golf journalist, for *Departures* in April 2012, sticking our pin on the world map.

• "To me, Cabot Links is simply the best golf I have experienced," Bob Weeks concluded in *SCOREGolf*'s June 2012 issue, after attending our official opening. One of Canada's most influential golf writers, Weeks made it seem like a patriotic duty to go to Cabot.

• Only a few days after the opening, *The New York Times* ran a long feature by Bill Pennington on the front page of the sports section, noting that the stylish resort with a true links course belonged to "a boutique category of oceanside golf architecture." A story of that length and prominence in the *Times* was tantamount to a national seal of approval; nearly half of our visitors are American. Pennington's reporting also added another element to the Cabot story; he described how strongly the resort was rooted in the local culture and community. He interviewed several Inverness residents to draw a composite portrait of a town that had a new "bounce in its step."

• "Cabot Links was built for golf, but the development is bringing an entirely new standard of service to Cape Breton, tilting its tourist map toward Inverness and the surrounding region . . . [and was] acknowledged from opening day as the best the island has to offer," Guy Nicholson wrote in the *Globe & Mail* on August 25, 2012, a second endorsement from this potent paper. Focusing on the resort's excellent

*Holing out at sunset, the 18th green can feel like a stage.*

amenities and its ambiance of "barefoot luxe," Nicholson was extolling the charms of Cabot—and of Cape Breton Island—to a crucial readership. By a significant margin, greater Toronto is Cabot's strongest market.

• In September 2013, *Golf Advisor* broached a new subject by calling Bandon "probably the ultimate guys' golf destination. On the other hand, Cabot Links strikes us as having much broader appeal, both to golfing couples and families where everybody enjoys the game. In part, it's the intimacy of the setting, but the larger factor is the Cabot Links lodging and dining experience, which is a distinct step up." Subsequently, several other publications made the same point. Cabot has even been included on lists of honeymoon destinations. It's not something we expected, but we've made adjustments to enhance the appeal to couples; king-sized beds, top-of-the-line linens and towels, heated bathroom floors, and state-of-the-art showers have been noted and appreciated. Over 25 percent of our guests at Cabot are women, almost twice as many as at Bandon.

On Facebook, starting in 2010, Ben was creating a new kind of archive that focused on the building progress at Cabot Links. Though Facebook had been around for a few years, it had begun to grow at warp speed, and Cabot Links was one of the first golf operations to fully exploit the platform. When I think of the expense and effort required to get photographs of Bandon Dunes printed and distributed in the 1990s, I'm grateful to have Facebook as a business tool (though I'd never go near it for any personal reasons).

The moment at which the Cabot story kicked into overdrive is easy to pinpoint. Even as Links was taking its bow, the media kept wanting to look up the coast, where Cliffs was under construction. Having experienced the rollout of several new courses, I realized that a strong groundswell was building. When Ben insisted on starting with the "town course," he was right for a reason neither of us had really foreseen. Without planning to, we'd staged a prolonged campaign for Cliffs by almost teasing everybody who came to Inverness. *Just wait till you see what's coming next. . . .*

Every writer wanted to be among the first to sing Cabot Cliffs' praises. Lorne Rubenstein, the dean of Canadian golf writing, played a few preview holes and reported in *SCOREGolf:* "Certain courses stir the imagination, and fire the mind, even during construction. . . . What a feat of the imagination. What a setting. What a course." Predictably, the article was accompanied by a photograph of the 16th hole, the par-3 situated on a promontory that points sharply into the Gulf, and the green—from the tee, a minuscule square of grass—seems suspended above streaked, whitish rocks that look like the molars of a giant. This thriller of a shot has to carry across the beach and thread through the massive, menacing jaw to a tiny spot of safety.

The 16th quickly came to symbolize the Cliffs experience—the excitement, the wow factor, the sensory overload. Whenever I see pictures of it, I recall Bill Coore wondering if it was even going to be possible to locate a green on that promontory, and Keith Rhebb, his associate, describing the challenge of building up the putting surface on jagged points of rock without driving his dozer over the edge.

Cliffs has eight holes on the ocean, and its inland holes defy easy descrip-

"IF I HAD TO PICK one spot anywhere to spend a summer, it would be in this old coal-mining town called Inverness on a beach fronting the Gulf of St. Lawrence. The proof is in the four caddies who carried my bag over four rounds there: a Scottish farmer, a junior high school principal, a practicing attorney and a renowned pediatric surgeon. Each made their way from far and wide to live or summer in Inverness so they could caddie and play the Cabot courses."

—JERRY TARDE, *Golf Digest,* 2018

OVERLEAF
*With a backdrop of evergreens and a bunker dominated by a gypsum boulder, the par-3 14th illustrates the character of the inland holes at Cliffs.*

tion. Bill's routing leads players through a series of "rooms," microenvironments that when strung together provide a tour of Cape Breton and its singular treasures. One hole bends along the reedy estuary of a river, the next enters a private alcove in the dunes, and the next leaps a ravine and heads up the hill into a forest of birch, spruce, and pine. So it goes throughout the course. I don't think anyone else has Bill's gift for teasing out the charms of a property and varying the mood of a golf course.

Without suggesting that Cliffs differs fundamentally from other Coore-Crenshaw designs, I will say that this site brought out the razzle-dazzle in them. At Cliffs, Bill and Ben didn't hold back, and the course is full of flourishes and fanfares. After an opening hole that's merely superlative, they designed a par-4 2nd that is a complete original. This is the first of many jolts of adrenaline. From an elevated tee, you try to figure out where to place a tee shot on a fairway shaped like a Y, branching to either side of a huge dune that looms up behind a marsh and in front of a partially hidden green.

No wonder Ron Whitten felt "giddy." Ron happens to be one of the most feared men in the game, the longtime architecture editor of *Golf Digest* whose reviews have caused meltdowns at several high-powered clubs. Over a career that now spans almost five decades, he has established and maintained a reputation for impartiality. He does not hand out glowing reviews lightly. But here he was at Cliffs, swooning and wondering aloud if he was witnessing the "second coming of Cypress Point," comparing our just-opened course to the century-old masterpiece that was, he added, "in my mind previously unmatched in its beauty, variety, and thrills." Though Ron questioned the unusual balance of holes—six par-3s, six par-4s, and six par-5s—*Golf Digest*'s panel ranked it head and shoulders above other contenders for the Best New Course of 2015.

Another important endorsement came from Matt Ginella—several of them, actually, since he made repeated trips to Nova Scotia and followed the course's development in print, video, and on TV. No one brings more gusto to reports of golf travel, and in 2013, on Golf Channel's *Morning Drive*, Matt narrated and starred in a video that reached the conclusion that Cabot was a "complex, beautiful, stand-alone destination."

He showered praise on both courses and called Cliffs the culmination of the Coore-Crenshaw partnership—maybe the longest in the game's annals—as well as my collaboration with them. (I'm not sure about that, since the Sheep Ranch was yet to come.) There wasn't a weak hole on the course, he said, and then recounted a conversation with friends in which they sat around a table comparing Pebble Beach and Cliffs, in a hole-by-hole match play. "Cliffs won holes 1 through 5. Pebble won holes 6 through 10. It was 5-to-5 going to the 11th tee. Cliffs won 11 through 17 and Pebble took the 18th. Cliffs wins 12–6."

Looking back over the articles and media coverage, I'm struck by how often the Cabot story diverged from the Bandon model. Ben and I always knew that it would—just not how, and where, Cabot would find its own style and identity. The emphasis shifted from the purity of the links to the fun and excitement of the two courses. The upscale appointments and amenities broadened the resort's appeal and became part of a larger story about a new, high-end tourism in Cape Breton. The intimate relationship between resort and town of Inverness was another theme, and the local culture, scenery, and lively music scene came to be seen as part of the allure of what the editors of *Golf Digest* called "the hottest destination in North America."

For me, the essence of Cabot is distilled in the finishing holes at Cliffs, a sequence that begins at the par-5 15th, which plays gently downhill from the highest point of the property toward an infinity green, bringing you to the edge of the cliff overlooking the Gulf. This late in the round, you might feel that your reserves of wonder have been emptied—until you step onto the 16th tee and encounter the shot I just described. Then, before you can catch your breath, you're on the 17th facing a drive across another stretch of beach to a rollicking fairway. And at last the 18th hole awaits you, revealing a landscape that compasses the sea, the distant Links, and the steeples of the town of Inverness, a vision of coastal golf that is invigorating and timeless.

# 12

# Cabot Saint Lucia

*Throughout his career, Mike [Keiser] has always been willing to give young people an opportunity. He hired David Kidd at Bandon Dunes. At Cabot, he took me on as a partner, and he trusted me. He gave me the confidence to reach for everything I wanted. I can't overstate how much that support meant. If you want to leave a legacy, be a mentor.*

—BEN COWAN-DEWAR

S INCE OPENING IN 2012, Cabot has moved from success to success, setting better marks each year for the number of rounds played, rooms booked, total revenue, and net profit. Ben was planning to build out the resort with an ambitious slate of new projects: a par-3 course, a third eighteen, custom housing at the Cliffs, a new clubhouse and spa.

Then, in 2020, the coronavirus pandemic brought these hopes to a standstill. In March, the Canadian government imposed a travel ban on foreign nationals, including Americans. Citizens were also restricted; the only people allowed into Nova Scotia were residents of the maritime provinces. Bookings were canceled, the restaurants closed, the courses stood nearly empty.

All plans were put on hold except for The Nest, a ten-hole par-3 course designed by Rod Whitman and Dave Axland on the high ground above Cabot Cliffs; it had a subdued opening in June. Discussions with Tom Doak about a third eighteen—he'd already done a routing—were set aside indefinitely.

It was painful to see Cabot Cape Breton turn into a ghost of itself when golf's popularity was soaring. At facilities all over the United States, the number of rounds played was higher than it had been for years—14 percent higher, to be exact. At Bandon, we had to close for six weeks in March and April; after reopening, the resort was solidly booked. When I tried to get a room for myself in October, I was told I'd have to wait until late November! But the only busy place at Cabot was the reservations desk, where the phones kept ringing and bookings for the 2021 season were far ahead of the usual pace. Cooped up and confined, golfers were obviously fantasizing about treating themselves to a special jaunt and planning in advance for when the pandemic would finally be behind us.

Even though Ben had many reasons to stress out, he was moving ahead with new projects. Having started out in the Great Recession at Inverness, he already had a playbook for getting through difficult times. A developer's faith in future prospects can never waver, which means always keeping an eye on the years ahead. Since 2016, Ben had been looking for a site in the Caribbean where he could build a warm-weather resort. Because of the seasonality of operations at Cape Breton, a winter-friendly destination would

enable him to run a year-round program that would make better use of key staff and resources, help build his customer base, and expand the Cabot brand. He focused on the West Indies, surveying projects that had been abandoned during the 2008 recession.

On the beautiful island of Saint Lucia, he found a parcel of land that checked all the boxes. Most important, this two-mile stretch of jagged coast-line was broken by promontories, cliffs, small inlets, sandy beaches, and crashing surf—the ideal ingredients for dramatic golf.

Inland, the land sloped steeply, as it does all over Saint Lucia; the island brings to mind Mediterranean hillsides where colorful houses are terraced into the slopes. Its iconic landmarks are the Pitons, a pair of volcanic silhouettes that rise almost vertically from the sea to a height of 2,500 feet.

The site's potential had not gone unnoticed. In 2007, the celebrated Raffles chain had announced its intention to open a resort with a luxury hotel, an enormous spa, five pools, and choice real estate. The golf course was a Nicklaus design, and Jack was so enamored of the property that he was calling it "my Pebble Beach." Preliminary clearing had begun, and several holes were roughed in before the development was scuttled. Then the land just sat there for years.

If you've spent decades looking for golf locations, you can get finicky and

*It's hard not to think of Cypress Point when I look at this rendering of Cabot Saint Lucia.*

jaded. But when I first visited Saint Lucia, I felt the old jolt of excitement. The land sprawled, twisted, and tumbled into that incredible blue-green Caribbean water. This was a setting of unsurpassed tropical beauty, and Ben and I were in complete agreement that we wanted the Coore-Crenshaw team to design the course. Bill Coore, who's worked on exceptional properties all over the world and weighs his words carefully, threw restraint to the winds when he saw this land at Saint Lucia. "It's just extraordinarily beautiful. It has the long views of Kapalua, and it's as spectacular as Cabot Cliffs or the Sheep Ranch. There's no question that it will be one of the most photogenic courses in the world."

But there was a question about how to make the project viable as a business. Even though the permits had already been obtained, the development was going to be hugely expensive. The acreage was suitable only for a single course. We started calling it Cabot Point, but we couldn't begin without addressing serious engineering challenges. On a volcanic island, the rocky ground would have to be capped with imported soil, and the steepest holes would require massive cut and fill. Obviously, Cabot Point wouldn't be a links course, and Coore-Crenshaw wouldn't be adhering to minimalist practices.

Nor could Cabot Point be a walking course; even resolute walkers might welcome a cart ride on a course where the opening holes of each nine climb up a significant incline. In the vivid description of *Golf Digest*'s Derek Duncan, they function like "the tense, clacking journey of a roller coaster mounting the ride's highest point, building hard-won inertia for later moments." My favorite holes are the 16th and 17th, par-3s that play point-to-point over the wild surf. I gave them both 10s, maybe the only time I've ever given my top score to back-to-back holes. In Bill's view, the challenge at Cabot Point was to design a course that's as playable as it is beautiful. Every golfer will want to play it once just to see the place—but a second round, much less over and over again?

Cabot Point is the cornerstone of Cabot Saint Lucia, a resort that will include a beach club, spa, two hundred residences, and villas for short term-term stays—all at the height of luxury, literally so with sweeping views over the golf course and the sea. The density of the real estate has been much reduced from what Raffles had planned. Ben wants the housing sited as it is at Pebble Beach—in private enclaves along the perimeter of several holes, never blocking a golfer's sight lines or interrupting the sense of playing against the backdrop of the sea.

The name itself—Cabot Saint Lucia—was chosen to evoke a place rather than a specific activity, a branding decision we had applied to Cabot Links (now Cabot Cape Breton, as noted previously). In effect, this new strategy is an expression of what evolved naturally at Inverness; with golf leading the way, the resort built a reputation for other amenities and activities, both on-site and off. Cabot Saint Lucia will offer the full panoply of island pleasures, with the level of luxury a few notches higher. Having seen the renderings that Ben developed with top designers, I didn't hesitate to become involved in Cabot Saint Lucia.

Here, of course, our roles are reversed. At Cabot Links, I was the major investor and senior partner; now Ben is the CEO and the prime mover. Our relationship feels much the same, though, as it was never shaped by titles or specific responsibilities, and we continue to exchange ideas as freely as we always have.

While watching this project take shape, I've contemplated the important differences between his situation and mine at his age. Considering the number of principals and moving parts as well as the number of investors, Cabot Saint Lucia is a more expensive and complicated venture than Bandon Dunes had been. Thirty years ago, I didn't need or want investors. Since I had enough money for a golf course, I was going to build one that suited my interests and preferences, nobody else's. After all, I was busy running a greeting card company in Chicago, and golf was still a part-time job.

For Ben, golf *is* his business, or its motivating force. Developing destination resorts is a full-time job, and he has to worry about repaying loans and delivering returns to his investors. He can't take the risks that I did and can't approach problems with the basic mindset I'd used, that golf comes first and everything else is a distant second.

Ben operates within a different financial structure and at another level of taste and sophistication, and thankfully he has a grand gift for it. My emphasis was on links golf, and his portfolio is moving toward superb courses in spectacular locations. Given his demonstrable talents, Ben's services are much in demand. At Revelstoke, in British Columbia, a place known as the holy grail of heli-skiing, Northland Properties—one of the largest hospitality corporations in Canada—is his partner with plans for a lodge, private residences, and a golf course that will make this a four-season resort.

I'm an investor and, to be honest, was attracted by the skiing as much as the golf. As a former ski bum, I'm still awed by deep powder and big moun-

tains, and I've made eight trips to Revelstoke. The town is surrounded by the peaks of the Selkirk and the Monashee ranges, the vertical drop is 5,600 feet, and the tree skiing might be the best on the planet.

Ben is a skier too, but his mission at Revelstoke is to build a golf course that reflects the magnificent surroundings. The obvious choice for its designer was Rod Whitman, an Alberta native who now lives in British Columbia and, since the debut of Cabot Links, has been recognized as the country's foremost golf architect. Two of the world's most majestic mountain courses, Jasper and Banff, are in the Canadian Rockies, and I expect Revelstoke's Cabot Pacific to rival them.

Overlooking the headwaters of the Columbia River, with broad natural benches projecting from the mountainside, the site provides far more room for golf than is usually found in such steep terrain. So Rod will be able to avoid the faults of most ski-area courses: steep slopes, narrow fairways, sharp drop-offs, stiff climbs between holes. He'll also be reunited with Dave Axland and Keith Cutten, who worked with him in Inverness, and their association has now been formalized as a partnership. The Cabot Links team is together again.

Cabot Cape Breton. Cabot Saint Lucia. Cabot Revelstoke. Ben Cowan-Dewar has planted his flag at some of the most sought-out destinations in the world, and the trajectory of his career is clear: the golf-mad kid who wanted to play all the great courses has discovered how he can add to their number. At the age of forty, he joined the select group of developers whose courses capture the artistry and splendor of the game.

## Rome, Wisconsin

---

2017 **SAND VALLEY**
Designed by Bill Coore and Ben Crenshaw
*Golf Digest,* Best New Course 2017

2018 **MAMMOTH DUNES**
David McLay-Kidd
*Golf Magazine,* Best New Course 2018

2018 **THE SANDBOX**, 17-hole, par-3 course,
Bill Coore and Ben Crenshaw
*Golf Magazine,* Best New Short Course 2018

# 13

# The Central Wisconsin Sands

*These dunes could be your ocean.*

—DEBRA MOSKOVITS, naturalist, Field Museum, Chicago

THERE IS NO OCEAN IN ROME, WISCONSIN. I pointed this out to my oldest son, Michael, when he urged me to consider central Wisconsin as the site of a new resort. My three requirements for a golf course have always been clear and non-negotiable: sandy soil, brilliant design, and an ocean. Michael is persistent, however, and Rome is now the home of Sand Valley, a destination that has brought public, links-inspired golf to the Midwest. If Michael and Chris, my other son, are able to fulfill their ambitions, Sand Valley might well be the prototype of a new kind of resort.

Michael and Chris were my partners in the initial stages of the project. Now they're in charge, developing Sand Valley in a manner that reflects the dreams, lifestyles, and cultural outlook of a different generation. When they were youngsters, I introduced them to the kind of golf that I loved best— walking golf on links courses at seaside locations. Of course, whenever we went to a place where there were carts, they wanted to drive; like most kids, they seemed to enjoy that as much as playing the game. Now they're both tall, all-around athletes, and they each have to spot me about three shots per side. I always encouraged them to follow their choice of sports and their own inclinations in choosing a career, but the golf business had long been a part of the family conversation. They'd joined me in walking courses with architects, sat in on all kinds of meetings, and worked as interns or junior staffers at Bandon or Barnbougle.

Still, it was a significant step for all of us to become partners in an endeavor of this magnitude, and none of us knew how it would play out. My own working habits had been forged to fit the needs and temperament of a part-time developer—remember, until 2005 I was still running Recycled Paper Greetings with Phil Friedmann. Once we sold the company, Phil and I shared the same new headquarters in Chicago, but by now we were ensconced in separate business and philanthropic interests. Happily, Len Levine's office was between ours—the perfect spot for our mediator, whom I considered my consigliere. Trained as a CPA, Len had become an astute financial strategist, and he'd handed off much of the routine number crunching to a younger colleague, Jon Kaull, who also has a high golf IQ. Add to this list Marianne Laughlin, my assistant, and there you have the core group

*With Chris and Michael at St. George's Hill on our trip to visit the heathland courses that inspired George Crump at Pine Valley*

of the Keiser organization—a term that's obviously a bit of a misnomer. We were semiorganized, but each new project brought new people into the mix and enabled us to form external partnerships to solve specific needs.

With this fluid, flexible structure, we could recombine and reconfigure the "organization" as needed. Instead of trying to fit developments into a predetermined model, we could tailor each one to suit the particular circumstances and make the most of individual talents. After my experience at Cabot and Barnbougle, I knew that Sand Valley would find its own character and identity as a resort, and that my partners would play major roles in the process. How would Michael and Chris respond to our new arrangement? What would they bring to it? And how would I respond? They wouldn't be simply partners. They were my sons, and the relationship couldn't be strictly business. Confident as I was in their work ethic and their grasp of our fundamentals, I was aware that father-son operations don't always run smoothly, and that it could be tricky to transfer direction and control from one generation to the next. I certainly didn't intend just to hand it over to them, nor did

I want anybody to think that's what was happening. My approach was to let them assume as much responsibility as they wanted, provided that at every step they showed me that they were equal to the new task.

As parent and senior partner, I wanted the project to succeed so *they* could succeed. Because they were entering the business on different terms than I had, they'd be vulnerable in ways that I'd never been. When I built the Dunes Club, I was already in my forties. Bandon Dunes opened when I was fifty-two. As an unknown, a maverick, I'd been able to fly mostly under the radar. Nobody would've paid much attention if I'd fallen flat on my face. Personally, failing as a golf developer would have stung, but I'd already won my trophy, so to speak, at Recycled Paper Greetings. My credentials as an entrepreneur were established. Michael and Chris weren't looking for a second career; they were launching their first. They were younger than I'd been and wouldn't be working in obscurity. They'd be viewed as insiders, not mavericks. As Keisers, they were stepping into a situation where a particular kind of golf course and a certain level of success would be expected, so their initial outing was bound to face intense scrutiny.

Well, it's no secret that Sand Valley opened with a bang and has kept right on going. I'm not giving anything away when I say that Chris and Michael have flourished, putting their stamp on every aspect of the resort. They're now making independent decisions there and initiating new projects of their own in other locations. They've really hit their own stride, and they've taught me that it's more important than ever to approach golf development with a sense of stewardship, a perspective that holds promise for the future of both the game and the planet.

It seems fitting and maybe inevitable that the seed for Sand Valley was planted by Tom Doak. In 1994, his *Anatomy of a Golf Course* came as a revelation to an Indiana high school student, Craig Haltom. An avid player and talented artist, Craig devoured the book and decided that his calling was to design golf courses. Following Doak's pattern of education, he went to Scotland for two years, got a master's degree in landscape architecture at the University of Edinburgh, visited as many historic venues as he could, and immersed himself in the game's traditional culture.

After returning to the United States, Craig embarked on a quest for the perfect site where he could design his own course. This was no hobby. For six years, in an organized, systematic fashion, he studied survey maps of the Midwest, looking for land that met his criteria for size, topography, soil, and landforms. Weekends were spent traveling with his wife, Becky, a botanist, to hike and appraise in person the possibilities he'd found. Though he regards himself as a down-to-earth realist, Craig realized that others could see him as a dreamer chasing the pot of golf at the end of the rainbow, but he didn't mind. He kept telling people about his search, confident that he'd find the place for his ideal course.

In Rome, Wisconsin, the topographical maps showed a landscape of ridges and valleys that were rarely visible from the straight roads that traversed the area. To most people passing through, there wasn't much to look at, just a monotonous stretch of red pine plantations that supplied the local pulp mills—row after row, on five-foot centers, a cornfield of pines, as it is sometimes described. However, like much of the Great Lakes periphery, this region had been scoured by glaciers, and Craig knew that in certain areas there were sand deposits running as deep as two hundred feet. He was particularly intrigued by a place known locally as the Bentley Hills. Here the topography was marked by rugged formations that had once been islands in a lake that had suddenly emptied out when an ice dam burst at the end of the last ice age, around eighteen thousand years ago. Suspecting that Bentley Hills might be what he was looking for, he mentioned it to a friend he'd made in Scotland.

At this point, my son Michael was drawn into the story.

MICHAEL: Greg Ramsay—the same Greg I'd known at Barnbougle— writes long-winded emails. I didn't hear from him often, but when I did, he went on for pages. Greg had a history with Craig. They had connected with each other in Scotland as two young guys with big ideas about doing something in golf, and they'd kept in touch.

Even in an email, Greg's a salesman, and the one he sent me about Craig Haltom and this amazing site in Wisconsin came at a time when I was starting to feel frustrated in commercial real estate. I'd seen my dad at work and done small projects of my own, converting warehouse space into residential units. I began to wonder if this property Craig had found might be my opportunity to develop something major.

MK: At Michael's suggestion, I met with him, Greg, and Craig at my Chicago office, and they made a case for their ideal course. Who knew central Wisconsin had sand dunes? Not I. Rome was a thousand miles from an ocean, but it definitely had plenty of sand. I like sand, and have deservedly been called the Sandman. When I hear about dunes, I have a hard time ignoring them. These Wisconsin dunes were evidently massive, and they were only a four-hour drive from Chicago. Without making any promises, I sent Josh Lesnik up to Rome on a reconnaissance mission, yet again asking him for reasons not to get involved. His report: theses dunes were definitely worth a look. So in the spring of 2013, Michael and I went to Rome to meet with Craig Haltom.

MICHAEL: Craig took us to a spot that locals called Kong, and we soon had our own name for it—the Volcano. It's one of the highest, steepest pieces of land for miles around. The area was a favorite with the ATVers. They'd ripped open big expanses of sand by doing their donut spins. These were the modern version of blowout bunkers. On the old Scottish links, the sandy areas were scraped out by sheep and sculpted by the wind. In Wisconsin, they were created by ATVs.

My dad liked what he saw, but wanted to know if there was enough land to build a destination resort, and that meant that there had to be good ground for at least two golf courses. He didn't have to mention the other possible deal-breaker—no ocean.

MK: Michael and Craig spent a lot of time together in the next few months, exploring a much larger expanse. Instead of thinking just about golf holes, Michael was assessing the site's potential from an economic perspective. Adams County had one thing going for it: the land wouldn't be expensive. Most of it was owned by timber companies, and nobody was buying red pines. Until recently, this had been the heart of a flourishing papermaking industry, with seven pulp mills running three shifts a day. All but two had closed, with those down to a single shift. The county, which included the towns of Rome and Nekoosa, was one of the most economically depressed in the state.

Michael was becoming more and more invested in the project, though we hadn't yet discussed in detail what his role would be if we went forward. My role, as I saw it, was to keep him from getting his hopes too high. I kept telling him that the most important thing in real estate transactions is knowing when to say no.

As it happens, I'm on the board of directors of the Field Museum, Chicago's showcase of natural history. When I mentioned the Wisconsin dunes to my colleagues, some of them surprised me by expressing an interest in seeing the country that in their circles was well-known as the setting for Aldo Leopold's *A Sand County Almanac*. A visionary whose work established the field of wildlife ecology and led directly to the creation of the American wilderness system, Leopold spent his summers in a cabin on the Wisconsin River. He used this area as a laboratory to study how the original ecosystem of the sand barrens and prairie had been all but destroyed by commercial exploitation. In fact, there's no Sand County in Wisconsin, but Leopold's book became a manifesto for American environmentalists.

I organized a picnic at Bentley Hills, and my guests from the Field Museum responded to the place with unbridled excitement. When they looked at the plundered landscape, they saw it through Leopold's eyes—as a place in need of renewal. Debbie Moskovits, a senior vice president at the museum, has also been one of the leading organizers of Chicago Wilderness, a group devoted to preserving the remnants of tallgrass prairie, oak savanna, and prairie wetlands in the metropolitan area, and she knew how to evaluate those elements in Wisconsin. She was able to see the dunes instead of the trees.

When I said the place lacked an ocean, she said simply, almost as a dare, "You don't need an ocean. These dunes could be your ocean."

MICHAEL: I'd never read Leopold's book. But when my dad and I got copies of *A Sand County Almanac* we realized that we were dealing with an American landscape that's hallowed ground for ecologists and conservationists. If we developed Sand Valley, we might be able to do something that transcended golf by helping restore this land. I know that people are skeptical whenever a developer says anything like that, but when I read Leopold, this unexpected opportunity was suddenly obvious. My dad felt the same way. When I'm asked if I convinced my father to do Sand Valley, the honest answer is no, I didn't. Aldo Leopold convinced him.

We got copies of *A Sand County Almanac* at the same time, and I stayed up late reading it. When we talked the next morning, we were both excited. By the end of that conversation, it felt as though the decision to go ahead had made itself.

*A SAND COUNTY ALMANAC* was published in 1949, a year after Leopold died while helping a neighbor fight a brush fire. A collection of sketches, autobiographical narratives, and natural history, the book is best known for its formulation of a "land ethic." "We abuse land because we regard it as a commodity belonging to us," Leopold wrote, stating one of his core beliefs. "When we see land as a community to which we belong, we may begin to use it with love and respect."

As a classic of American nature writing, *A SAND COUNTY ALMANAC* rivals *WALDEN*. The book has been translated into fourteen languages and sold over two million copies, and it remains a source of inspiration and ideas for policymakers and conservationists. At Sand Valley, we've put copies of *A SAND COUNTY ALMANAC* in our guest rooms, and we aspire to the ideals that Leopold articulated in quotes like these:

> "A thing is right when it tends to preserve the integrity, stability and beauty of the biotic community. It is wrong when it tends otherwise."
>
> "Conservation is a state of harmony between men and land."
>
> "All ethics so far evolved rest upon a single premise: that the individual is a member of a community of interdependent parts. The land ethic simply enlarges the boundaries of the community to include soils, waters, plants and animals, or collectively the land."

MK: We closed on the land December 31, 2013. *A Sand County Almanac* might have tipped the balance, but many other things were falling into place. Now, if need be, I can be patient when I believe in a project—I've been trying to build a course in Ireland, on the Dingle Peninsula, for almost fifteen years. Coul Links, in Dornoch, Scotland, has been on the verge of getting approved for five years. But except for the lack of an ocean, the signs were auspicious at Sand Valley. Michael had taken the lead in negotiating with the property owners and started building good relationships in the community. The land was cheap, as I said, and there didn't appear to be any organized resistance to what we were preparing to do. On the contrary, the leaders in Adams County and throughout the region were welcoming. They saw that a destination resort could help them create jobs and kick-start the local economy.

Michael undersells his role in persuading me. I wasn't interested in being the patriarch of a golf dynasty, but I was fascinated to see my son discovering his passion and testing his powers. He's always had a marked intensity, and once attracted to something—like the mountain climbing—he locks in. He wants to learn everything. In the months since he'd first heard about this location, Michael had been steadily drilling down.

As a veteran of several golf projects, I know that it takes somebody willing to be absolutely dogged and single-focused to make them happen. The developer has to be relentless. He's starting from scratch. No one else cares about his project—and why should they? He has to overcome their inertia or resistance, their doubts and suspicions. Every day, he has to try to convince people who've never met him that what he intends to do is something that will benefit them. He not only has to believe but to communicate that belief to others. I was that person at Bandon Dunes as Ben was at Cabot, and Michael was ready to take on that role at Sand Valley.

Chris was also ready to get involved. He was already working in the golf business, running his own start-up, and he was in the loop when we started talking about Wisconsin. Chris is more reserved and soft-spoken than Michael. Growing up with three older siblings who had strong opinions, he learned early on to listen, watch, and pay close attention. A natural analyst and good with numbers, he's somebody who likes to gather information and use it to figure things out, to solve problems logically. Moreover, Chris's experience in media and marketing dovetails nicely with his brother's talents.

CHRIS: Dad never tried to steer me toward the golf business. I've been playing and talking golf with him since I was three years old, but I was always encouraged to do what I believed in. Growing up, I often heard my dad talk about business, but it seemed to me that he spent just as much time on philanthropy. He and Mom were both active supporters of education programs, and that's the direction I first followed. After graduating from Georgetown, I taught and coached for two years at Chicago Jesuit Academy, an all-boys school where every kid was on a scholarship. I believed in the mission of that school and loved working with kids who were trying to overcome odds that were stacked against them. What I didn't like was the predictability of the job, knowing exactly where I'd be and what I'd be doing every hour of every day.

From seeing Dad at work, I knew that his days were anything but predictable, so I went to work at Bandon Dunes, where I took over the online store. It needed an overhaul, and sales tripled within a year. My own business, Vanguard Pro Shop, grew out of that, providing similar online services to private clubs and destination resorts. Then Sand Valley came along, and it was no contest. If I was ever going to join Dad and Michael, this was the right time. My partner was willing to buy my share of Vanguard, and I was now working full-time for Keiser golf, doing many of the same things I'd been doing—I was just doing more of them. There wasn't any announcement, and I didn't have a title. That might sound vague, but we talked to each other often enough—and to Len Levine and the people at KemperSports—that we were able to address problems without assigning anyone to a specific lane.

MICHAEL: I was in full beta mode, living in Wisconsin and learning everything I could. I met with the dirt bikers, the snowmobilers, the shooting clubs, the Chamber of Commerce, the Rome Development Authority. For a while I lived in a converted motel and ate hundreds of pizzas from Pritzl's, the local gas station and convenience store. Then I spent several months living in a tent—a six-hundred-square-foot tent, so I wasn't completely roughing it. I had a shower shed, too, and my girlfriend, Jocelyn, a psychologist, came up from Chicago to visit on weekends. This wasn't the courtship she had imagined, but the camp was on a quiet road, hidden away in the pines, and we heard birdsong when we woke up. I had never felt so excited about the future and so grounded at the same time. Jocelyn is now my wife, and we have a son, Tommy, and a daughter, Winifred.

MK: To me, the models for this project were obvious, two great American inland links courses built on sand and with truly historic design: Pine Valley and Sand Hills. I'm not sure who suggested combining them into a single name, but there was never any serious alternative. This destination would be called Sand Valley. It was our way of paying homage.

We all liked the Sand Hills logo, which looks like a branding iron, and wanted the Sand Valley logo to have that same style. One day Josh

Lesnik had a few hours to kill in an airport, and he sketched out a few designs—and after an artist had refined the concept, we had a bold logo that looks like a check mark or a heart.

My deal with the boys was that I'd be actively involved in launching the project, which included buying the land and raising the money to build the first course. For everything else—infrastructure, accommodations, restaurants, equipment, and all the other costs—Michael and Chris would have to secure the funding. I did tell them that I would be the lender of last resort, emphasis on *last*.

Early in the process, we spoke to each other on an almost daily basis and figured out each new task as it came along. In financial matters, we had Len to advise us and Jon Kaull to track and crunch the numbers. KemperSports provided expertise and stability. In another key partnership, Craig Haltom took part in every aspect of constructing the course as one of the top operatives at Oliphant Construction, which handled the major earth work. I was in charge, but as Michael Corleone says in *Godfather III*, all the ships were sailing in the same direction.

The initial land purchase amounted to 1,300 acres. I bought it with Barry MacLean, a Chicago friend who has extensive business ties in Wisconsin; he wanted to be involved with a project that could revitalize the area. We leased the land to Michael and Chris, an arrangement that lessened their tax burden; after all, they'd have to meet many other financial demands. In a project like Sand Valley, buying the land is just a down payment—a fraction of the total investment.

With input from Len and my friend Jim Murphy, we decided to raise capital by attracting a group of investors. A serial entrepreneur who's launched many businesses and led several philanthropic efforts, Jim has long been a mainstay of the Chicago golf community; he helped us figure out how to structure and present our idea.

We were doing something I'd never considered at Bandon Dunes, so we had to work through a couple of objections. First, how could we bring in investors without compromising our commitment to public golf? Second, how could we create a financial structure that wouldn't be a hassle for all concerned? I was determined to avoid contractual arrangements that were overly cumbersome and invited conflict or litigation.

The answer was to adapt the precedent set by George Crump. I had just read Andrew Mutch's *Crump's Dream,* and as a developer I could relate to his efforts to raise enough money to build Pine Valley, especially since I don't like asking for financial help. A group of his friends got together and composed a letter that was more of a personal appeal than a business proposition. Their goal was to find "200 to 250 good fellows, who are fond enough of the game and sufficiently interested in a plan of this kind to buy one share of stock, at $100 per share. . . . It is not an investment. If you buy a share of stock, you will very probably never get your money back, but it will be very well spent just the same."

If Pine Valley had done it, then so could Sand Valley. In 2013, we couldn't be that blasé about making a return on capital, and we'd need to ask for a lot more than $100. We set the threshold at $50,000 and told potential investors that they'd be recognized as "Founders." As such, they could play golf for free at Sand Valley, and their accompanied guests would receive a 50 percent discount. For lodging, food, and any other activities or services, the Founders would be treated like everyone else. In Len Levine's opinion, the key to the whole concept was bragging rights. People wanted to get in on our next resort.

MICHAEL: Our letter went out first to the directors of the Western Golf Association, and we had a great response. I made visits to several clubs to present the Founders Program, and even though we started out hoping to find one hundred investors, we ended up with 173. Their names are on the Founders Wall in the Sand Valley clubhouse.

The packet we sent out included some pictures and maps of the area, as well as brief summaries of its economic, geologic, environmental, and cultural history. But it contained no business plans, no drawings or descriptions of any golf course or buildings, and most important, no promises about any kind of financial performance. After ten years, investors would have the right to ask for their money back, but we were under no legal obligation to return it. What we were offering was basically a handshake agreement.

When I showed this proposal to other people in the golf business, some of them laughed. They were amazed that we ever sent it out and even more so that we had such a strong response without making promises or guarantees. We were asking people to trust us, and if we

OVERLEAF
*The low-growing vegetation at Sand Valley evokes the British heathland courses, but the plants and grasses are native to the American prairie.*

made any money, we'd send them a check. They didn't own an interest in the resort or any company affiliated with it. I was keenly aware that Founders were joining because of my dad's involvement. He was putting his name on the line, and he was trusting me to come through. There was no way I was going to let him or the investors down.

Some Founders have never come to Sand Valley, and others come as often as they can to enjoy their free golf. They often come in groups, and they bring guests. The only problem is that our tee sheets are so full that it's not always easy to fit them in.

MK: There's been only one bad apple in the bunch, a guy who thought that being a Founder entitled him to special privileges. He got obnoxious at Bandon Dunes and threatened the staffer who tried to calm him down. When Michael heard about this, he returned the guy's money and let him know he was an ex-Founder.

MICHAEL: George Crump influenced us in another way, too. In 2014 we made a family trip to England and played some of the heathland classics that Crump visited on his 1910 tour of British, Scottish, and European courses. My mom went with us and walked those beautiful courses when Dad, Chris, and I played. Sunningdale, Swinley Forest, Walton Heath, and St. George's Hill are inland courses, one generation removed from the original Scottish links, and built on light, sandy soil with low-growing vegetation. They're mature now and look as though they've always been there. As the first major wave in the spread of golf from Scotland to England, these heathland courses still stand as brilliant examples of how the design and playing conditions of the links can be adapted to inland properties. That's what Crump did at Pine Valley, and what we wanted to do at Sand Valley.

MK: I've always been a believer in returning to the source. The links courses are what first inspired me, and for almost every project since I've relied on them and sent my architects and their associates to visit them, too. Bill Coore once described me as a "living American connection to links golf," and that's one title I'm proud to accept.

The purpose of these trips is not only to make note of specific features of the links but also to soak up their atmosphere and personality. Golf courses are artistic creations that can endure and evolve over the decades, acquiring a character that can't be easily described—but you can feel it through the soles of your shoes when you're on a great links or heathland course. Hallowed ground doesn't become sacred overnight. This happens over generations, a process that takes thousands of rounds, each adding its tiny bit to the aura of permanence and continuity. No other game places us so fully in the footsteps of our ancestors. Playing on classic courses changes your frame of reference, extending it backward in time and pushing it forward into the future. For Chris and Michael, I wanted this to be part of the preparation for building Sand Valley.

MICHAEL: Not long after buying the first piece of land, we had an opportunity to buy another seven thousand acres. Not that we needed it—we already had enough land for three or four golf courses. The owner was a lumber company that wanted to unload the property, and after having the timber appraised I realized that we could pay for the land by clearing it and selling off the pines. I envisioned those seven thousand acres as an area where we could make a statement about our ambition to restore the sand barrens. This was a chance to do something on a large scale. Getting rid of the red pines would be the first step in a process of regeneration. The pines were planted so closely together that the canopy kept sunlight from reaching the ground and stifled the growth of any native vegetation.

We took out more than three million trees. In the old days, the clearing would have been done by loggers with saws and axes, and it would've taken several months. Today, a vehicle that looks like an excavator does the job. Instead of a bucket, it's equipped with a mechanism that cuts a tree at ground level, trims off the branches, and cuts it into twelve-foot lengths, all in fifteen or twenty seconds. Now the land is cleared except for a few oaks and jack pines.

MK: In 2008, my daughter Dana gave me a book called *Second Nature*, by Michael Pollan, and wrote this inscription: "Some ideas to consider for the gardener in you." I wasn't sure that there *was* a gardener in me, but the book gave me a new way of thinking about nature. Pollan contrasts the "wilderness ethic," in which nature is allowed to take its course, with the market ethic, in which land is used and manipulated to achieve economic ends, regardless of the consequences. Neither approach provides a basis for a sustainable, long-term, human relationship with the land. A middle way, a garden ethic, begins with accepting the fact that human beings must substantially alter nature in order to survive. This doesn't mean that the gardener should therefore go out and conquer nature. "The gardener's conception of his self-interest is broad and enlightened," Pollan writes. "Anthropocentric as he may be, he recognizes that he is dependent for his health and survival on many other forms of life, so he is careful to take their interests into account in whatever he does."

The more we got to know the area around Sand Valley, the greater potential we saw for restoring the sand barrens. We wouldn't have to buy the entire county. Other users of this land—hunters, hikers, birders, naturalists, even the ATVers—shared some of the same goals. Why not have a consortium of owners, all of them gardeners in their own way, contributing to a common goal of reviving the community of native plants and species? I proposed a number: What if we could restore an area of one hundred thousand acres?

MICHAEL: Before building a single hole, we hired an ecological consultant, Jens Jensen, to survey the resort site and create a master plan for its restoration. Though Jens isn't a player, he immediately saw how the golf and the restoration efforts could dovetail. In total, about six hundred acres of the original tract were set aside to be managed as prairie or sand barrens; in some places the goal was to preserve a native landscape that had survived, while in others Jens attempted to re-create what had been lost. One of the first things you notice on arriving at Sand Valley is how the dunes roll right up to the doorstep of the clubhouse—that's some of Jens's most visible handiwork.

Walking the property with Jens was an education. The Wisconsin sands aren't a single landscape but a continuum. The sand barrens and blowouts blend into areas of prairie covered with low-growing plants, and these flow into stretches of savanna, where scattered black oaks and jack pines flourish in open meadows. When the land was being cleared, we found and preserved remnants of these different habitats, and Jens used them as the anchors of the restoration plan.

I won't forget the morning in the spring of 2015 when I was out in a place where the pines had been cleared. A year earlier, this spot had been dark and lifeless, hidden beneath a grid of pines that blocked out the sunlight. Now the flowers were popping up out of the slash, and birds were fluttering and singing. The sun was shining, and it hit me to my core—this is what we're doing, we're bringing this land back to life.

Ever since, I've tried to live up to my thought that morning. I'd like to approach everything we do as restoration.

*The rough-hewn Sand Valley clubhouse*

14

# Sand Valley

*The key to being a good golf course architect: first of all, having a love and appreciation for the game of golf, and what it's provided for so many countless millions of people through its 500-year history.*

—BILL COORE

T O BUILD THE FIRST COURSE at Sand Valley, we chose Bill Coore and Ben Crenshaw.

They'd be coming straight from Cabot Cliffs, a course that some were calling their masterpiece. Bill's my age, and Ben's a few years younger; they've made the turn onto the back nine of their design career, but their courses have only gotten more daring and original. Instead of repeating themselves, they seem intent on proving that the cardinal principle of their design credo—take what the land gives you—leads to constant innovation and invention.

One of the pleasures of working with them is watching the alchemy as they transform a piece of ground into a work of art. Another is the friendship that has grown over the years. Bill and Ben are among the true gentlemen of golf, and we've worked together so often that our days in the field are now like playing a round with familiar partners. I've spent more time with Bill, who's taken the lead role in their design work. Sand Valley would be our fifth course together (with Sheep Ranch the sixth).

Bill and I first met at Sand Hills in the mid-1990s, but we didn't really get to know each other until he built Bandon Trails—a course that crosses a ridge and sprawls over hundreds of acres, including land that Howard McKee wanted to reserve for other uses. It seemed that every time Howard drew a line on the topographical map to set the course's boundary, Bill would find a reason that he needed to cross it. Their conversation was a spirited tug-of-war, and they worked out a negotiation style that included a lot of good-natured needling.

They liked to needle me, too. We often had dinner together while Bandon Trails was under construction, and when we talked politics, the two of them were on the same side, left-leaning, ready to join forces against me, a conservative. They were a formidable duo—Howard the intellectual stalwart, armed with data and comprehensive arguments, while Bill was the sly, courteous, dumb-as-a-fox storyteller who made his points with parables and anecdotes. This was in the early 2000s, when political jousting didn't necessarily lead to animosity. In those conversations, we learned more about one another's perspectives and values—values that in many cases turned out to be not so different even when our politics were at odds.

In 2007, when Bandon hosted the USGA Mid-Amateur Championship, the competition was played over two courses, Bandon Dunes and the brand-new Bandon Trails. Sadly, Howard McKee was not able to attend. After several cycles of remission and treatment, he was in the final stages of his battle with colon cancer. At the ceremonial dinner to kick off the tournament week, his absence was deeply felt by Bill and me and Lindy, who to this day cannot walk around the resort without thinking of Howard. The three of us were seated at the same table. Bill and David Kidd were scheduled to give remarks after the meal, and I advised Bill to speak first. Nobody should have to follow David, one of the most entertaining after-dinner speakers in golf.

I can't remember exactly what Bill said, and I doubt that he can, either. His speech wasn't written out, and it turned into a tribute to Howard. What the hundreds of USGA officials and tournament competitors made of it, I don't know. Bill's voice was close to breaking as he tried to contain his emotions. Beside me, Lindy's eyes had teared up, as did mine. Howard had taken such pride and delight in the creation of Bandon Dunes that it seemed impossible he was no longer there to guide us, to goad us, to inspire us all with his grand ideas and infectious laughter.

That night solidified another friendship. In Oregon, Nova Scotia, Chicago, and Scotland, Lindy and I have spent time with Bill and his wife, Sue Hershkowitz-Coore, who's a highly regarded expert in communication skills. She knows me well enough to tease me about my one-sentence emails— which she sees, by the way, because I have to go through her to get to Bill, who's never had an email address.

Bill has accompanied me when I've inspected new properties, and he's investigated places in Scotland and Ireland as my proxy. I always ask him to take Sue, knowing that if she wants to go, he can't refuse. After a couple of trips to Durness, a northernmost point of Scotland, they reported that this landscape was spectacular but wild, windy, and desolate—too remote even for me!

And we spent years trying to win approval for another Scottish project that was dear to my heart—Coul Links, near Dornoch. No place in Scotland holds sweeter memories for me, and Royal Dornoch, a gorse-framed course where golf has been played since 1616, has always seemed like the ideal links, a combination of historic town, whitecapped sea, and soulful golf. At Coul, I'd hoped to build a companion links, and Bill was beside me every step of the way, sharing the high hopes and then the deep disappointment when our plans were rejected by the Scottish government. After devoting myself to bringing links golf to North America, I wanted to return to Scotland and build what would be the capstone of this links legacy.

It was not to be. God bless Dornoch.

I realize that there's almost never been a period in the last fifteen years when Bill and I haven't been working together on some project, and I can't imagine my career without him. Every time I play a course that we built together, I remember at least a few of the thousands of conversations we had, the hunches, the false starts, the adjustments, the drawings in the sand. Some golfers can make their way around a course without thinking for one second about the people who created the hole they're playing. For the owner, every feature on a course comes attached with a story.

BILL: When Mike called me to say he'd found a site in Wisconsin, I said, "Mike, last time I looked at a map of Wisconsin, there wasn't any ocean." He laughed, but this was no small thing. At Sand Valley, he was breaking away from a proven formula of oceanside links. That's what he'd always built, and what was expected from him. But if he had any doubts about it, I never saw them. He seemed completely confident that building a course in the middle of Wisconsin was the right thing to be doing. Mike makes even significant decisions seem almost nonchalant.

MK: Bill does his routings the old-fashioned way—he starts walking. He's so gifted that a lore has grown up around his process. I've heard people say that his secret is to find the animal trails in the woods and follow them, assuming that they'd found the best routes through a piece of property. I think he's as good at routing a course as anyone in the history of golf design.

BILL: It's true that I will sometimes follow an animal trail. I think anyone walking through woods or thick brush tends to do that—the deer have already made a path. What I'm really trying to do on my first visits to a site is to find a natural way to get from one place to another, without thinking about any golf holes. I want to find out what's unique about the property, what parts of it you'd notice if you were just out taking a walk.

I've taken the lead in doing the routings for our company. When we started out, Ben had playing commitments, and I had time to spend in the field, and it's evolved from there. I'm usually the one who's out there on the site, lumbering around. When Ben and I talk about routings, I outline the options and we make decisions together. I use topos [topographical studies] as a rudimentary tool—I make notes on them, and I can halfway tell where the slopes are, but I have to actually see the contours before I can start drawing a hole.

I have a method for working on a routing at home or in a hotel room. I have my templates, paper shapes that are cut to scale—a short par-3, a long par-5, a dogleg par-4, and so on. Sue calls them my paper dolls or my "little men." These are basic shapes I've carried with me for years, and they're just about worn-out by now. I lay them out and arrange them so that I can see the general layout. A good routing will form a pattern that has balance and coherence. When the design is off, the pieces look awkward and disjointed, and you don't have to be an architect to see the difference. One glance at the little men and Sue can tell whether or not a routing is coming together.

In golf design, there are three major elements: the routing, the greens, and the bunkers. The routing is like the skeleton of the human body. It provides the sequence and variety of holes, obviously, but it also gives the course its shape and proportions. If the routing isn't right, the course will never feel right.

MK: After watching Bill do this so many times, I've learned to pay attention to what happens between holes. It's easy to focus on individual holes and ignore how they're linked together. Bill doesn't. He spends hours trying to figure out the best way for players to move from a green to the next tee. At the very least, the transition should be smooth and convenient. There's some stagecraft involved, too. What do you see on the short walk? How does the next tee frame the hole you're about to play? You're entering a new space, and Bill often encourages you to pause at the threshold.

BILL: The entire Sand Valley site was densely wooded, and for once we didn't have any dispute about clearing the trees. I said, "Mike, you won't believe this, but it's all right with me if you go ahead and cut them all down." Usually, I like to clear in a three-step process: cut the center line, then widen it out to include the whole fairway, and then do selective cutting along the edges, keeping the best trees. At Sand Valley, we did end up tagging a few mature oaks and pines to save, but the main clearing was carried out on an industrial scale.

MIKE: I'm not a fan of trees on golf courses. Links courses have survived for centuries without them.

BILL: Our problem at Cabot Cliffs was to combine many different landscape elements—dunes, marsh, forest, seaside cliffs—into a cohesive routing. Here, once the trees were removed, we saw that the ground was more of a piece. It was actually quite repetitive, a pattern of ridges and valleys. We had to avoid building a course where every hole looked the same, with a fairway down in a valley. We had to figure out how to get up, over, and across those ridges to give the holes individuality and variety.

MK: I confess that I had lingering doubts about the area. Could the dunes really be our ocean? Could Sand Valley stand up to the inevitable comparisons to Bandon Dunes? I was never exactly sure how to refer to this landscape—a prairie? Sand barrens? It wasn't on anyone's list of the hundred most beautiful places in America. But once the plantation pines were removed, a hidden world began to emerge. The golf course was opening up a vast, peaceful, primordial landscape.

BILL: On each new job, the crew changes. Our guys don't work exclusively for us, and sometimes they have their own design projects. We mix and match, depending on who's available. At Sand Valley, we had some veterans—Dave Axland and Rod Whitman, who'd been working on Cabot Cliffs. Dan Proctor was there, and Tony Russell came in from Oregon to help out. Jim Craig, another longtime member of the crew from Fort Worth, also joined us in Wisconsin.

JIM CRAIG: I say I've been working for Bill since I was five years old, but it was really more like twenty-five. I started out as a bag boy at Shady Oaks, in Fort Worth, Ben Hogan's club, and they kept moving me around to different jobs until, eventually, I got up on a dozer and started doing small shaping jobs. When Bill and Ben came to Shady Oaks to redo some of the greens, they noticed my work and asked if I'd come work with them at Talking Stick, in Arizona. I said, "Heck, yeah." After a week or so, Bill took me to lunch at a Denny's and he asked me if I really wanted to do this kind of work. He was warning me about the life of a shaper. He said it would keep me on the road. I told him I thought it would be cool to work on something that would last, something you could point to years later. I already knew that this is what I wanted to do with my life. Bill said, "Well, you might want to start planning ahead."

BILL: The Sand Valley property was so large that I spent several days walking it before starting on the routing. I was just trying to decide where to locate the course. Craig Haltom was my guide—he'd studied the entire place and drawn his own routings for a couple of different courses. He had detailed, computer-generated plans and beautiful hand renderings of individual holes, and I wanted to use some of his ideas if I could. I staked out a loop to the north of what's now the 1st tee, on some of the steepest ground on the site. Jim came along when Ben and I walked it.

JIM: For Bill, it was a stroll in the park. He walks everywhere and he's in shape. Ben and I are smokers, and when we walked that loop and got back up to the top of the Volcano, I was leaning over with my hands on my knees, coughing up Marlboro Lights.

BEN: When Mike says he's found a good site, I know it will be unique and I know it will be sandy. It is a blessing to work with sand. A golf course built on sandy soil is going to have good drainage and firm turf. For the designer, it's ideal—you can mold it and shape it exactly as you want. I'm a hopeless perfectionist, and sand lets me focus on the fine details, tweaking until I get it just right.

MK: As Bill walked the property, he was tempted by some of the lower ground. The two spots I liked the most were high points—the Volcano, and the ridge where the 5th tee is now located. There's a wonderful view up there, and the 5th hole is a downhill par-3 where your tee shot seems to hang in the air forever.

BILL: My problem was how to get the golf to climb up there. The solution was to make the 4th hole a long, uphill par-5. When we first staked it out, Mike had his doubts, and I said, "Mike, we're building this hole to get you up to that view. You need to give it the benefit of the doubt." I think he likes the finished hole—it's a good par-5, and the walk's not that hard.

MK: The other high spot was the Volcano, where we first saw the property. Every time we visited, that's where the walk started and ended.

BILL: No question, the Volcano was the prominent feature of the land. It was appealing, and I understood its importance to Mike and Michael—it was a direct link to their first excitement about the place. But there was a flip side. The terrain was steep, and the crest of the ridge wasn't very big, either. A clubhouse wouldn't fit up there. If it was going to be the focal point of the course, I'd have to figure out a way that golfers could negotiate those slopes without feeling they were constantly hill climbing.

MICHAEL: On Bill's first routing, there was a short par-3 on top of the Volcano—a fantastic little hole, but it was the 11th hole. Because of the way things had evolved, beginning with Craig's discovery of the Volcano, I really wanted the course to begin and end there. That's where Craig sold us on this project, and I wanted to keep the energy of that spot. Bill heard me out, then said, "I prefer my routing, but only 51 percent, and if you feel that strongly, I can make a few changes."

MK: When Bill settled on the routing, I went to Wisconsin with Josh Lesnik and Len Levine to walk it. The whole place was in an early construction state—heavy equipment, dust, ground so broken up that we had to ride in utility vehicles to get to the course. When we reached its farthest southern point where Bill wanted to place the 7th tee, someone asked, "Do we own this land?"

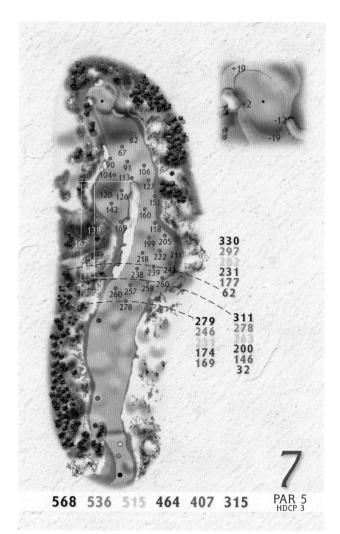

**JIM:** When they started talking about it, Bill and I walked on ahead. The decision about buying more land was above my pay grade.

**MK:** Bill Coore, land grabber. On every course we've done together—Cabot Cliffs, Bandon Trails, and Sand Valley—he's seen a way to build a better hole by crossing a boundary line. When the goal is to build courses that will rank among the best, you can't economize. I can name several courses where a single weak hole is regarded as a serious blemish. The classic example is the 18th at Cypress Point.

**BILL:** We probably could have made the hole work on the available land, but it would have been cramped. The green site was there, but with two big dunes on the left and a tight boundary on the right, the hole would have been long and narrow. After Michael bought the land and had it cleared, there wasn't a tree left—there was nothing at all over there. It looked like a bomb had gone off and leveled everything. We needed to define that right edge, and Jim and I thought a big blowout might work, something like the natural blowouts at Sand Hills. So Tony Russell got up on his dozer and built the huge chasm that now borders the fairway. It's one of the biggest expanses of sand on the course, and Jens Jensen and his crew worked on it, putting in native plants and grasses. Jim Craig did the grading and contouring, and the 7th now lets the golfer figure out the best way to get to the green. That extra width made that hole a lot more interesting to play and to look at.

MICHAEL: As it turned out, we had to acquire an additional eighty acres so that Bill could build the 7th. The timber companies don't sell one acre at a time; they only sell in units of forty acres. We owned over a thousand acres, and Bill wanted more. How can you say no to Bill Coore?

"SAND VALLEY is not an imitation of Pine Valley, America's top-ranked golf course, although the two bear similar traits. Sand Valley has wider panoramas, larger expanses of visible sand, fewer pines and bigger targets on each hole. Nor is it Sand Hills, that central Nebraska private retreat that truly began the Coore-Crenshaw epoch in golf architecture. Their Sand Hills design was as minimalist as humanly possible; their Sand Valley design involves more manipulation of the land: sculptured fairways, hand-carved sand scars, invented green sites, all done with such sophistication as to mislead most into believing such features were there from the beginning."

—RON WHITTEN, announcing the selection of *Golf Digest*'s
Best New Course of 2017

MICHAEL: The Founders' investment was paying for the golf course, but when construction began in 2015 I was still actively looking for additional sources of funding. We were going to need roads, a clubhouse, lodging, restaurants, maintenance buildings and equipment. Chris and I didn't want to borrow from Dad, and we didn't have the resources that he'd had when he built Bandon Dunes. Commercial bank financing wasn't a viable option. We were going to have to be inventive about finding backers. One possibility was to go to local government agencies to see if they could help. When I suggested this, my dad and Len Levine were skeptical—and that gave me additional motivation to succeed. Their attitude was "I'll believe it when I see it."

LEN: I think Michael sometimes felt in an awkward position in our discussions. Mike and I had been working together since the early 1980s. Our offices were side by side, and we could finish each other's thoughts. Michael had to deal with that dynamic. By nature, I'm cautious and always look for the downside. I don't automatically jump up and click my heels when I hear a new idea. I don't with Mike, and I

OPPOSITE
*The course guide shows the importance of that extra room on the right. On both the drive and the second shot, the golfer can now devise his own strategy for dealing with that long, slightly angled bunker that is the major hazard.*

didn't with Michael. Did I have doubts about what he was proposing to do? Yes, I did. He was biting off a lot.

MICHAEL: Rick Bakovka, president of the Central Wisconsin Regional Economic Growth Initiative, took an interest in our project, which was quickly turning into the largest capital investment that anyone was making in this part of the state. Rick visited the site, did his due diligence, and decided that Sand Valley could be an engine for the economic revival of the area. He had all the best traits of a local politician—he was enthusiastic, tireless, and persuasive. He helped me shepherd a TIF proposal through the Rome Community Development Authority. TIF stands for Tax Increment Funding; basically, the program enables a municipality to lend money to a developer who has a project that will benefit the municipality by increasing the tax base. Though the program is popular in Wisconsin, there was no precedent for granting TIF funds to a golf destination. That didn't stop Rick. He believed in the potential of Sand Valley, and in June 2015 Rick and I were in Madison, the state capital, when the Wisconsin Legislature passed Assembly Bill 123, authorizing the town of Rome to lend us $13 million—funds that were designated for construction of a clubhouse and a second golf course. The citizens of Rome were now major stakeholders in Sand Valley.

BILL: At Sand Valley, it was apparent that Mike was handing off more and more of the overall responsibility to Michael—and to Chris, too, though he wasn't there as often. His confidence in them was well founded. From my perspective, the transition went as smoothly as it could. There was never a time when I thought, *Uh-oh, there's going to be a problem when Mike gets here.*

MICHAEL: I was working with Rick on the TIF proposal, and I was talking to architects, kitchen designers, and dozens of different vendors as well as the media people who'd started coming to Sand Valley for a first look. At that stage of the development, the understanding was that Chris and I would take the lead on the non-golf aspects of the resort, and run all big decisions by our dad.

I spent a lot of time with both Bill and Ben, on the course and after work. Since Bill lived in Wisconsin for a few months, I got to know him well and started to think of him almost as an uncle. I wanted to hear his stories and soak up his wisdom about people, about life. When I had ideas about the golf course, I'd mention them first to my dad, and if he liked the idea he'd bring it up with Bill.

CHRIS: Michael was totally immersed in the Sand Valley project, and I was still based in Chicago, working on projects that involved all our resorts. My wife, Biz, and I have two daughters, and Biz—short for Elizabeth—wanted an advertising career that was easier to pursue in the city. Besides, we both grew up in Chicago, and I had a good model—my dad—for how to do work at distant locations from a city office. Sometimes I did feel a little frustrated, though. Neither Dad nor Michael ever seemed to have a single doubt that Sand Valley would succeed, but I saw the budget and knew how much money we were spending every week. I'll admit that I was nervous.

MICHAEL: Jens Jensen, our ecological consultant, was on-site every two weeks or so, working with Bill and his crew, or with Craig Haltom, who was supervising the large-scale earthmoving. One important element of the restoration was reintroducing native vegetation to the margins of the golf course, the roughs and the sandy areas, as Jens had done at the 7th. Some areas were reseeded, and others were managed to stimulate the native seedbank. Another technique was "chunking"—using an excavator to lift large, intact chunks of native vegetation from an area that was going to be converted to maintained turfgrass, and planting it in the sand. Chunking is a quick way to introduce mature plants to the sandy expanses, and it's been done extensively on all the courses.

JENS: Michael wanted to see as much sand as possible. He'd say, "We're selling sand," and the sand was a major part of the visual presentation. I'd never worked on a golf course before—I don't think many developers bring in an ecologist or try to think of a site holistically. The Keisers did, and so did Craig, and so did Bill. He grasped right away that I was looking at the site as a mosaic of different native plants and habitats, and we discovered how we could make this work both practically and aesthetically. We gave a lot of attention to the areas of rough, adding texture and color, trying to knit together the course's various elements.

MICHAEL: By October, most of the holes had been roughed in and we had an outing for the Founders. A dozen of them showed up to play dirt golf, hitting shots off small mats. Gary D'Amato, a sports columnist for the *Milwaukee Journal Sentinel,* was also part of the group. Gary was completely on top of the project, a journalist who was able to put all the angles of the Sand Valley story—the golf, the politics, the business, the community concerns—into context.

"SAND VALLEY . . . could be the most ambitious golf project ever undertaken in Wisconsin. If all goes according to Chicago developer Mike Keiser's plan, someday there will be five courses and lodging on 1,500 acres . . . a resort that would provide hundreds of jobs in depressed Adams County. . . . Hundreds of thousands of red pines have been harvested, revealing a wondrous sand barren—a prairie-like habitat that once formed the bed of a prehistoric lake. The land tumbles and heaves to the horizon in all directions. Who knew that such a place existed in Wisconsin?"                              —GARY D'AMATO

BILL: In the background that day, while people were looking at the golf holes, the ATVs were buzzing around. I didn't mind too much. I had the idea that if they hadn't opened up those big areas of sand, Mike wouldn't have bought the land and Ben and I wouldn't have been building a golf course here.

MK: Bill and Sue were living in Wisconsin that summer, and he was out on the course every day, not just walking and directing the crew; he still gets up on the Sand Pro—the smallest of the earthmoving machines, about the size of a riding lawn mower—to do the final grading of every green. He started as a shaper, and he still wants to put that finishing, personal touch on every green.

His work ethic is shared by the whole crew, and their product feels hand-crafted. I think every golfer senses at some level how much care and attention has gone into every detail. A Coore-Crenshaw course is a finely made object.

BILL: Golf course design is more about editing than authoring. Over the years I've worked with many talented associates who are designers in their own right. We give them initial concepts and tell them, when they start working, to feel absolutely free to deviate from this at any point they see something that could be better. They come up with things that we never would, and our courses benefit from that collaboration.

MK: I'm not going to dispute Bill's description of his working method, but I would add that when he edits, he doesn't stop being an artist.

MICHAEL: I got to know several members of Bill's crew pretty well, especially Jim Craig, probably because we're such manic workers. Have dozer, must work—that could be Jim's motto. The two of us talked about the course every chance we got, and Jim was in daily conversations with Bill and Ben. I realized that this was another way that I could get my ideas into the discussion.

CHRIS: I was there on the walk-through when the group—my dad, Bill, Michael, a few others—was discussing whether fescue should be used on the greens. I don't know much about turf, but I could see that Rob Duhm, our superintendent, wasn't happy. He didn't say anything, but his body language was shouting, *No!* I didn't say anything at the time, either, but afterward I brought it up. I thought we needed to hear more from Rob. He had his say, and the greens at Sand Valley are now two strains of creeping bent grass. Sometimes, as an observer, I think I can facilitate the conversation.

MK: In the summer of 2016, Bill was diagnosed with tonsil cancer—a dangerous cancer if it's not detected early. Fortunately, Bill's was, and the treatment was successful. He was almost apologetic about it, but it sent a shock through all of us. Bill doesn't assert himself, but when he's on a project, he's out there in every kind of weather. There's no question about who's in charge.

JIM: Bill might have missed a few weeks, but he'd walked that course so often that all the details, all the connections, were filed away in his mind. He sees everything. I liken him to Ben Hogan, who said, "The golf swing is nine-tenths over at setup." That's how Bill is. He is so well prepared, his fundamentals are so solid, that he's not going to make a bad swing.

MICHAEL: That June, during the last push on the course, I got a text from Jim. He'd gone back to Texas for a week off. He sent me a selfie, and at first I didn't know what I was looking at. It didn't look like Jim. His head was shaved, with a big gash running down the middle. His head had been split open like a coconut, then stapled back together.

JIM: About a week before that, I'd been talking to Michael, and when I stopped talking I had no idea what I'd just said. My mind had gone blank. I knew that something was wrong. I was due for some time off, and when I got home to Fort Worth, I went to see my doctor. He's an old-school doc, the kind who usually says, "Nothing's wrong, just put some dirt on it." That's not what he told me this time. He said, "You need to go to the emergency room, right away." I got a CAT scan and then they put me in the MRI machine. My wife, Shea, was waiting there with a doctor when I got out, and the doctor said I had a mass in my brain. A tumor. I said, "All right, what do we do now?" He said, "Take it out." I said, "When?" And he said, "Tomorrow."

MICHAEL: Six weeks later, Jim was back in Wisconsin and back up on his dozer. We urged him to take it slow, but we were all in overdrive as the last holes were being built. Every decision had a ripple effect. In a period of a few months, we completed the 17th and 18th holes, rerouted the entrance road, relocated the clubhouse, altered the footprint for the second course, and staked out the par-3 course, the Sandbox.

BILL: The 17th was always a linking hole. We had an obvious natural green site at the 16th and we had to get from there to the 18th tee. At one point I thought the 17th could be a short par-4, but then I realized that we needed a par-3. All right, where do we put the green? My first idea was to tie it into the face of the dune that was standing there. Mike looked at the hole and I thought maybe we could make it work. Then, after Mike left, Jim and I started looking around behind the dune where there was a big hole filled with bushes and a few straggly little pines. Mike likes infinity greens and punchbowl greens, and we started wondering if he'd be okay with putting the green down in the hole. I showed Michael what we were considering, and he was completely supportive. Before Mike's next visit, we cleared the site out, but I wasn't sure what he'd think—the putting surface wasn't going to be visible from the tee. We had a blind par-3. There were a bunch of us out there—me, Michael, Jim, Craig, maybe a few others—when we showed it to Mike. He heard me out, and then he said, "I like bowls."

BEN: At the 18th, a medium-length par-5, we started with a wide expanse and a long upslope. The question was how to place the bunkers and position the green to make it inviting. When the wind is right, an aggressive player has a good chance to get home in two. The slope on the left is built up to feed a ball toward the putting surface. I wanted the player who takes a risk to have a chance to make an eagle. The 18th is a great gambling hole that might decide a match.

BILL: Ben must have spent two full days in that area, just pondering. He came up with the idea of putting that giant bunker in the face of the slope, an obstacle that made the second shot a whole lot more interesting. Zach Varty, a young shaper who'd just started working for us, built the big bunker. The smaller bunker to the right of the green was always there—it was a wide place in the trail that the ATVers used to get up to the top of the hill. We just left it as it was.

On one of his site visits, Mike suggested adding a back right area to the green. We'd already staked out the green, and he drew a line in the sand with his foot, making the putting surface quite a bit larger. At first, Ben and I weren't sure about it—this addition didn't seem to fit with the contours around the green. Jim Craig and Ryan Farrow got to work and tied all the contours into one another. Now the pin is often placed back there, and people watching cheer when a ball rolls back there and swings toward the hole. The 18th is a good example of how a hole gets better with collaboration.

MK: Preopening, Sand Valley was generating a lot of buzz, and the pressure was on Michael to get the whole place up and running. To his credit, he didn't try to force decisions about the lodging and the clubhouse. First things first, and golf came first. People were going to come to Sand Valley for the golf, not for a fancy clubhouse or luxurious rooms.

CHRIS: We're frugal. That's something Dad has stressed for as long as I can remember. The great example is the old Pacific Dunes clubhouse, the double-wide trailer with the clock tower. It didn't stop anybody from coming to play golf. We did need someplace for people to stay, and the first cabins we put up were custom prefabs, built nearby and delivered to the resort.

We had one of the greatest turnstands in golf—Craig's Porch, named for Craig Haltom, located on top of the Volcano, looking out over the golf course and the sunset. The building itself looks kind of like a farm shed. Out front, right above the 18th green, there's a terrace with a few tables and a row of unpainted Adirondack chairs, and in the late afternoon they're always filled with people watching others hole out. There's a lot of cheering and commenting. It sums up the Sand Valley atmosphere—informal, congenial, comfortable, down-to-earth.

And affordable. That's important. At Sand Valley—at all our resorts—we want to make sure that guests come away thinking that the experience was worth it. We want to give them value for the money they spend. The green fee at Sand Valley is less than at other top resorts, including Bandon. Sometimes small things make a big impact. At Craig's Porch, the daily menu is posted on a chalkboard and the bargains haven't changed.

OPPOSITE
*No. 18 at Sand Valley*

Nye's ice cream sandwiches in nine flavors, the egg-cheese-bacon breakfast sandwich for $3, beers for $2, pulled-pork tacos for $1.50. People might not remember how much they paid for their room, but they remember the $2 beers.

MK: When Sand Valley opened officially in 2017, we were considering a clubhouse location somewhere on that same ridge. One option was a temporary clubhouse, a tent structure. David Kidd was already at work on the second course, Mammoth Dunes, and he was pushing a location in the vicinity of what is now his 3rd hole. To build there would have meant destroying an oak savanna, one of the most intact remnant landscapes on the property. Though we tentatively decided to use that spot, it was one of those decisions that leave the door open, and we kept looking.

MICHAEL: The entry road wasn't completed when we opened, and the pro shop—the place where our first guests paid their green fees—was a repurposed shipping container. I had worked in a single-wide trailer when Barnbougle Dunes opened in 2004. I had no intention of rushing to build a large clubhouse, and no money to build one. Golfers showed up in droves, and they felt as though they were in on the discovery of a cool new place.

# 15

# Mammoth Dunes

*Golf architects have been taught over the last hundred years to create golf
courses that are defensive against the golfer, and I'm considering that this could
fundamentally be wrong. The very basis on which our profession is grounded
could be wrong. A course can be playable—it can be ragingly good fun—and still
be challenging.*

—DAVID KIDD

L IKE IT OR NOT, David Kidd and I were joined at the hip. The young,
unknown architect and the unknown developer had collaborated to
build a course that shook up the conventional wisdom about American golf.
At Bandon Dunes, we'd caught magic in a bottle . . . and hadn't worked
together since.

I won't say that success had spoiled David, but it certainly brought out
the wicked side of his talents as an architect. A natural showman, he's incapable of building a boring course. My favorite of his post-Bandon designs
is Nanea, one of the best courses in Hawaii. When Lindy and I visit the Big
Island, we play there as often as we can. Nanea would easily be a Top 100 if
the owners allowed course raters to see the place—but they don't. They are
content to keep it as their own private preserve.

Following Bandon, David's best-known designs are also his most con-
troversial. An architect who pushes his imagination to the limit, he's built
courses that are over-the-top—extravagant, complicated, imposing, and just
too damn tough. Tetherow, his home course in Bend, Oregon, is so punishing that it soon had a nickname: Death Row. His most notorious design,

the Castle Course at St. Andrews, had some of the steepest, wildest, most unfortunate greens I've ever seen. Both courses have been softened since they opened.

David knew what I thought of these courses. An architect can get away with a high degree of difficulty at a private club, where members have years to figure out its defenses. Sometimes, a hole with an extreme feature—the Devil's Asshole bunker at Pine Valley comes to mind—can even become a part of club lore, a love-hate feature of the course. Resort guests play a course once or twice, and they're not likely to be feeling love if they have to climb down a ladder into Satan's bowels.

Personally, I enjoyed David, and I was glad that his offices weren't far away. When he wasn't off in some remote corner of the world adding to his global portfolio, David often popped over from Bend to Bandon Dunes, piloting his own plane. David left his fingerprints all over the resort, not only as the brash young architect of the first course but also as the shrewd wordsmith who gave us our motto: *Golf as it was meant to be.* He came up with that phrase when he was writing out the script for a wake-up message that we used in the early years. In those days before smartphones, the first words our guests heard in the morning were delivered in David's rich Scottish brogue. Now, when we want to roll out the red carpet for a group visiting Bandon Dunes, we frequently invite David to speak to them. Put him in front of a microphone, and David knows how to win over a crowd. He's witty, engaging, and provocative, an irrepressible storyteller with a deep knowledge and affection for the game.

In 2014, when I asked him for yet another speech, David proposed a quid pro quo: he'd come to Bandon Dunes if I'd visit Gamble Sands, the course he'd just built in Brewster, Washington. I'd been hearing good things about it from people I trusted, most importantly from Michael, who'd seen Gamble Sands before it opened. When he tried to convince me that David had turned over a new leaf, l gave him a hard time for becoming such a Kidd cheerleader. But he was so insistent that I decided I should see the course for myself.

On a blue-sky September day, I played Gamble Sands with David, Josh Lesnik, and Michael. My first reaction was to gush at the beauty of the location. Spread across a high, sandy plateau, Gamble Sands has glorious views of the mighty Columbia River, the rocky slopes of the Cascade Mountains, and the expansive orchards that thrive in this part of Washington. David,

I had to admit, has a flair for creating courses that look right at home in vast, wide-open spaces. Immense fairways, gigantic greens, and sandy areas blended with the surrounding expanse of high desert chaparral. Gamble Sands had the scale and sublimity of a seaside links.

Starting on the 1st tee, David pointed out design features that he'd crafted to enhance the playability. Friendly fairway contours, receptive greens, sparse rough, roomy green surrounds, manageable recovery shots, unobstructed sight lines—this place was huge but not frightening. Gamble Sands was a course that made you want to swing freely.

On the scorecard I kept that day, I followed my usual practice of ranking each hole on a scale of 1 to 10. Anything higher than 5 is respectable, as I said earlier, and the front nine at Gamble Sands racked up mostly 8s and 9s—a stretch as good as anything David had ever done, even at Bandon Dunes. Though the back nine got slightly lower marks, the course finished with another flourish, an 8 and a 9. After the round, I sent David an email with my scorecard attached and shared the collective opinion of our group: a grand slam home run.

That round was a kind of audition. David knew that work would soon begin at Sand Valley, and he wanted to design a course there. What I saw at Gamble Sands convinced me that he'd returned to the principles that had guided him at Bandon Dunes. Back then, I'm not sure he could have articulated them; he was still in his twenties, and both of us were working largely on instinct, trying to build a links course. "I didn't know what I didn't know," David has said, but links golf was in his blood, and he knew plenty. He was high-spirited and confident, brimming over with energy and ambition and ideas, and he built a whale of a links.

He had blossomed at Bandon Dunes, and at Gamble Sands I saw the handiwork of an architect who'd returned to his roots—a new David, a mature professional who could explain in micro-detail how and why he'd sculpted the features of this course. He'd dissected his design philosophy, breaking it down step by step, supplementing instinct with analysis, backing away from the difficulty that had become a trademark of his work and embracing an approach that emphasized playability.

Gone was the taskmaster of Tetherow, replaced by a David who was described in a magazine article as preaching a "gospel of fun."

I knew him well enough to respect his drive and determination. The twentysomething David who designed Bandon Dunes had been boisterous,

*David Kidd
in a relaxed,
contemplative mood*

unruly, cocksure. He and his crew had closed the local bars, and they got into more than a few scrapes. The new David is lean and trim, a fitness freak who trains daily on state-of-the-art bicycles and competes in triathlons. He still sips a glass of Oregon pinot noir at dinner, and he still has a personality that can dominate a room, but in midlife he has become more patient and disciplined.

At Gamble Sands, he'd applied that discipline to his work. Though the course shared many features with Bandon Dunes, it was by no means an imitation. Plenty of people carry on about putting the fun back into golf; David had figured out how to make it happen. In fact, I cautioned him about talking so openly about his new ideas in interviews and articles. Some of the information seemed proprietary. Why wouldn't other architects just copy him?

He shrugged off that worry. "They won't. Golf design is still a traditional profession. People don't want to change."

After Gamble Dunes, David was back in contention. For the first course at Sand Valley, the obvious choice was Coore-Crenshaw. For the second, given the scale and openness of the site, I thought that the new David could do a terrific job.

There was a hitch. Tom Doak was also aware of the work under way at Sand Valley, and I'd all but promised him the job. He expected to build the second course. He'd even sent out a Christmas card with a picture of Sand Valley, proclaiming that his work here would soon begin. As it became clear that the Coore-Crenshaw course was a real winner, we began to consider the timing of an official announcement of the next architect—and I realized that some stakeholders, including me, weren't fully ready to commit to Tom. Several other designers had visited the site, and in informal discussions we'd speculated about the possibility of setting up a system that would give them a shot, and also allow several stakeholders to participate in the selection process.

Meanwhile, Tom had worked with topo maps to come up with a routing, then visited Sand Valley with an associate and walked through it. Inadvertently, I had set the stage for another episode in the Kidd–Doak rivalry.

The competition between those two went all the way back to the mid-1990s, when both David and Tom lobbied for the commission at Bandon Dunes. David got the job, and after the ecstatic reviews rolled in, he expected to do the second course as well—but I picked Tom. The decision wasn't a mark against David; for all kinds of reasons, I thought it would benefit the resort to have a different architect. Yet it cast them once again as rivals, and when David and Tom met for the first time in the Bunker Bar at Bandon Dunes, they eyed each other warily. David said to Tom, "I left you a gimme," not exactly a conciliatory remark. Tom went out and built Pacific Dunes, a course that was as unlike David's as he could make it, setting up a head-to-head comparison that still sparks animated discussion among Bandonistas. In course rankings, Pacific Dunes has generally placed higher than Bandon Dunes, though guests at the resort, judging by the number of rounds played on each, rate them almost equally, with Bandon Dunes having a slight edge.

One golf writer referred to their relationship as a "faux competition." Knowing the two of them, fully aware of how ambitious and talented and competitive they both are, I don't think there is anything "faux" about it.

The plot thickened in the fall of 2014 with the release of Tom's updated *Confidential Guide to Golf Courses*. The first volume rated the courses of Great Britain and Ireland on the Doak Scale, in which 10s are rare and 3s are given to average courses, as we've seen. Rarest of all is a rating of 0, awarded to "a course so contrived and unnatural that it may poison your mind, which I cannot recommend under any circumstances."

Only one course received a 0—David's Castle Course.

That was the background for our deliberations about the second Sand Valley course. After talking to Michael, Chris, and several others who make up the Keiser kitchen cabinet, I decided to make it a real competition, a bake-off. We would invite three architects—David, Tom, and Rod Whitman, who teamed up with Dave Axland—to come to Sand Valley, spend as much time on the property as they needed, and submit a routing. David and Rod seemed happy to be asked. Tom definitely wasn't.

Michael was in charge of the rules and logistics. After the designers had drawn their routings, the names would be removed and the plans evaluated by the members of the kitchen cabinet. On a frigid winter day, with snow still on the ground, twelve of us walked all three routings, starting with David's—though we didn't know it was his. We scored each hole on a scale of 1 to 10. For the first few holes, Len Levine asked me for guidance about how to decide on a number. "How many 10s should I give?" he wanted to know. I told him that there were only a handful of 10s in the entire world. He thought I'd discount his ratings since he was new to this process, and there were experts on that walk, including Mike Davis, the executive director of the USGA, but I also wanted to hear from retail golfers. When the numbers were tallied, David Kidd won the bake-off handily. After almost two decades, we'd be working together again.

MICHAEL: For a long time I had serious objections to my dad's habit of grading each hole when he walked a course. I thought it was like grading individual notes in a piece of music, not listening to the melody, missing the overall effect. But I've come around. It's easy to rationalize a weak hole—if you know you have a 10, you can find an excuse for a 3 or 4 on either side of it. As long as you don't forget that the course has to work as a single composition, the hole-by-hole numbers are useful tools. Why not try to make each hole a 10? It will never turn out that way, but it's a scoring system that keeps the pressure on. I've seen holes improve because of it.

DAVID KIDD: I was overjoyed to get the job at Sand Valley. I considered Mike a friend and a mentor, and his criticism of my work wasn't something that just rolled right off my shoulders. It stung. The opinions that mattered most to me were Mike's and my dad's—and they both let me know when they thought I'd made mistakes.

My dad, Jimmy, introduced me to golf. He's the one who first put a club in my hand, and then a rake for the bunkers. I grew up thinking of golf as both a game and a profession. My dad enjoyed my success as much as I did. No matter where I was building a course, he'd come have a look. He's told me more than once that he thought a green needed to be plowed under. He can read me, and he knows when to speak out and when to hold his tongue. A son can read his father, too, and there were times when he didn't say much—but I could see the disappointment in his eyes.

The knock on my work was that the courses were too difficult, too extreme, too punishing. Every golf architect has critics, and I was consciously pushing the envelope. I didn't expect everyone to love my courses. I'm proud of all of them, including Tetherow and the Castle Course, the two that have attracted the most criticism. Anyone who plays those courses or bothers to read the reviews—not just punch lines but the whole review—knows they're both gorgeous to look at, and that they both have memorable, exciting golf holes. One of the problems with reviews and ratings is that a golf course gets reduced to a single number or a sound bite, leaving out the hundreds of details that make up an actual round of golf. I defy anyone to play the Castle Course without being blown away by the whole situation, with the North Sea on one side and the steeples of the Auld Town on the other. On some lists, the Castle Course is rated one of the best in Scotland. A zero? I don't think so.

I've often thought that criticism of my work comes with a subtext. Some of the most vocal, opinionated reviewers of golf architecture post on the *Golf Club Atlas* site, and their attitude toward me had to do with the fact that I wasn't Tom Doak. To that crowd, Tom's a god who can do no wrong and I'm the anti-Doak. And then there's been a nagging question about whether I'd peaked at Bandon Dunes. That was my best-known course, the one that thousands of people had played. Was it a one-off? Was I a one-hit wonder?

Some of that skepticism was because people just hadn't seen much of my work. I've built several ultra-private courses, and I've worked in places that aren't on the map for American golfers, like Fiji and South Africa. Even Gamble Sands, which won Best New Course honors in 2015, was well off the beaten track. It didn't have near the visibility that a course at Sand Valley would have.

I had something to prove at Sand Valley. The top priority was to build a course that would work for Mike—that would be a draw for the resort. Beyond that, I wanted this course to make a statement. I'm competitive, and I'm ambitious. I want to be at the top of my profession. For almost my entire life, I have lived and breathed golf, and I want to leave my mark on the game. I grew up in an environment where people honored the memory of men like Old Tom Morris, who built Machrihanish, where we spent our summers, and James Braid, who built Gleneagles, where my dad worked for so many years. I wanted to be remembered in the same way. I wanted to build courses that stood the test of time.

In my personal life, I had driven myself hard to meet goals that seemed out of reach when I set them. In my professional life, I hadn't been as focused and disciplined. Even the greatest golfers need to do more than rely on native ability; they have to strive to improve. The same applies to the golf architect who wants to stay on top of his trade.

In 2009, during the Great Recession, I had some down time and I spent a week at Bandon Dunes with two of my associates from DMK Design, Nick Shaan and Casey Krahenbuhl. We were on a mission. We played all the courses and then, over dinner, we analyzed the golf from every point of view we could think of—strategy, aesthetics, operational, maintenance, everything down to the nuts and bolts. We were trying to deconstruct the entire experience to get a complete answer to the fundamental question: What makes golfers love this place? What's the magic elixir at Bandon?

I talked to the caddies—they're the ones who know what really happens out on the course. I interrogated them about how golfers played the courses, what they liked, what they didn't like, where they had trouble, what they complained about. The first thing I learned was that the average score was about 100. Not 90, which is the "official" USGA average. 100! I'd been living in a fantasy world. I'd been worrying about how to create a challenge for golfers when the last thing they needed was more challenge. They were their own challenge. I'd been trying to make courses tougher when I should've been thinking about how to help the players. I should've been working for the golfer, not against him.

That was a seminal moment. When I realized that I'd been over-estimating golfers my entire career, it sank in that I'd gone over to the wrong side of the equation as a designer. I hadn't been thinking about the ordinary player, the person Mike has always referred to as the retail golfer. That's been his mantra—the retail golfer, the retail golfer, the retail golfer. When he looks at a golf course, he sees it from their point of view. He thinks about what it feels like to look for a ball in the rough, or to four-putt, or to find yourself in a bunker where the chances of getting out are basically nil. When we were building Bandon Dunes, his advice never varied, though he said it in many different ways: Keep it simple. Don't make this any harder than it has to be. He wasn't asking me to dumb it down. He still wanted every hole to "sing." He just didn't want the song to be a funeral march. "Simple" golf could be challenging and elegant, and it meant, above all, giving all golfers a chance to play their best game.

Now when I hear someone talk about a "test of golf," I think, what horseshit. Since when is "test" a term of praise? In any other context, "test" means boring, tedious, stressful. For too long, golf courses have been judged with criteria like "resistance to scoring" or "defending par." For a golfer trying to break 100, making a par on any hole is a small victory. Surely it's not the architect's job to deny him that pleasure. Yet I had to admit that in some of my designs, that's exactly what I'd been doing. My intention was to make the golfer hit a great shot, not to make him suffer—but the result was often that he couldn't pull off the shot, and he did suffer.

A course for the retail golfer can call for precise shots, and it can have heroic shots. At Bandon Dunes, there are both. Mike likes the razzle-dazzle. You can get into all kinds of trouble at Bandon Dunes, but here's something else we discovered on that trip: you can almost always get out. Yes, there are a few places where you can lose a ball in the gorse, but nearly always you can try the heroic shot—and even if you don't succeed, you can keep playing the hole. You haven't lost a ball, you're not out-of-bounds, you're not in a water hazard, you're not in a situation where you have to stop, break the rhythm of a round, flail away at some impossible shot, take a penalty, or just pick up.

That's the tradition of the links: find your ball and hit it. You might not make a par, but you can finish the hole, usually with the loss of only a stroke or two. The penalty isn't overly severe. Bad shots don't ruin a round, and they might even set up a manageable recovery shot that will be a highlight. Net effect: golfers keep their hopes up. They have fun.

I'd lost sight of how all the little things we'd done at Bandon Dunes, from the tee through the green, kept the golfer in the game. After that 2009 visit, I was ready for a reset. On the next courses I built, at Huntsman Springs, in Idaho, and Mukul Resort, in Nicaragua, I dialed back the difficulty. My mindset was that my job as a designer was to entertain, and I had some new material to work into my performance. A few years later, when I designed Gamble Sands, I was feeling confident about this new approach, willing to take greater risks and push it even further.

Mike and I have talked a lot about this new philosophy, and he was so enthusiastic about Gamble Sands that I thought he might offer me the first course at Sand Valley. But he called me on Christmas Eve in 2014 to tell me that he'd decided to go with Coore-Crenshaw. They've been his go-to architects, and I thought, *Okay, my turn is coming.* Then, a year later to the day, he called again on Christmas Eve 2015. I saw his name on the caller ID and thought I was about to get a great big glittery gift. Instead, he told me that there was going to be this competition, this bake-off. He was inviting me to do a routing—not what I had in mind.

But I was still in the running and determined to make the most of the opportunity. I spent a week at Sand Valley working on that routing. My competition and I hadn't been given any restrictions on where we could go on the property, and each of us chose to focus on a different area. The most dramatic feature was a big, V-shaped ridge, and I headed straight for that. Maybe it's just my personality to go for the most spectacular site, but Mike likes drama too. A golf course built up and over and around that ridge was going to have some fantastic holes, but there was one huge problem. It was easy to see how the ridge could be crossed once in eighteen holes—but how could I get back? Where was the second crossing? The others didn't want anything to do with the ridge, and I understood why. The routing wouldn't work if I couldn't get over the ridge and back without a steep climb, or resorting to an elevator or some kind of shuttle. On my routing the elevation changes—the distance that golfers would have to climb—were something like 512 feet. That might sound like a lot, but the issue isn't the total amount. What also matters is the angle of the gradient, the steepness. I had to find a way to cross the ridge that would be as gentle as possible. I think I succeeded. Now, when I ask golfers to tell me which hole has the biggest climb on the course, most of them don't have the foggiest idea. The answer is No. 3, a double dogleg par-5 that rises about fifty feet, but they don't even notice. The rise is so gradual that it looks and feels almost level.

The ridge was what made the difference in the bake-off.

Working with Mike wasn't the same as it had been at Bandon Dunes. He was still in charge of the project, and reserved the right to bless each hole before it was grassed. He didn't visit the site very often, maybe three times during the first summer that I was there. The next summer he came only twice. The day-to-day supervision was left to Michael, and it became clearer and clearer that the baton was being passed.

Michael was running things at Sand Valley. The clubhouse and the lodge were being built at the same time, and he had a thousand things to do, but whenever he could get away, he was out there on the course with us. He was far more involved in the daily discussion of the architectural details than Mike had ever been. At Bandon Dunes, a lot of my communication with Mike went through Pete Sinnott, the construction supervisor, or his on-site representative. But when Mike came out to Oregon for his site visits, I never forgot that he was the boss. He's concise, decisive, quick to reach conclusions. Though he does a lot of looking and careful listening, he comes across as the alpha—how could he not? That's what he'd been in every project since he was twenty-one years old. Mike was my dad's age, a father figure. He delivers his opinions with authority, and it took me a while to realize that he wants people to stand up to him. He's open to other views. It's not his way or the highway.

Michael was younger than me, and our discussions were wide-ranging, about theory and design principles as well as specific, practical matters. Our ongoing discussion was about striking a balance in the design, giving the 100-shooter a chance to play fun shots and giving the 70-shooter all he can handle.

Everyone who comes to Mammoth Dunes is struck by its gigantic scale. Most courses are built on two hundred acres or so; Mammoth Dunes spreads out over an area of almost five hundred acres. On the holes on the backside of the ridge, a golfer can start to feel lost in a vast, open prairie. An average course might have twenty-five or thirty acres of fairway; Mammoth Dunes has eighty-five acres. Altogether, including greens, the course has 120 acres of maintained turfgrass. Some fairway landing areas are more than a hundred yards in width. As a general rule on American golf courses, greens average between five and six thousand square feet; at Mammoth Dunes the average is over ten thousand. I haven't calculated the size of the sand pits, but some of them must be at least five acres. They're as big as meteorite craters. The dunes themselves are—well, they're mammoth!

Incorporating the slopes into the course's design was a technical challenge. To minimize the amount of earth we had to move and still keep the slopes playable, we used a detailed topographic map overlaid with a program on AutoCad. There's much more exposed sand now than when we began. In the field, we did a lot of "melting," shaving down the landforms, taking off some of the pronounced edges as we tried to tie them into a unified landscape. And the guys on my team got to be expert at chunking.

To determine the playability of certain holes, we went to a less technical tool—a basketball. We did play some dirt golf, but that only tells you what a ball's going to do in the air. If you want to know what it does on the ground, you need a basketball—not a soccer ball or a volleyball, but a firm, fully inflated basketball. Roll it on the dirt and it will do exactly what a golf ball will do once the surface is grassed.

As a sand-based course with tight fescue turf, Mammoth Dunes has some fantastic rolls. The best might be at the 14th, a downhill, drivable par-4. This hole has its own story. The designer of record is actually Brian Silvernail, winner of the 2016 Armchair Architect contest that was run by *Golf Digest*. A graphic designer who has a side business designing computer golf games, Brian knew a lot about digital design. What he didn't know was how design worked on the ground, but he got a tutorial when he came to Sand Valley for a weekend. With his plans as our template, we made the adjustments in the field to fit the hole into the steep slope. One feature we're proud of is the tee at

"NO DESIGN IN MEMORY so successfully melds strategy, playability and spectacular aesthetics. Mammoth Dunes plays like an inland links, with emphasis on the ground game. The ball darts here and there, and it's up to the player (and perhaps his caddie, on this walking-only course) to solve the puzzles the contours present. Enormously roomy, rumpled fairways allow golfers to choose their own path to the target, amid vast areas of open sand and gargantuan greens. While the landing areas are plenty wide, finding the spot that provides the most advantageous angle into the green is paramount."

—THE EDITORS, *Golf Magazine,*
describing their choice for Best New Course of 2018

270 yards. Too many so-called drivable par-4s are reachable only for the golfer who can carry the ball 300 yards, but the 14th at Mammoth Dunes gives most players a chance to take a whack at it. Any well-struck tee shot will just keep rolling, rolling, rolling. We never timed it out, but when we rolled that basketball, we must've watched for fifteen or twenty seconds as it trundled toward the green. Shorter hitters will have just as much fun as bombers on this hole, watching their tee shots rolling merrily down the fairway.

The only complaint I've heard about Mammoth Dunes is that it's too easy. Well, there is a safe route. On many holes, this is so obvious a route that it's impossible to miss. But the smartest way to play the hole is often hidden and involves a considerable amount of risk. I don't want to defend par—I want every golfer to make a few of them—but I do want to defend birdie. Bradley Klein, an editor at *GolfWeek* and a rigorous critic of golf course architecture, saw right away what I was doing. He recognized the challenge that was presented to the better player. After saying that the course was inviting to those who aren't overly worried about posting a score, he wrote, "At every turn, the slopes, angles, and ground features have a purpose that has strategic value if you are trying to make par (or better) and care about your score. That principle gets established early for anyone who looks carefully."

I'd like to think that Mammoth Dunes could be Exhibit A in the argument that a golf course that is fun to play can also have a backbone.

*Many say that
the drive on this
downhill par-4 is
their favorite shot at
Mammoth Dunes.*

MICHAEL: After the success of the first course in 2017, my dad stepped back a little and turned his attention to some other projects. He and Bill were getting started on the Sheep Ranch, and they were also working together on Coul Links in Scotland. He was still in touch with the progress at Mammoth Dunes, but Chris and I took on more day-to-day responsibility.

David Kidd was on-site about half the time, and his lead associate, Casey Krahenbuhl, was the full-time project manager. He got just as fired up as I did about the place's geology and cultural history. It was Casey who built the Cellar Bunker on the 7th hole, using a stone wall from a house in the community of émigrés from Bohemia (a large region of the present-day Czech Republic) who had established settlements throughout the upper Midwest.

David and Casey had visited Pine Valley with me and my dad, and David made a second trip with Dad, Chris, and me. In our early conversations about the visual presentation of our course, we referenced Pine Valley and the heathland courses, but as it began to take shape, we thought more and more in terms of a regional landscape, of sand barrens and savannas. I'd been able to find old, grainy photos showing how this landscape had looked before the tree plantations covered everything. Jen Jensen would drive up twice a month from Madison, spend an afternoon in the field, have dinner with us, and then spend the night, sometimes on the couch at the house David was renting at Lake Arrowhead.

Because of that tall ridge and the steeper slopes at Mammoth Dunes, there were better trees and more undisturbed native vegetation than at Sand Valley. For the lumber companies, it was easier to plant the red pines on flat land, so they didn't bother with the slopes. One spot had some little cactus growing in it, brittle prickly pear cactus that produces a small yellow flower in the spring—cactus, this far north! The strategy for restoring the landscape was to use these remnant areas as anchors and work outward.

Jens was also handling the landscaping around the entry road, clubhouse site, and lodgings, though some visitors might think these areas had never been touched. They're sandy, and the plants are native. We want our guests to know from the moment of arrival that they are in the Central Wisconsin Sands, a place with a distinct geological and ecological history. In every possible detail, we wanted Sand Valley to be authentic.

CHRIS: As a group, we had considered several clubhouse sites, and I thought we'd decided to go with the one that both Michael and I originally preferred—on the high ground where Craig's Porch sits. Mentally, I'd already checked that off the list. But then we switched gears. Dad preferred the lower site. I was turned around and frustrated. Len, who's been a mentor and confidant, has been through this before. He knows that Dad likes to let the creative process evolve even after the stakes have been put in the ground.

MICHAEL: Mike Angus, our land planner, suggested the site we ended up using. For operational purposes, this was a better location— spacious, accessible, a natural hub. One drawback was that David would have to reroute his course—as a matter of fact, the Mammoth Bar in the clubhouse now sits exactly where he had originally placed his 4th green. In his first adjustment to the routing, he had several fairways running side by side behind the clubhouse. In its own way, this would have been impressive, but we would have had an almost continuous stretch of turf five hundred yards wide—and that was too much.

Then David came up with the idea of creating that enormous gash of sand that now lies between the 1st tee and the 18th fairway. What's more, he used that material to build up the terrace that's now behind the clubhouse. It was a genius idea. His changes gave us both that enormous sand pit that defines the view and a broad green terrace that easily accommodates the putting green, a bocce court, fire pits, and an elevated 1st tee.

DAVID: I can't help it, I've become a closet master planner. I couldn't stay out of the discussion about where to put the clubhouse, and that location makes Mammoth Dunes the mothership of the resort. I like how the golf seems to flow right into the building. The huge putting green is hard up against the clubhouse without a single strip of grass or pathway in between. You can almost putt while you're sitting on the porch. The 1st tee is just steps away. You can roll a practice putt, look up, and watch one group hitting their drives and another finishing up on the 18th green. Everything converges in that one area.

CHRIS: In coming up with an aesthetic for the buildings, we followed the principle of all Keiser resorts. We try to make every element of the design, from the infrastructure and buildings down to the fabrics and furnishings, express a sense of place. Michael took the lead in working with Northwork Architects, and all the structures at Sand Valley are derived from the vernacular architecture of the Midwest, using the tin roofs, wooden siding, and the shapes of barns, farmhouses, cabins, and other familiar farm buildings.

We also made comfort a priority. I visited showrooms all over Chicago, and I must have stretched out on hundreds of mattresses before settling on the right one. The same with chairs, and the same with showerheads—we tested more than twenty, and the ones that didn't make it ended up in what we called the showerhead graveyard.

MICHAEL: Chris and I seem to gravitate to roles as Mr. Inside and Mr. Outside, but it's more complicated than that. We've both been involved in all phases of the development, and I had a lot of input at the Mammoth Bar, which we built first and worked on together. Later, at Aldo's, our high-end restaurant, Chris took the solo lead. At the entry, guests see some historic photographs of settlers in this area, and of dunes and sand barrens. The most prominent artwork hangs above the mantel, a portrait of a distinguished older man. He's clearly a person of substance. Since Sand Valley's a golf destination, it would be natural to suppose that he's some sort of golf figure—a champion, or maybe a golf architect. He's neither one. That's a portrait of Aldo Leopold. Chris and I commissioned it, and we like having Leopold in the place of honor.

CHRIS: No one is completely sure who first came up with the name Mammoth Dunes. David Kidd thinks that Dad might have been the first to say it. He does a good imitation of Dad's deep voice, saying to him, "David, these dunes are *mammoth*." In any case, Mammoth Dunes ended up on a list with other possible names and logo concepts.

Michael and I both thought Mammoth Dunes was a perfect double entendre. The dunes were huge, and "mammoth" tied into the prehistory of the place, a time after the glacial dam burst and wooly mammoths roamed in North America. Michael and I knew that the logo would be really cool. Dad wasn't convinced that a shaggy, extinct beast was the right choice, but this time Michael and I had the final say. Not to rub it in, but we were right. Items with the Mammoth Dunes logo fly off the shelves in the pro shop.

**DAVID:** I like watching people arrive at Sand Valley. They've been driving for hours when they finally pull up in front of the clubhouse, and the adrenaline is starting to flow. On the entry road, they catch a few glimpses of the dunes and the golf course. As they unload their golf bags, they see the breezeway between the pro shop and the clubhouse, and a lot of them head toward it before they go inside to register. That breezeway is like the portal to a magic kingdom. They walk through it and boom! It's all right there in front of them, a huge amphitheater filled with golf. I've stood there and watched people shaking their heads and grinning like mad. They pull out their phones and start taking pictures. They've been at Sand Valley for two minutes, and they're already happy.

## 16

# The Short Game

*One of the more pleasing trends in modern golf is the return of the short course, and the elevation of pitch and putt golf in America from an afterthought to a key part of operations. . . . They are generally as well built, and maintained, as any full-length tracks. Such consideration was once unthinkable, but this modern era is all about fun and there are few better ways to spend an hour late in the day than playing a bunch of expertly shaped par threes.*

*—Planet Golf USA* (2020)

W HEN BILL COORE was routing Bandon Trails, he looked longingly at the land that lies between the present first tee and the Pacific Ocean, a fine dunescape that sloped down to the beach. Bill often says that a piece of ground feels like golf, or looks good for golf, and he kept trying to figure out how to incorporate this thirty-acre parcel into his routing. The contours were ideal and the views were stunning, but he couldn't find a way to get in and back out without creating too much disruption. So he stayed out.

Fast-forward seven years. Many Bandonistas were getting on in years, and they weren't as keen as they'd once been to walk thirty-six holes a day. I mentioned to Bill that I'd been thinking about a par-3 course, which might work as a breather, an opportunity for people to take a load off their aching knees and still play a little more golf. We immediately agreed that those dunes we hadn't been able to use at Bandon Trails would provide perfect terrain for a set of short holes.

Bandon Preserve, thirteen gorgeous holes terraced above the sea, now occupies that tract of land. Why thirteen? Because that's how many holes Bill was able to find in the dunes. I didn't care how many holes he built as long as it wasn't nine or eighteen. We were doing something different, and there was no reason to make the course conform to a conventional number. No hole is longer than 160 yards, and they all have views of the Pacific Ocean. They also meet the standard Bill and I had set: every one of them is good enough to deserve a place on the big courses.

At Bandon Preserve, some of the usual rules are suspended. There's no limit on how many golfers can play in the same group as long as they keep moving and don't slow down anyone else. Caddies and guests can play together, and often do; it's not unusual to see groups of eight, a foursome playing a match with their four caddies. At the Preserve, families can play together—husbands and wives, mothers and daughters, grandparents and grandchildren—on roughly equal terms. On a hole 100 yards long, a beginner has a fighting chance against a scratch player.

Since Bandon Preserve opened in 2012, it has been so popular that we've added par-3 courses at other Keiser properties. The Preserve's success is often credited with making short courses cool again, sparking a "mini-revolution" of alternative courses, not only par-3s but variations on the nine-hole course. In the last few years, many leading resorts have added short courses by top designers, including Pinehurst (The Cradle, designed by Gil Hanse); Big Cedar Lodge (Top of the Rock, by Jack Nicklaus); and Pebble Beach (the Peter Hay course, by Tiger Woods). This small-is-beautiful trend has gained enough traction so that *Golf Magazine* published a first-ever ranking of the Top 100 short courses in the world.

Par-3 courses have been around for a long time. Despite a few gems like the famous one at Augusta National, they've had a mostly humble history. Ron Whitten has referred to them as "the sand lots" of golf, and Bill Coore, who played them growing up, acknowledges that they were seen as "second-class citizens—where you went if you couldn't get on a big course." Modest, local mom-and-pop operations with do-it-yourself designs, the par-3s had the virtue of being affordable and accessible, places where beginners could learn the game and youngsters could play all day for a few bucks. The important innovation at Bandon Preserve was that these short holes offered real golf. Design, construction, and maintenance were all at the same level as on our regulation layouts.

At Bandon Dunes, we've also added a gargantuan putting course, the Punchbowl, an acre and a half of short grass with fantastic contours. One model for the Punchbowl, of course, was the putting course at St. Andrews, the Himalayas. Another is the Thistle Dhu, at Pinehurst, a rollicking piece of ground where golfers can amuse themselves for hours with a putter and a ball. Get the ball in the hole—it's the essence of golf.

The Punchbowl isn't a practice green. It's an eighteen-hole course, laid out to guide players up, over, and around the outrageous mounds that were designed by Jim Urbina and Tom Doak. No one who plays the Punchbowl will ever call me a leveler of greens! Every morning the superintendent lays out a new challenge, cutting fresh cups and marking the tees with waist-high metal stakes that include the indispensable cupholder. The Punchbowl gets most of its play in the evening, after golfers have walked thirty-six. There's no rule that you have to drink a Frosty while playing the Punchbowl, but almost everybody does.

At Sand Valley, twenty acres were earmarked for smaller-scale golf—a driving range, a putting course, maybe a combination of the two. Situated

*Bill Coore and Jim Craig at the Sandbox*

close to the entry road, just north of the 18th hole of Mammoth Dunes, this parcel occupied a strategic spot, but with all the other construction going on in the summer of 2016, I hadn't really focused on it.

MICHAEL: Ideas about how to use that land had remained in flux along with the location of the entry road, the clubhouse, and the lodges. As the buildings were sited, it looked less and less suitable for a driving range: we couldn't have people hitting golf balls into the guest rooms. I wondered if we could do something different, like maybe a putting course—not just a single continuous putting surface like the Punchbowl, but an actual course with several greens. A par-2 course.

As the Coore-Crenshaw team was just finishing up at Sand Valley, Jim Craig and I started kicking this idea around, and decided to try it out before anybody had a chance to tell us we couldn't. Not all of the TIF money had been spent, and it wouldn't cost much to let Jim rough in enough of the course to show people what we had in mind. At first we agreed that he'd have three weeks to work on it, but that soon stretched out to six weeks.

OVERLEAF
*The Punchbowl at twilight*

JIM: We had a lot of names for that course. One of the earliest names was 22, like a .22-caliber bullet. That evolved into 20 2s—completely unheard of. Nobody had ever built a golf course with twenty par-2s. Nobody knew what a par-2 was, anyway. That's what you see in putt-putt golf. We were thinking of a course that could be played with only a putter. The idea was that anybody of any age who could roll a ball with a putter would have fun on this course.

MICHAEL: The land was mostly flat. The elevation change from one end to the other was only two feet. We brought in some fill from a lake we were building, and soon there were mounds, ridges, little valleys. For Jim, this was all he needed to turn his imagination loose, and he was on a creative high. Some nights I thought I'd have to drag him off the dozer.

MK: The first time I saw the short course was in September. Bill and I had arranged to be on-site for a last walk-through of Sand Valley. Michael said he had something else he wanted to show us. I could see that somebody had been working in that area, clearing and pushing sand around, but I hadn't paid close attention.

JIM: When Michael called me and said his dad and Bill were here, and he wanted to show them what we'd been doing, I didn't feel a hundred percent ready, but this was it. No turning back now. We all met at the entrance, where Craig Haltom had cut an opening in a sand ridge that separated the area from the road and the buildings. The first thing that happened was that Senior—that's what I call Mike, not to his face, but it's how I think of him—looked at it and said, "That's a big gouge."

Uh-oh. We weren't off to a good start. He didn't say much when we walked the 1st hole, and then we looked at the 2nd, where the green is tucked into a dune, and he seemed to like it. Then we get to the 3rd hole, with the double plateau green, and he says, "How much can we charge people to play this?" I took that as a good sign.

BILL: After we'd seen a few holes, Mike asked me what I thought, and I said it was outstanding. I was completely surprised. Not by the actual work that had been done—I knew Jim had plenty of design talent. It was the scale of the work, the thought and imagination that had already been applied to the holes that were out there. Jim and Michael had been busy. Not all twenty-two holes were completed, but you could see that this little course could be phenomenal.

MICHAEL: Bill and Ben got involved after that, and they were into it as much as Jim had been. They made more than just tweaks. Bill saw places where greens could be consolidated, and also continued the process that Jim had already begun of adding length so that holes could be played through the air, not just on the ground. That had been the original concept, a course for putting only, but we scrapped the idea of a par-2 course and went to a legitimate, challenging par-3. For anyone who wants only to putt, there are still putting tees on every hole, marked by a trowel and located close to the greens. Some people even play the whole course from the back tees with a putter.

BEN CRENSHAW: On many of those holes, we'd talk to Jim and then just let him go. When we came back, he'd nailed it.

BILL: At the Sandbox, we could do things that we'd never get away with on a regulation eighteen-hole course. When someone is hitting a wedge into a green, you can ask for a nearly perfect shot. But out here, the idea of what's "fair" changes completely. That's what was so much fun—we were able to do things we'd never been able to do anywhere else. We could take every concept to its limit.

BEN: J. L. Low was one of the first people who wrote about golf architecture (*Concerning Golf*, 1904), and I've never forgotten his words: "Undulation is the soul of golf." On a course like the Sandbox, we could really play with the undulations. The holes are short but they're designed so that you can hit all kinds of different shots. You can run the ball onto the green, pitch it, drive it in low, with spin. A good golfer can play boldly, cagily. Every player has a chance to hit some really fun shots.

JIM: Once Bill and Ben got involved, the ideas really started flying around. We ended up with some original greens and some of the famous template greens—a Road Hole green, a Biarritz, a Redan, an Alps, a Lion's Mouth, a Punchbowl, and one that seems to be a favorite, a Double Plateau. Bill says it looks like two big matchboxes are buried under the green.

BILL: One afternoon Jim and I were walking with Ryan Farrow on a section of the course where there was nothing, just a flat piece of land, a few pine trees, stakes marking the location of the tee and the green. I asked Jim, "What are we going to do here?" Neither of us had any idea. I said, "All right, Ryan, this is your hole." The next day he was out there working on a green that is unlike any of the others, sloping up toward a narrow back, with a center ridge and front flairs on the left and right, a neat green with pin positions that can really change the strategy of this 115-yard shot. The 12th is the Ryan Farrow hole. It's satisfying to see the young guys come up with their own designs.

BEN: Jim has a video of me working on the Road Hole on a day when there's snow on the ground. I made an extra trip to Sand Valley just so I could keep working on the Sandbox. When I was a kid, I didn't like to practice on the range, but I could spend hours chipping and putting, and that has never changed. Now I get to design greens, and the fascination is still there. On a green every fine detail matters—the hole is only four and a half inches wide. I like working on small things, miniature things. There's an art to getting a green exactly right.

BILL: Once we started consolidating some of the greens, we weren't completely sure how many holes would end up in the course. The number went down from the original twenty-two, and for a while it looked as though we'd probably end up with nineteen. Ben liked that number. But we kept tinkering with the tees and looking at greens from different angles, and finally decided that the best number was seventeen. That seems right for a course like the Sandbox, where the idea is to have fun.

MICHAEL: The Sandbox has become an integral part of the Sand Valley experience. I own one of the houses not far from the Sandbox, and I keep my putter standing near the door so I can go out on the spur of the moment and play a couple of holes. At the start of the pandemic last March, my son Tommy and I went out to the Sandbox to "putt." He had some plastic clubs but had only hit them once. We stepped onto the 15th green and he lagged one to five feet. He stood up to the second putt from the same spot and rolled it into the center of the cup. I paced it out and it was forty-seven feet! It was clear he was a natural. Two minutes later, he was much more interested in playing in the bunkers. Since then I've tried to remember that my excitement watching him putt far exceeded his. When we're on the golf course we spend most of our time playing in the bunkers, and we only swing the clubs when he insists.

# 17

# The Lido

*The Lido is the finest course in the world. It is a standing miracle, the wonder of which will never fade. Our golfing ancestors could have desired nothing better.*

—BERNARD DARWIN

W E COULDN'T HAVE SCRIPTED a better reception for Sand Valley. While it wasn't remote by Bandon standards, Sand Valley felt worlds away from the nearby cities of Milwaukee, Chicago, and Minneapolis. Visitors responded to the sand barrens as though they were discovering a new American landscape, then went home and told their friends about it. When the beauty of its location becomes a talking point, a destination resort has made a giant step toward success. Truth to tell, I was a little surprised myself at the visual impact of the massive dunes, and I still marvel at the scale of the place every time I go there.

The accolades came quickly. The Sand Valley course was named the Best New Course of 2017. A year later Mammoth Dunes was selected as the Best New Course of 2018. The Sandbox also opened in 2018, and it was the icing on the cake. All three courses were solidly booked for most of the six-month season, and the number of rounds in 2019 totaled sixty thousand. The judgment of both the raters and the retail golfers was in: the golf was great, the place was spectacular, and the price was right. More than one journalist called it the Bandon Dunes of the Midwest, proof that the "Keiser method" worked. And now, of course, there was more than one Keiser.

A strange thing began happening to me on my visits to Sand Valley: I could relax. On a short trip in September 2019, I stayed two nights and played three rounds of golf with a group organized by an old friend and classmate, Warren Gelman, who has a lifetime appointment as our commissioner. Michael refers to us as the Buffalo Boys. We played at least one round of golf each day on a big course and then, as seniors, topped it off with a round at the Sandbox before sitting down to a long, convivial dinner at Aldo's. During those three days I did talk a little business with Michael, and one afternoon, instead of playing the Sandbox, I led a short tour of the site where Tom Doak had staked out a new course we were calling Sedge Valley. Otherwise, I simply enjoyed myself on a buddy trip.

I had nothing to worry about. I can't pinpoint an exact moment when Chris and Michael took over, but for all practical purposes Sand Valley is now their resort. They're the ones who should take a bow for all that's been accomplished there—and, I would add, in a very short period of time. At the

*My two sons: brothers, partners, developers*

outset, I gave them a helping hand, and they ran with it. I might have fretted too much about giving them such a responsibility, and no doubt there were times when they silently wished that I'd just step aside and let them do their thing.

When we started working side by side, I thought they might gravitate naturally to roles as Mr. Inside and Mr. Outside. Chris was focused and analytical, interested in branding, sales, and communication. Michael clearly had a passion for building and an appetite for being in the field. Now, five years later, with Sand Valley thriving and expanding, I see them as developers who've established their own creative partnership. Together, they make decisions about matters both large and small, working in a fashion that I recognize. In fact, they both describe their work with an analogy that I've used—they compare themselves to movie producers who oversee every detail of the operation, from raising the money to hiring the key people to setting the prices and, yes, selecting the showerheads.

Let me be completely clear: Michael and Chris are now doing projects on their own.

We discuss them together, but they initiate and develop them. They have big plans for Sand Valley, and their ambition doesn't stop there. For the last two years they've also been working on a separate project in Colorado, near Denver, where Michael has just signed a contract for the land. He envisions multiple courses; Bill Coore and Jim Urbina have already done routings. If everything works out perfectly, Michael and Chris could open four golf courses in four years. Four in four years! I never traveled at that speed.

The vicarious pleasure runs deep when you're watching your sons move strongly into careers that afford them the scope in which to exercise their talents. As I write this, they are setting out to finish something that I dreamed of years ago—they're building the Lido.

CHRIS: We had such a good 2019 season at Sand Valley that we decided to start construction on Sedge Valley, an eighteen-hole course, ahead of schedule. Michael and I had been talking with Tom Doak about the kind of "short" course that he'd been wanting to build for years. Tom has always rejected the idea that yardage is a genuine requirement, and we thought that a smaller course would be a perfect complement to Mammoth Dunes. Sedge Valley would be only about six thousand yards, with a par of 68 or 69, but the individual holes had the length and scale of any regulation course.

In spring 2020, we had to reevaluate our plans. Before our season opened, the first wave of Covid-19 was beginning, and we had no idea what to expect. We didn't know whether the resort would be able to open at all, and we were counting on that revenue to help fund Sedge Valley. With a lodge, clubhouse, and restaurant, the new course was projected to cost $27 million. Other support was expected from the town of Rome, and they were also reconsidering their 2020 budget. With so many uncertainties, we decided that we had to hit pause.

To keep our momentum going at Sand Valley, though, we looked at the other projects in the pipeline. One of them, the Lido Conservancy, wasn't dependent on resort revenue. We'd be introducing a completely different business model. The Lido was conceived as a private club, and the project had a real estate component. We could finance this course with the sale of lots and memberships.

MICHAEL: Our thinking about the resort has been in constant evolution. We've invited several architects to visit the property and share ideas with us, and we pay attention to what guests like. Both Chris and I fit Warren Buffett's definition of an entrepreneur as somebody who wakes up thinking, "How can I delight my customers?" The popularity of short courses led us to the Sandbox, and then we started thinking about what we called a "precision" course, and that led to our conversation with Tom about a short course. We're soon going to do a putting course with David Kidd. There's no formula for how to build out a resort so that you offer a golf experience that's fun, varied, memorable—you don't do it by building eighteen-hole "championship" courses one after another.

MK: Their decision to go ahead with the Lido came as a surprise. After all the years I spent trying to interest people in doing a Lido, I wasn't sure that anyone would ever find the right circumstances to make it work. For a developer with a strong sense of tradition, it's the ultimate project—the resurrection of the lost masterpiece.

MICHAEL: I remember when my dad was thinking of building a Lido at Bandon Dunes. He did his own in-person market research, asking everyone, "What do you think?" If he has a catchphrase, that's it. He asks people what they think, and he means it. He really listens to their answers.

He got a disappointing response. The Lido might be the most lamented lost course in golf history, but to retail golfers—if they've heard of it at all—it's just a footnote. Architecture junkies like my dad and me revere Charles Blair Macdonald, a giant in American golf, renowned both as a player and a designer. When the Lido opened as a resort course in 1917, many considered it one of the three best courses in the country, as good or better than Macdonald's most famous course, National Golf Links, and a little more difficult. It had also been far more expensive to build. The course occupied a flat, marshy stretch on the south shore of Long Island, with a few holes right on the Atlantic. Macdonald had to dredge a channel for two million tons of sand to spread over the site and then, on top of that, he added many more tons of organic matter so grass could grow. In effect, the Lido was the first entirely manufactured golf course in the game's history.

The resort struggled through the Great Depression, and the course closed in 1942. Since then, the Lido's mythical status as a place of vanished glory has grown stronger and stronger. It's like the lost city of Atlantis, or the castle of King Arthur. I still remember sitting in meetings where Dad was talking to Jim Urbina and Tom Doak about the Lido—it gave me goose bumps to hear them talk about bringing this amazing course back to life. But his project turned into a tribute course, Old Macdonald.

CHRIS: After talking to our closest advisors and friends, Michael and I decided to go ahead with the Lido Conservancy. Michael's been the driver. He identified and purchased the land, worked with the architect, set the timeline, and obtained the funding. My most important role has been to challenge him with questions and to make sure that we don't get ahead of ourselves.

MICHAEL: The land for the Lido is right across the road from the entrance to Sand Valley. Part of the motive to buy was defensive—I didn't want someone else building three hundred houses over there. These 880 acres are flatter than the land we used for the Sand Valley and Mammoth Dunes—no hills, no giant dunes. Any course built on that parcel would have to be something very different, a low-profile course like St. Andrews.

I make that comparison deliberately. This is what really excites me about the Lido—I think the original was more like St. Andrews than any American course. Macdonald became infatuated with golf when he was a student at St. Andrews, and all his courses show some of that influence, but the Lido had many, many characteristics of the Old Course. Huge greens, double fairways, fearsome bunkers, fairways that were wrinkled and rumpled everywhere even though they were man-made. Usually, people associate the Lido with Long Island and don't make the connection with St. Andrews. Admittedly, there are some glaring differences, but I see it as Macdonald's most deliberate effort to create a classic links.

At first, the idea just sat on the back burner. I didn't see how this could work as a public course. For one thing, it was just too difficult. The Lido had blind shots, cross hazards, and bunkers with sheer walls that rise fourteen feet straight up. It had intricate greens and strategic features that nobody was going to figure out in a single round. The original Lido was a resort course, but when Macdonald built it, he was tempted by the owner's promise that he'd have "complete freedom" to build his "greatest holes." The result was a dramatic, challenging course that seemed just right for a membership that would relish the opportunity to spend years trying to solve all its puzzles.

My fascination with the Lido tied in with a desire to expand the conservation effort at Sand Valley. I'd read about the growing number of successful people who'd made a lot of money and built big, expensive houses, shrines to themselves. They had their mansions—now what? When they looked around for something else to do, something more fulfilling, many of them turned to conservation projects. For the same amount of money that they'd just spent on a palace, they could build a smaller, perfectly comfortable house and restore fifty or a hundred acres of land around it. The long-term strategy at Sand

*The flowering prairie*
*at Sand Valley*

Valley has always been to put more land into a conservation program, and to get other people committed to the restoration of the sand barrens.

That was the origin of the Lido Conservancy. After working with a land planner and Jens Jensen, we came up with a site plan that included nineteen homesteads, varying in size from five to twenty-five acres. On each one, roughly an acre is designated for the house, garage, and any other structures. The remainder of the land in each homestead will be part of the conservancy, maintained just like the conservation areas on the golf course.

In broad outline, the plan is to restore 316 acres of savanna and woodland, 172 acres of prairie, and 132 acres of sand dunes. The golf area, comprising the course and the lakes, will total about 215 acres.

Some of the houses will have views of the golf course, but the closest will be set back about 150 yards. They'll have very little visual impact, if any, on the golfers, and the other houses will be completely out of sight. Ideally, the homeowners will think of the prairie as their back-yard. We aren't developing lots or some lavish subdivision to generate big profits. The goal is to sell as many lots and club memberships as we need to cover the cost of the course—about $18 million, significantly less than the projected all-in cost for Sedge Valley.

The lots have sold more quickly than we imagined. When I talked to potential buyers, I kept hearing the same complaint: Sand Valley courses are always full. It's tough to get a tee time. Members at the Lido will be guaranteed tee times on their course, and a concierge to assist them in booking tee times at the other courses. They won't have special privileges, though. Sand Valley's a public resort and we didn't want to create a special caste.

In fact, our plan is to set aside certain times for public play at the Lido, so resort guests will have an additional course to play. This kind of accommodation has often been looked down on in the U.S. But Muirfield and Royal County Down are two of the world's great courses, and they set aside times for visitors. It hasn't hurt their reputation. I hope we can make it work here.

I sometimes say we aren't building a replica, we're building *the* Lido. I wasn't interested in creating an impressionistic version, with holes that were kinda-sorta like the originals. I didn't believe that we could build the real thing until I saw the computer renderings of the Lido that were done by Peter Flory.

Peter is one of the country's top hickory players and an expert on NLE—no longer existing—courses. His hobby is creating digital 3D models of lost courses, and he's a monster researcher. After thousands of hours of poring over every available bit and scrap of data, Peter had models of the Lido that were exact down to the inch. When I saw his brilliant graphics, it felt like I'd opened a time capsule.

Peter's work pushed our concept into the realm of possibility. When I told Tom Doak about the renderings, he didn't believe me at first. Then, after studying them, he agreed to take the job, on one condition: he would build the Lido as long as it was clear that it wasn't a Tom Doak design. This was going to be the strictest restoration ever, a Charles Blair Macdonald design, with Tom as the contractor and construction supervisor.

TOM DOAK (from the brochure for prospective members of the Lido Club): I've been adamant that no project should be called the Lido unless it's a faithful re-creation of the original course, and I've doubted that anyone could gather enough information to do it, and resist the temptation to "improve" it. When I saw Peter Flory's attempt at reproducing the Lido in a gaming format, I changed my mind. He's done the research and gathered all the available data about the old course, and Michael Keiser Jr. is serious about wanting to re-create the course as it was, not a sanitized version. . . . I know there will be skeptics, and I look forward to the challenge of making them admit they were wrong.

MICHAEL: When the backer of the original Lido ran short of money, Macdonald was unable to build four holes as he'd planned. Peter thought those holes on our Lido should be built according to Macdonald's intentions. Tom and I took the position that we should build them exactly as they'd existed on Long Island for twenty-five years, integral elements of the course that so many people had played. Anyone who's been involved in a restoration project knows that this is a fundamental issue: What is the definitive version of a golf hole? How do you decide? Where do you freeze the frame and say, "Here! This is the true and authentic hole, the one we must replicate."

**TOM:** This project has taught me a new respect for contemporary technology, and I was once a math geek. Before studying golf architecture at Cornell, I spent a year at MIT, thinking I'd become an engineer. I was interested in technology and computers. Then I went to work for Pete Dye, who had absolutely no use for them. This was in the 1980s, and I accepted what Pete said. I avoided technology for years.

Forty years later, I've come around. I've learned to use computers when I do routings. The design programs are easy to use and much, much better than those early ones, but I had no idea it was possible to do what Peter Flory did. The detail in his renderings is amazing. He was able to reproduce not just the approximate sizes and shapes of the features of the Lido but the exact angles and undulations, the depth of the bunkers, the relationship of the greens and fairways. I've worked on several Macdonald/Raynor courses, and I'd never realized what I could learn right away from Peter's images. All the greens are five feet higher than the fairways. They're horizon greens, and that couldn't have happened by accident. Macdonald wanted you to see only the green, with nothing behind it, when you were planning your approach.

I thought we could build the holes that Peter had rendered, but a big step was missing—we needed a grading plan. In my first conversations with Michael, I told him I didn't know how to bill him because I'd never done anything like this. We were going to have to reverse engineer the course, translating the renderings of the holes into a grading plan. I thought we'd have to do it by hand. As it turned out, Michael found a young guy who was a computer whiz. No problem—he designed a program and generated a grading plan that is precise and complete.

With that plan, we can build a Lido that is very close to an exact replica. The only changes necessary are in the spacing between holes, where tees and greens are close together. We'll add a few yards to make the course safer.

**CHRIS:** With the Lido we're going in a new direction, and we're sensitive to that. The Lido Conservancy will be adjacent to Sand Valley, but it will be a different place, a private club with its own clubhouse, maybe a small lodge. It will have its own atmosphere and personality. Sand Valley is always going to be a public resort, and as long as we stick to our fundamentals, I think we can introduce new concepts.

MK: I can't wait to play a round on the completed Lido. The symbolism is impossible to miss—Michael and Chris are completing something their father had conceived of many years ago. They're going about it in a way that the old man never could have, using state-of-the-art digital renderings and grading plans calculated by a made-to-order algorithm. Even though their site isn't on the Atlantic Ocean, it's far better than the one I was considering at Bandon; it's flatter, and they have enough land to reproduce the exact size and shape of the original footprint. They're taking a stricter approach, too. I wanted to change those four holes back to what Macdonald drew.

I wish I'd had the nerve to build it—and then immediately think that it's probably best that I didn't. This Lido will be more authentic.

I've seen myself as a steward of the game, committed to throwback golf and all that implies—to maintaining traditions, customs, and values that have been nurtured for centuries. As a developer, I've aspired to be a custodian of the game. Leave things a little better than you found them, my father used to say. Chris and Michael heard me repeat Pap's lesson countless times, and they obviously intend to make stewardship the cornerstone of their own developments. With the Lido Conservancy, they've taken on a project that's worth doing both for the good of the game and the place where it's played.

Their application for permits lays it out clearly: "the Lido Conservancy will restore 850 acres of timberland back to its original Sand Barrens landscape." This has been a consistent theme at Sand Valley, and this conservancy will enable Michael and Chris to continue building a base of stakeholders who will actively further these efforts. Michael believes Sand Valley could someday have other similar conservancies, and that the resort might grow to six or seven courses. Bigger than Bandon Dunes! He and Chris envision a place that could become a destination for young families—like theirs—who want to spend time outdoors and recognize a shared responsibility for this land. Though golf would remain the core activity, Sand Valley might become a new kind of "national park" that offers a full range of outdoor pursuits.

To quote Aldo Leopold, "What more delightful avocation than to take a piece of land and by cautious experimentation to prove how it works. What more substantial service to conservation than to practice it on one's own land?"

Make no little plans! Chris and Michael share my willingness to entertain big ideas. Whenever I fly out to Bandon and the plane comes in low over the Oregon Dunes, I still fantasize about a links sixty miles long, an otherworldly course that might take a week to play from one end to the other. My sons have their own vision of a time, far in the future, when the whole of the Central Wisconsin Sands, more than a million acres, has been transformed by golf. It could become a landscape where golf courses flow naturally in and out of prairie and savanna, a domain to be protected and enjoyed. Like me, Chris and Michael are developers who bring a passion for using their spoils to reestablish both a healthy local economy and a healthy ecological system.

This goes far beyond our original aspiration to bring one hundred thousand acres into a restoration program, and why not? Some people questioned our sincerity when I first mentioned that number, but now it seems within reach. Michael and Chris expect to purchase additional land that will enlarge the resort's footprint to more than twelve thousand acres. Separately, I've made a pledge of $5 million to the Wisconsin Nature Conservancy to purchase and set aside as many as five thousand acres. This land won't be part of the resort, nor will it be used for golf. It doesn't necessarily have to be close to Sand Valley. What matters is that these funds be used to secure another piece of the Wisconsin Sands that can be enjoyed, perhaps as a park, while the prairie and sand barrens are undergoing a renewal. As a practical environmentalist, I support projects that attract people to natural wonders and win them over as allies in conservation.

I've started thinking of these ambitions as the Jack Pine Project, named for a lonely, woebegone tree that stands just north of the 4th green at my first course, the Dunes Club. Unlike stock Christmas trees, each jack pine is different, and this one sticks in my mind as a representative of the unappreciated "junk" foliage that's been removed wherever lumber companies were operating. Many other species native to the sand barrens have also been struggling. I've started reading bulletins from the Wisconsin Department of Natural Resources, and I'm rooting for a long list of threatened and endangered species: the Kirtland's warbler; the badger, the official state animal; the prairie chicken, once harvested by the tens of thousands, now found only in

*Lupine and Karner blue butterfly, two species we are trying to protect at Sand Valley*

a small area of restored grassland; the Karner blue butterfly, which depends on the blue lupine to complete its life cycle (at Sand Valley, volunteers gather lupine seeds, which are then sown in promising areas to give this butterfly a fighting chance).

Could Sand Valley become the prototype of a new kind of conservation zone, a park where both public and private forces are devoted to the essential work of restoration, where golf is the engine that helps a region reinvent itself on a new foundation that's sound economically and environmentally? Like every developer, I've been portrayed as an enemy of nature, and Michael and Chris will undoubtedly run into some of the same mischaracterization. But I see them as leaders in the golf industry's movement toward adopting sustainable practices.

It bears repeating that all three of our North American properties have helped to heal degraded land. At Bandon Dunes, generations of miners had plundered its resources, and the invasive gorse had made the property a terrible fire hazard. Cabot Links was built on a toxic site that had once been a coal mine and railyard. Sand Valley emerged where plantations of red pines had once obliterated a rich ecosystem.

The earliest links were absolutely "sustainable" in that they were simply part of their natural location. Sandy soil, dunes, a flock of sheep to mow and fertilize the turf—all that was required was to scoop out a few small holes. Presto! A links! Today, a golf course is vastly more complicated, but the same principle applies: the more it belongs to its natural location, the healthier it will be. Anyone hoping to build a course that will last for generations must pay heed.

. . .

I wish I had a crystal ball in which I could see the future of the game. I've read many articles on the subject, and thought about it in painful detail as I've weighed options about the future of Bandon Dunes. After pouring my heart and soul into that place, I want it to remain in the hands of people who appreciate it. Some buyers of golf properties could ruin it, and they would do so happily, believing they were making splendid improvements. It makes me shudder to think of a twenty-story hotel standing on the cliffs at Five Mile Point, its new name written in gold-plated letters so large they can be read from ships at sea; or carts scooting all over the place (though I acknowledge that as boomers age, more and more of them will have medical reasons to ride in carts); or, God forbid, the fairways lined with a solid wall of condos. I can imagine a new owner so hell-bent on hosting a major event that he ignores another bedrock principle: the courses at Bandon weren't built for the pros. They were designed for retail golfers, the ordinary men and women who love playing the game just as it has been played for centuries.

In 2009, in the depths of the Great Recession and on the advice of Len Levine, I had Bandon Dunes appraised. Len is always a wise, reasonable, dispassionate voice, just what I needed to hear at the time. "Never let a crisis go to waste," he counseled, and he was right. An appraisal of Bandon Dunes would reflect the depressed real estate market. The resort could only increase in value, and I didn't want to hang on to it so long that my children wouldn't be able to afford it. So instead of making Bandon Dunes a part of my estate, I decided to sell it to Michael, Chris, Leigh, and Dana. Though my daughters aren't golfers, they've grown up knowing that Bandon Dunes is a fixed point on our family's map, a source of both wealth and well-being. Even before the boys proved themselves at Sand Valley, I was confident that the children, as a group, would know how to maintain everything that was best about Bandon Dunes.

Having begun his career in an accounting firm whose clientele consisted almost entirely of owner-operated businesses, Len had firsthand experience with the many financial, legal, emotional, and Oedipal issues that can arise in any generational transition. He summed up this process with another piece of accountant's humor: "I spent years making you rich, and now I am going to make you poor."

Mind you, I have no intention of retiring, and believe I still have a few courses ahead of me. Recently, Bill Coore went to Scotland to check out a site not far from Coul Links. According to my sources, the Scottish government has felt some remorse about nixing my project, and they might be willing to consider this alternate site. Bill says it has promise, and soon I'll go and see for myself. Maybe I will include a side trip to Lofoten, a Norwegian archipelago in the Arctic Circle, a place of northern lights, crystalline fjords, and snow-covered mountains. There's already a golf course there, whose owner believes that it could, in the right hands, become one of the most magnificent in the world. And while I'm over there, I should probably take a look at the dunes of northern Denmark, which Michael describes as the equivalent to those in Scotland.

And then there's a stretch of California dunes, big enough for five courses, on the decommissioned Vandenberg Air Force Base, not far north of Santa Barbara and within a half-day's drive from major population centers. For the last five years, my partner, Owen Larkin, and I have been negotiating with the Air Force to build a resort that could become a remarkable golf destination. Vandenberg already has one unique attraction: Elon Musk now uses part of the property to launch his SpaceX rockets. So imagine a golfer out among the dunes, playing an age-old game and standing over his putt in deep concentration—when he hears a roar, looks up, and sees a rocket rising into space, on its way to Mars!

Alas, this project has run into so many obstacles that I recently wrote to Owen: "I've run out of time. I'm 76, and we've been working on this for over five years. . . . I have decided to cease my financial support and wish you all the best on your own. If you are finally able to win approval, my sons Michael and Chris would welcome the opportunity to partner with you."

The future projects that most excite me would take me back to where it all started—to Bandon. The resort has been so busy that we haven't been able to keep up with the demand. As the need for more lodging became glaringly obvious, the next question was unavoidable—should we build another golf course, so soon after the Sheep Ranch? A full course? Another par-3 course?

Why not both?

On a fine May day in 2021, after talking this through with Chris and Michael, I was out in the field with David Kidd, walking a piece of land about ten miles south of the resort. Twenty-four hours later, David had come up with an absolutely gorgeous routing for a course that is tentatively called New River Dunes. The first twelve holes were 9s on the Keiser scale! Meanwhile, Tom Doak has been looking at a stretch of sandy ground just south of the Preserve, and we'll soon be building another par-3 course—with thirteen holes, we think, though the final number could change. Permits are expected to be in hand by the end of 2021, and construction will begin soon. This short course will be located right beside the Preserve—yet another pairing of a Doak design with one by Coore-Crenshaw.

For the moment, though, the anticipation is blissful. I'll be back at Bandon, working with David Kidd and Tom Doak. The most interesting chapter is always the next one.

# Epilogue

L INDY SAYS that I have one gear: forward. As usual, she's right. I am impatient. I hate to wait. On the golf course, I've usually had to slow down to match my partners' pace, though lately I've noticed that the others seem to be moving faster. Maybe I've lost a step. For my entire working life, I've operated on a tight schedule, trying to fit everything in, not just business but also my family, the golf, the philanthropic work. It's more natural for me to look ahead, sometimes years ahead, than it is to glance in the rearview mirror. Working on this book has been a different kind of exercise for me, an extended look at the past.

The pandemic kept me at home. For most of 2020, Lindy and I sheltered in place at our lake house in New Buffalo. Thankfully, we're close enough to the Dunes Club to walk over whenever we felt like playing a round of golf, which was often. We're lucky to have this refuge, and not be locked down in Chicago. I do go into the office now and then, but usually I work from home, making my calls out on the porch where the cell signal's strongest. I do not Zoom. Most days I walk five or six miles. I feel like I've been on a long, long vacation.

Like billions of others, I'm ready for this tragic pandemic to end. One of the few silver linings has been the surge of interest in golf. I've read that many fallen-away golfers have returned to the fold, and new golfers are discovering the benefits of the game—fresh air, open spaces, exercise, and an escape from the worry and pressure that weigh so heavily on everyone.

I'm a missionary for golf, and I probably ascribe too many special virtues to the game. Good friends have chided me for this, pointing out the obvious: golfers as a group are no better or worse than anyone else. I'm well aware that golf has its share of cheats, weasels, snobs, and scoundrels. Nevertheless, if approached in the right spirit, I continue to believe that the game is a teacher of valuable lessons. No doubt I am guilty of nostalgia, but when I try to assess the principles that have guided me, many of them can be traced all the way back to the East Aurora Country Club, where I learned to play as a boy. Indulge an old golfer and hear me out.

First impressions are lasting, and my first impression of golf was that it was a walking game, played with caddies. When I was a youngster in the 1950s, the first carts showed up at East Aurora, a noisy, smelly, gas-powered fleet. Some golfers preferred them. Strange as it might seem today, there was once a stigma against riding. That was only for the old, the lazy, the unserious.

*Lesson: If you want to play golf the right way, you walk.*

Aged ten, I started caddying at East Aurora CC, and spent the next five summers hanging out at the club with a group of buddies who shared my great ambition—to break 50 for nine holes.

*Lesson: Humility. No one ever masters the game.*

The pro, Don "Wink" Winkelmas, kept an eye on us. He gave us a few pointers about the golf swing, and, just as important, sent us out as bag-toters. It goes without saying that East Aurora was a modest, local club; a snootier kind of place never would've allowed members' kids to caddie.

*Lesson: If you want to be remembered fondly, do someone a favor. Thank you, Wink.*

As far as we were concerned, the arrangement was perfect. We could earn a few bucks, play golf to our hearts' content, and eat delicious hamburgers for lunch. Green grass, blue skies, idyllic summer days. Maybe East Aurora was nothing special, but to me it was paradise.

*Lesson: Cherish the time you spend in the freedom of the outdoors.*

Spiked shoes, steel shafts, persimmon woods, balata balls—these and many other features of the game as I first knew it have faded away. The caddie endures, I am glad to say. For me, caddies are as integral to golf lore as cowboys are to the tales of Texas, or Sherpas to the stories of Mount Everest. Without caddies, everything about the game would be different—the optics, the pageantry, the atmosphere and pace, the narratives of determination and success, friendship and trust.

*Lesson: Support the cause of caddies whenever possible.*

To be a caddie or to have a paper route: both jobs were so commonplace in the 1950s that they were almost a rite of passage, a ritual of American boyhood. I wanted to work almost as much as I wanted to break 50.

*Lesson: When work and play are closely allied, the work ethic takes root.*

For the next five years, I learned the game as caddies do, hitting thousands of shots, imitating the pros I saw on black-and-white TV, watching people of all shapes and sizes, with wildly different skills and personalities, navigate the tight, hilly course.

*Lesson: The golf swing is not one-size-fits-all.*

Arnold Palmer, Ben Hogan, and Sam Snead were my first golf heroes, and they'd all been caddies. To me, these caddies-turned-champions are representatives of an era when American golf had a strong grassroots appeal. They all had distinctive swings. They were proudly self-reliant. They were full-blown characters who played the game with a style and attitude that were inimitably their own.

*Lesson: Play your own game.*

As a caddy, in addition to my first lessons as a wage earner, I was learning that there are as many ways to play golf as there are human beings. Put a man or woman in front of a golf ball with a club in their hands, and their personality will reveal itself. The caddy, standing by quietly, has an unobstructed view. Sometimes the show is a melodrama, with gusty emotions, fits of temper, quarrels with the gods, ranting and club throwing. Far more often, though, personality traits are expressed in small, ordinary, habitual gestures. The way a golfer behaves on a green—how he marks his ball, lines up his putt, takes his stance, positions himself, moves in relation to others—provides sufficient material for a full character analysis. The caddie also sees the private moments, how the golfer deliberates and talks to himself and how he talks to others. The impressions add up quickly. Is she cheerful, tense, cautious, or disciplined? Impulsive? Resilient? Stoic? Is this one aware of the others or too absorbed in his own game to pay attention? Optimistic, or delusional? Is he always trying shots beyond his ability or does he play within himself? Does she give her best effort on every shot or just go through the motions? Does he cheat, God forbid? Is he a needler? Is the needling friendly or is he a gamesman? Is he having fun? Does he want the group to have fun? And, finally, is he or she generous?

*Lesson: To caddie is to enroll in a course on reading people.*

In theory, caddying is unskilled labor, as low as it gets in the hierarchy of work. The basic job description: show up, keep up, and shut up. If you want to be a good caddie, though, you must have patience, communication skills, a strong work ethic, relationship skills, and respect for people who are very different from you. You have to figure out how to get along with them. You have to suspend judgment. You cannot complain. You have to know when to speak and when to keep your mouth shut. You have to be able to do something that goes against every instinct in a teenager's body: put others first.

*Lesson: Shut up and listen. Respect others.*

You might think your golfer's a knucklehead, and you might be right about what he's doing wrong. So what? It doesn't matter. Your job is to help your golfer, whether he shoots 128 or 68. You're not being paid to judge or to correct anybody's swing faults, let alone their behavior. Your task is to watch and listen. You have to understand your golfer. What does he want? How can you help? In every business I've run, that's been the cardinal principle. Find out what people want, and try to provide it.

*Lesson: Respect others. Repeated here for emphasis.*

When I became a developer, I was still trying to do what a caddie does: make sure that my golfer has a banner day. I've heard from thousands of people who've had such days on a course I built. For them, that course will forever be associated with a glorious day that stands out brightly from the succession of dull, ordinary days. I still remember those caddie days, for heaven's sake, and the thrill I felt when Mrs. Holsclaw, after paying the standard fee of $1, gave me a fifty-cent tip.

That's all anyone can ask of the game, that it provide us with indelible moments that give shape to our lives. One more verse from Wordsworth: "There are in our existence spots of time / That with distinct pre-eminence retain / A renovating virtue." I won't forget the afternoons spent playing wilderness golf here in New Buffalo, roaming around with a few irons and balls in the small patch of woods that eventually became the Dunes Club.

Then, after I'd worked up the nerve to build my first course and the club opened, it became the site of many rounds of father-son golf, and Chris still remembers the high fives when, age seven or so, he finally hit a drive that carried the sandy waste area in front of the first tee. He wasn't much older when we played a round in Brora, in the far north of Scotland, where he and a cousin took endless delight in hitting shots from the cow patties and the sheep droppings that were scattered all over the course, those fairways doubling as pastures.

Later still, at Royal Dornoch, there were evenings when the three of us, Chris and Michael and I, couldn't call it a day and lingered around the greens in the long Scottish twilight, chipping and putting until it was too dark to see. The day when Michael fully understood the magnetic pull of an ancient course, he says, was also at Dornoch, when we played the big

*At New Buffalo, we not only played wilderness golf. We played beach golf, too. Here I am with seven-year-old Michael.*

*With Chris in Scotland. That's a full-body smile.*

course in the morning and followed that with two rounds on the shorter Struie Course, carrying our own bags, absorbed by the game and the place. On such days you can lose track of time, but the hours are being recorded in your heart and soul.

With Michael and Chris, I didn't try to make the course into a classroom or instruction session. I didn't try to correct their swings—well, maybe now and then I couldn't help giving a tip. But I always tried to instill in them the fundamentals of fair play and respect for others. They quickly mastered the etiquette and protocols of the game. Most of all, I encouraged them to enjoy themselves. As boys, they were already good golf buddies, and I hoped that would last for a lifetime. Many unspoken communications passed between us on those rounds, and lasting bonds grew from that companionship. On the course, loving the game and each other, we could connect in a way that came easily.

I've built several golf courses that I hope will last for centuries. As a developer, I was trying to create a successful business, certainly, but every golfer knows that the game is bigger than any course or any business. In a world of increasing complexity and accelerated change, golf courses serve much the same purpose as those remnant areas at Sand Valley, preserving a living connection to nature. Yet another mystery of the game is that it has remained an idyllic pursuit, offering those who play it an abundance of great, simple gifts. To move freely across a beautiful landscape, seeing the sparkle of sunshine on the sea, enjoying the company of family and friends with the breeze at our backs—golf makes us happy to be alive.

Now, as ever, I hope to hand on this beloved game with its pleasures intact.

# Acknowledgments

This book is the result of a collaborative effort. Early on, I decided with my cowriter, Steve Goodwin, that if told only from my perspective, the narrative would be limited and far less interesting than a story that incorporated many voices. In all my golf projects, I've benefited from the insight and talent of many partners, colleagues, and associates—why shouldn't they have a say in this book? Thus, several chapters now read as oral histories, and even the short quotes are the tip of an iceberg—the visible part of a longer, ongoing conversation. Everyone named in this book spoke patiently to me and/or Steve so that our chronicle would be as complete and balanced as possible. I can't list all their names here, but I'm grateful to all those who've helped me build resorts and golf courses—and who've now helped me share the story of their evolution.

Many who aren't named in the book also made important contributions. Chief among them is Jim Seeley, who was associated with Bandon Dunes first as an advisor from KemperSports and later, until his death in 2019, as the executive director of the Wild Rivers Coast Alliance; he guided the resort's efforts to preserve the ecology and economy of Oregon's south coast. His successor, Marie Simonds, has continued this important work. We relied on her husband, Jeff Simonds, the director of golf, for information about competitions and tournaments. Don Crowe, the general manager, arranged schedules, meals, and accommodations to make our work as congenial and productive as possible. His assistant, Lee Ann Remy, who's also the Bandon Dunes archivist, had a knack for leading us to the documents and photographs that we needed—even when we didn't know exactly what we were looking for.

Mary Schamehorn, the longtime mayor of Bandon, shared her insights and knowledge about the community. For the backstory of land transactions, we turned to Bob Johnson, the realtor who's been instrumental in putting all the pieces together at the resort.

My assistant in Chicago, Marianne Laughlin, facilitated the writing process in innumerable ways, and she was part of the group that gathered the illustrations that add so much to the book. Michael Chupka, the director of communications at Bandon Dunes, knew where to find the best pictures and didn't rest until he'd secured them. He had dedicated counterparts at the other resorts: Brandon Carter at Sand Valley and Beth MacLellan at Cabot Cape Breton. Sara Mess tracked down the images from Doakgolf. The photographers themselves, particularly Evan Schiller, Christian Hafer, and Jeff Marsh, went above and beyond to provide us with the shots we wanted.

Sarah Perrin, at Knopf, was endlessly patient in coordinating this effort and in guiding us through the stages of manuscript preparation.

Our agent, Rafe Sagalyn, played a key role in shaping the book's strategy. Gary Fisketjon acquired the book at Knopf; his knowledge of the game and passionate belief in this story were invaluable in helping us develop and articulate our ideas. The fine hand of Jonathan Segal, our editor, is evident throughout the book; he has deftly steered us toward precision, economy, and clarity, keeping us on track and on key.

Finally, and most of all, I want to thank the retail golfer—not the abstraction, but the thousands and thousands of living, breathing golfers who come to the resorts and play the courses. They come in all shapes and sizes, young and old, male and female, duffer and pro, and they come in all seasons and play in all weathers. Many of them have told me in emotional terms how much they enjoy the courses at Bandon, Barnbougle, Cabot, and Sand Valley, and they thank me for building them. My response is that I should be thanking them. Over and over again, I am deeply rewarded by their love for links golf.

# ILLUSTRATION CREDITS

## PERMISSIONS CREDITS

Grateful acknowledgment is made to the following for permission to reprint previously published material:

Tom Doak: "Doak Scale, from 0 to 10." Reprinted by permission of Tom Doak.

*Links Magazine:* Excerpt from "Golf Architecture's Most Important Courses" by Darius Oliver, originally published in *Links Magazine* on April 26, 2016; and excerpt from "Bandon Dunes Celebrates Its 20th Anniversary" by Graylyn Loomis, originally published in *Links Magazine* on October 23, 2019. Reprinted by permission of *Links Magazine.*

Darius Oliver: Excerpt from "Barnbougle Dunes Golf Links," originally published in *Planet Golf* (www.planetgolf.com). Reprinted by permission of Darius Oliver.

Josh Sens: Excerpt from "Now 20 years old, Bandon Dunes has proven itself to be much more than a pioneering one-off" by Josh Sens, originally published on GOLF.com on September 4, 2019. Reprinted by permission of Josh Sens, senior writer at GOLF.com.

Jerry Tarde, o/b/o himself and Discovery Golf, Inc.: Excerpt from "Best New Course 2015: Cabot Cliffs" by Ron Whitten, originally published in *Golf Digest* on November 9, 2015. Copyright © 2015 by Golf Digest, a division of Discovery Golf, Inc. Excerpt from "Golf Digest's Best New Course of 2017: Sand Valley" by Ron Whitten, originally published in *Golf Digest* on December 8, 2017. Copyright © 2017 by Golf Digest, a division of Discovery Golf, Inc. Excerpt from "Canada's Briga-dune?" by Jerry Tarde, originally published in *Golf Digest* on January 18, 2018. Copyright © 2018 by Golf Digest, a division of Discovery Golf, Inc. Reprinted by permission of Jerry Tarde, o/b/o himself and Discovery Golf, Inc.

Mike Keiser is the founder of Bandon Dunes. His business career began in 1971, when he and a college roommate successfully launched Recycled Paper Greetings. In his second career as a golf course developer, he's built award-winning resorts and spectacularly beautiful courses from Tasmania to Nova Scotia. He has lectured on management at the University of Chicago, and he lives with his wife, Lindy, in Chicago, Illinois.

Stephen Goodwin is the author of *Dream Golf: The Making of Bandon Dunes* as well as two other golf books and three novels. He served as the director of the Literature Program at the National Endowment for the Arts and cofounded the PEN/Faulkner Foundation. He taught literature and creative writing at George Mason University and now lives with his wife, Robyn, in Vineyard Haven, Massachusetts.

## A NOTE ON THE TYPE

The text in this book was set in Miller, a transitional-style type-face designed by Matthew Carter (b. 1937) with assistance from Tobias Frere-Jones and Cyrus Highsmith of the Font Bureau. Modeled on the roman family of fonts popularized by Scottish type foundries in the nineteenth century, Miller is named for William Miller, founder of the Miller & Richard foundry of Edinburgh.

*Composed by North Market Street Graphics, Lancaster, Pennsylvania*
*Printed and bound by Mohn Media, Gütersloh, Germany*
*Designed by Maggie Hinders*